LANGUAGE, RELIGION, KNOWLEDGE

For Tony,
One of the four Americans who might conceivably find some of this stuff interesting,
all the best,
Jim

ALSO BY JAMES TURNER

Reckoning with the Beast:
Animals, Pain, and Humanity in the Victorian Mind

Without God, Without Creed:
The Origins of Unbelief in America

The Liberal Education of Charles Eliot Norton

The Sacred and the Secular University (with Jon H. Roberts)

JAMES TURNER is director of the Erasmus Institute and the Rev. John J. Cavanaugh, C.S.C., Professor of Humanities at the University of Notre Dame.

LANGUAGE, RELIGION, KNOWLEDGE

Past and Present

JAMES TURNER

UNIVERSITY OF NOTRE DAME PRESS
Notre Dame, Indiana

Copyright © 2003 by
University of Notre Dame
Notre Dame, Indiana 46556
http://www.undpress.nd.edu
All Rights Reserved

Manufactured in the United States of America

Library of Congress Cataloging-in-Publication Data
Turner, James, 1946–
Language, religion, knowledge : past and present / James Turner.
p. cm.
Includes bibliographical references and index.
ISBN 0-268-03356-0 (cloth : alk. paper)
ISBN 0-268-03357-9 (pbk. : alk. paper)
1. Universities and colleges—United States—History.   2 Universities and colleges—United States—Religion—History.   3. Language and languages—Study and teaching (Higher)—United States—History.
4. Catholic Church—Education—United States—History. I. Title.
LA226 . T87   2003
378.73—dc21

2002013376

∞ *This book is printed on acid-free paper.*

To my teachers

> Bernard Bailyn
> Donald Fleming
> Oscar Handlin
> Neil Harris
> Samuel Thorne

> Forsan et haec olim meminisse iuvabit

Contents

Introduction   1

PART ONE   HISTORICAL STUDIES

CHAPTER ONE
Language, Religion, and Knowledge   11
in Nineteenth-Century America: The Curious Case
of Andrews Norton

CHAPTER TWO
Charles Hodge in the Intellectual Weather of   31
the Nineteenth Century

CHAPTER THREE
Secularization and Sacralization: Some Religious   50
Origins of the Secular Humanities Curriculum, 1850–1900

CHAPTER FOUR
The "German Model" and the Graduate School: 69
The University of Michigan and the Origin Myth of
the American University (written with Paul Bernard)

CHAPTER FIVE
The Forgotten History of the Research Ideal   95

PART TWO CONTEMPORARY INTERVENTIONS

CHAPTER SIX
Catholicism and Modern Scholarship: A Historical Sketch   109

CHAPTER SEVEN
The Evangelical Intellectual Revival   121

CHAPTER EIGHT
The Catholic University in Modern Academe:
Challenge and Dilemma   129

CHAPTER NINE
Catholic Intellectual Traditions and Contemporary   143
Scholarship

Notes   157
Index   196

LANGUAGE, RELIGION, KNOWLEDGE

Introduction

John Maynard Keynes mused at the end of the *General Theory*: "Practical men, who believe themselves to be quite exempt from any intellectual influences, are usually the slaves of some defunct economist. Madmen in authority, who hear voices in the air, are distilling their frenzy from some academic scribbler of a few years back."[1] Keynes's observation hits even closer to the mark in our day than in his, for universities now more nearly dominate the life of the mind. Higher education and university-based research are among the most powerful forces shaping our world. To understand higher learning, how it took its present form and where it may be headed, is imperative. The book in your hands probes only a few sensitive spots in higher learning, but it both explores historical origins and plots future trajectories.

The term "higher learning" is more apt than "higher education" because the frame of reference here extends beyond colleges and universities. True, most of the ensuing chapters focus on higher education in this strict sense. But not all; and the concern in every case is less with academic *institutions* than with academic *knowledge*—erudite discourses grounded in specialized bodies of information. In the last two centuries academic knowledge has most commonly made its home in universities, but it was and is by no means pent up there.

Consider two historical figures who appear in this book. Andrews Norton and Charles Hodge helped to place education for Protestant ministers on a firm institutional ground in the United States, yet this achievement has nothing to do with their presence here. Norton had shaken the dust of Harvard Divinity School off his sandals long before the episode at the center of chapter 1. Both men attracted numerous readers, and the great majority of them had no connection with higher education other than perhaps having been graduated from a college. Yet, if the university did not always shelter Norton's career or supply his and Hodge's audiences, it did provide the essential stuff of their work. Erudition gave their writings a distinctive stamp—and considerable authority among educated men and women. When Norton and Hodge stepped outside the institutional walls of higher education, they still thought, spoke, and wrote the language of higher learning. This is the sort of distinction I am pointing out when I say that higher learning, not higher education, is the primary subject of this book.

What will you find out about it? The five chapters of part 1 examine varied aspects of the history of higher learning in the United States. The four chapters of part 2 analyze certain problems in higher learning today, three of them venturing solutions. The reader will discover that, even as a critic of the present, I cannot help but think as a historian.

This is not such a bad habit. A lot of hand-wringing goes on in print about present ills of higher learning, and I do my share in part 2. But there are surprising blind spots in our historical knowledge of how higher learning got to where it is today. Part 1 aims to improve our hindsight. Historians have taught us much about the evolution of institutions and practices in colleges and universities, less about intellectual developments. A handful of superb books and a larger number of workmanlike studies do investigate the intellectual history of higher education and academic knowledge. Yet much more remains to be explored. A few essays cannot discover a massive amount, but those in part 1 do poke into some particularly dark corners.

Written over fifteen years and on varied occasions, the historical chapters do not pursue one topic with the singlemindedness of a bloodhound. They are more like a mutt that returns time after time to worry its bone—in this case gnawing on different edges of four problems in modern academic history. No essay treats every one of the four themes; no essay ignores all of them.

The first topic is the influence of language study in the history of knowledge. Before the late–nineteenth century, all sorts of academic inquiries into language and literature were grouped under the broad umbrella of "philology," a word now grown so obscure that many well-educated Americans go blank when they hear it.[2] Those who recognize it commonly take "philology" to mean grammatical and etymological scrutiny of Greek and Roman texts. This was indeed among the term's nineteenth-century meanings, and not the least notable. But "philology" then also referred to biblical criticism; theoretical linguistics; literary criticism and literary history; inquiry into the history of a language or languages (including comparative grammar and etymology); the study of "exotic" tongues (such as Amerindian or Polynesian languages); and even unbridled speculation on the origin and evolution of language.

Philology towered over higher learning during the nineteenth century. In the forms of biblical criticism and classical scholarship, it reigned as queen of the sciences in German universities through the first half of the century—a time when these universities provided the prime example of erudition for the rest of Europe and America. New disciplines as diverse as anthropology and art history spun off from philology or copied its methods.[3] When American undergraduate education was reformed in the last quarter of the century (leading to today's curricula), philology animated the new humanities, then the heart of liberal education.[4] The most spectacular philological coup was the reconstruction of Indo-European, the lost ancestor language of the major tongues of Europe and India: an achievement as widely trumpeted as Darwin's and far more generally admired.[5] Yet until very recently American historians have paid more attention to football than philology.[6] No competent scholar would dream of similarly ignoring the natural sciences. Several of the following chapters begin to atone for this baffling sin of omission by tracing a few of the tracks of philology in other fields of knowledge.

The second theme weaving in and out of these essays is historicism. Philological research in ancient texts requires careful attention to historical contexts. As suggested in chapter 6, historical contextualization by biblical and classical philologists nurtured historicism: the inclination to regard the ideas, institutions, and behavior of a people as the product of its history. This attitude came to maturity in the nineteenth century, an Age of History. Schemes of historical development pervaded thinking in fields from biology to theology, from philosophy to ethnology, from sociology to law. Obsession with history, though, is not necessarily historicism. The latter has its own story, much of it still untold. A handful of essays can hardly aspire to comprehensiveness, but the studies in this book uncover aspects of historicism's fortunes both in erudite discourse and in educational developments.

A third theme is the advance of disciplinary specialization and its doppelgänger, the fragmentation of academic knowledge. Both became conspicuous in the United States in the two decades prior to 1900, inspiring argument and confusion. They found their natural home in the new graduate school, and chapter 4 untangles some knots in its history. But coping with the consequences of specialization and fragmentation was a problem far from unique to graduate education. Indeed, offsetting their effects first came to seem urgent in the undergraduate curriculum. After all, higher education showed its most public face and earned its bread and butter in the college classroom. Chapter 3 focuses on this touchy domain. It looks at how specialization and fragmentation intersected with another controversial development: the splintering of the Protestant framework that traditionally encased American colleges.

Religion and its retreat from academe supplies the fourth and most insistent theme of these essays. For a long time, historians of higher education pretty much ignored religion. In the last decade or two they have panted to make up for lost time. To call religion a cottage industry within the history of higher learning hardly does justice to the hubbub. Amid smokestacks belching and machinery clanking, the essays here would seem only a few widgets tumbling off the assembly line. But they show at least some marks of original artisanship, exhibiting features not delineated by earlier historians. One essay shows how religious and linguistic anxieties combined to produce an epistemological crisis in learned circles in Boston in the 1830s: a seemingly provincial story with large implications. Another looks at how a leading Protestant intellectual responded when orthodoxy collided with historicism, a reaction exposing a fault line in American Christianity. A third chapter examines specific reshaping of college curricula to counter the "secularization of the academy," revisions responsible for the prominence of the humanities in American education.

Taken as a whole, the essays in part 1 do not present one coherent history; but they give overlapping, crisscrossing perspectives on a single story, radiating out from these four themes like the intersecting circles of ripples flowing out from four pebbles tossed close together into a single pond. And the story is not a minor one. This is why it makes sense now to bring these essays (but not others of mine) together between two covers, even though all were written as occasional pieces.

Their (re)publication here also owes something to a peculiarity of my scholarly temperament. I think in terms of writing books, not articles.

A lecture or conference paper gets composed often because some friend twisted my arm; and, once delivered, it generally sits in my files unless that friend or another asks to print it. Although most of these chapters have earlier appeared in print *somewhere*, these somewheres are sometimes where few readers of history would look. If these pieces, collectively, are worth considering by other students of history—and I have come to believe they are—making them into a book is the only realistic way to make them accessible.

Born as occasional essays rather than out of research for a monograph, all the historical writings here share another trait. All are more or less speculative. I by no means deem this a bad thing; speculation, if firmly grounded, can open up new perspectives. But it does give them a special flavor, one that may turn a more austere historian's stomach. The usual process is the following: an essay rests on respectably solid knowledge of a particular case, interesting, I hope, in itself; on the basis of that case, I extrapolate broader conclusions that, if true, would alter our view of some matter of historical importance. To exemplify: good archival research supports what I write about the University of Michigan; but, admittedly, what is true at Michigan may turn out to be false elsewhere.

In every case, I believe my speculations to be legitimate—that is, more likely true than false and important enough to justify the trouble of finding out. After all, the nineteenth century is a field I have tilled for a long time, particularly those sections of it where academic knowledge once flourished. Even my flights of fancy take off from familiar ground. But I have not done the monographic research and, on most topics treated here, do not mean to. My fondest hope is that another historian will. I do not mind at all being shown wrong. I mind terribly letting big historical problems go without at least a stab at a solution—even if all I accomplish is to supply some future researcher with a poorly drawn sketch map.

The chapters of part 1 share something else. They were all delivered in larval form in the seminar of the Centre d'Etudes Nord-américaines (CENA) of the Ecole des Hautes Etudes en Sciences Sociales (EHESS) in Paris. Over the last decade I have had the privilege of settling in as a sort of permanent guest at EHESS. CENA, my home-away-from-home there, has in a relatively short life grown into a remarkable center for scholarly exchange among French and American historians of the United States. The faculty permanently affiliated with it—Jean Heffer, François Weil, Pap Ndiaye—rank among the most knowledgeable and acute American historians of my acquaintance. But their intellectual environment differs from that of American historians in the United States: they daily interact in a sea of *non*-Americanists; they observe the United States from a European angle of vision; they are together responsible for all doctoral training in American history, not merely one subspecialty. Perhaps for these reasons, they are broader in outlook than United States–based Americanists, unhobbled by the provinciality that too often lames American history.

Reactions in CENA seminars to my work in progress have pushed me to think more expansively and more imaginatively, to make connections with historiographies beyond those of the United States. If the historical essays in this volume have any special virtue, it is a certain breadth of view, often deriving from comments made in Paris. One has to walk away from the tree one is staring at before one realizes there is a forest. Too often, American historians lack this clarifying separation between themselves and their subject. There is now a move in professional historical circles to "internationalize" American history. This would be greatly to the good if talk extended to action. As of now, history departments in the United States balk at such tiny steps as serious foreign-language requirements for their graduate students in United States history.

So far, patient reader, you have sat through a prolonged dissection of the peculiarities of the first five chapters of this book. You may wonder how the quiet historian of part 1 became the ranting propagandist of part 2. The connection between historian and polemicist is, in fact, pretty direct, the explanation correspondingly brief. When in the middle and late 1980s I began working on the history of higher learning, I uncovered—so I thought—roots of certain present dilemmas. My historical excavations suggested no obvious solutions to current problems. (History rarely does, unless subjected to the rack; and then it lies.) But they did clarify some losses and gains.

Prominent among both debits and assets was the fading of religion from academic work. The gains from the secularization of knowledge (to use a hopelessly protean phrase, for which no good substitute exists) probably do not need rehearsing. They include the removal of religiously based restraints on inquiry (mind-forged manacles at least as often as external ones); the opening of new ways of thinking; and the eventual admission to full academic citizenship of scholars once marginalized, in the United States notably Jews and Catholics.

Inevitably, a secularized academy finds it harder to see the losses from its secularization, but they came to seem real to me. The losses included the fragmentation of knowledge explored in my historical writings. But I also observed the marooning of research, especially in the human sciences, on a kind of island of modernity; secularization cut research off from millennia of sometimes acute thinking about persisting human problems just because the thinking proceeded from theistic assumptions. I saw no reason why gratitude for the gains from secularization should prevent us from trying to recoup the losses as best we could without returning to quasi-ecclesial hegemony.

So, when presented a chance, I began to speak out on the present state of religion in intellectual life and to commend what seemed to me opportunities worth seizing. Talking about the role of religion in higher learning provoked derisory hints that I do something about it. In 1995 I moved from the University of Michigan to the University of Notre Dame, partly with "doing something" in mind, though just what remained vague. In 1996, together with a philosopher from Yale tolerant of a historian's foibles, I undertook to moderate a three-year national argument among scholars and administrators called the Lilly Seminar on Religion and Higher Education. In 1997 I became the director of a new research institute aiming at encouraging the use of Catholic intellectual traditions (as well as those of other Christian churches, Judaism, and Islam) in otherwise "secular" scholarship. Such activities, as much as the historical research that first piqued my interest in religion and higher learning, supply the broad context for the essays in part 2. More precise contextualization can await the essays themselves.

Presented on diverse occasions over the course of two decades, the essays in both parts have their own irreducible particularities as well as share the common themes broached above. Rather than homogenize everything into a factitious contemporaneity, I have chosen to let each piece stand pretty much as originally written. This includes the scholarly apparatus, although I did add a handful of citations to call attention to recent publications that I want readers to know about. I silently corrected a few solecisms and misleading phrasings: in this respect, too, eschewing a foolish consistency. There are hobgoblins aplenty to haunt any sane person at the start of the twenty-first century without adding another. Both the reader and I owe a large debt to Ingrid Muller for her intelligent and attentive editing of the manuscript. The staff of the University of Notre Dame Press sets a high standard of competence and efficiency; it has been a pleasure especially to work with Barbara Hanrahan and Rebecca DeBoer.

Two of the essays and this introduction were written under the looming presence of the high peaks of the Sangre de Cristo range in northern New Mexico. Somewhere around eleven or twelve thousand feet our scribblings fall into perspective.

El Prado, New Mexico
May 2002

PART ONE
Historical Studies

CHAPTER ONE

Language, Religion, and Knowledge in Nineteenth-Century America

The Curious Case of Andrews Norton

Scholars of "the Enlightenment" (which historians nowadays regard as plural, diverse Enlightenments) know that a great load of intellectual baggage was piled atop speculation about language in the eighteenth century. Writings about the origin and nature of language carried analyses of the development of consciousness, the evolution of culture, the limits of human knowledge, and other fundaments of the human sciences. When these linguistic suitcases were eventually unpacked in the nineteenth century, the contents were parceled out to disciplines as various as philosophy, anthroplogy, physiology, and, to be sure, linguistics.

But when did the unpacking occur, and were the contents dispersed everywhere uniformly and at the same time? At least since the studies of Henry May in the 1970s, American historians have appreciated how deeply Enlightenment, especially its Scottish variant, penetrated the culture of the new American republic and how long Enlightened habits of thought cohabited in the United States with younger, romantic or Victorian, ones. A few scholars have noted specifically the persistence of linguistic speculations redolent of the eighteenth century.

Chapter 1 pursues these hints and explores a revealing episode in the entwined American histories of language, religion, and knowledge. This episode, I suggest, may reveal one link in a chain of American thinking about language that is now largely buried but was once of far-reaching influence. When I wrote this piece, I was musing mostly to myself; surprisingly, French scholars proved interested. I hope publication in English might provoke other historians to find out how much truth my speculations contained.

During the late–eighteenth and nineteenth centuries, philology—the study of language—sent its generative currents through the intellectual life of Europe and America. It animated forms of knowledge all over the academic countryside. The evolutionary tree, now covered with Darwin's leaves, grew originally in comparative linguistics. Lewis Henry Morgan forged the anthropological concept of kinship on the anvil of philology. Until the nomothetic natural sciences usurped its throne in the last third of the nineteenth century, philology (broadly defined) possibly provided the dominant model for erudition.[1]

Possibly—for we are only beginning to glimpse how pervasively language study, in its heyday, gave structure to scholarship. Since its legacy survives in some of the ways in which we still construct knowledge, the excavation of nineteenth-century philology becomes an effort simultaneously at historical reconstruction and contemporary self-understanding.[2] Some of the impetus for this research doubtless derived from the writings of the French post-structuralists of the 1960s, with their special concerns for the shape of knowledge and the shaping force of language. But in form and method recent historians of philology and language theories have bypassed postmodernism's funhouse mirrors. It is through the traditional lenses of intellectual history and *Wissenschaftsgeschichte* that scholars have begun to survey the philological terrain in Europe.[3]

America has gotten only a glance now and then.[4] The neglect is understandable: the giants of philology were all European. Yet language study in America, at least until midcentury, displayed two features of distinctive interest. One was its frequent embroilment in theological controversy, the other its persisting recurrence to philosophical problems. The theological inclination owed a lot to the origins of American philology in biblical scholarship, the philosophical to the continuing resonance in America of the Scottish Enlightenment, and both to the shaping of American intellectual life by Reformed Protestantism. These distinguishing characteristics seem to have faded in the second half of the nineteenth century, as their causes receded.

Indeed, by the 1850s or thereabouts the broad river of American language study was starting to divide into distinct currents. One spilled into classical philology, whose most distinguished figure was Basil L. Gildersleeve (1831–1924) of Johns Hopkins University and whose adherents clustered around the American Philological Association (founded 1869). Another flowed into English, German, and Romance philology, represented most eminently by Francis J. Child (1825–1896) of Harvard and contained in the Modern Languages Association (1883). A third carried students of "oriental" languages, outstanding among them the Sanskritist William Dwight Whitney (1827–1894) of Yale, who found their professional home in the American Oriental Society (1842). (Naturally, the orientalists took special interest in European efforts to reconstruct the putative ancestral Indo-European language, but apparently no Americans actually worked in that line.) Yet a fourth was biblical criticism, so roiled by theological storms that only a minority of its practitioners joined the Society for Biblical Literature and Exegesis (1880). Though all philologists in some sense, these diverse groups had before 1900 drifted almost beyond hailing distance of each other.[5]

The story was very different earlier. Then, biblical scholars might argue with bankers about the origin of language, and theologians quarrel with orientalists about its epistemological limits. That much is clear. But how common were such discussions about language? How extensive? Did they display any larger pattern? Did they relate to European scholarship on language? Or to the later contours of American academic philology? Did they entangle themselves in the large questions of religious faith and epistemological uncertainty that haunted Americans and Europeans in the nineteenth century? Can they help us in excavating the fossil bones of American intellectual life, in reconstructing the skeleton hidden under the well-padded flesh of Victorian knowledge?

Large questions, these. Answers will come slowly, uncertainly, and only when we have explored much more of philology and its environs in America. But sometimes a little story, an anecdote even, can set us to sniffing down interesting trails. Such a story can already be told. It concerns Andrews Norton.

Of all the minor characters in American intellectual or religious history, Andrews Norton must rank as one of the least understood and most abused. Norton was one of the three leading biblical scholars in America before 1850, an important conduit for the flow into the United States of German theology and philosophy.[6] Yet he is remembered, if at all, chiefly as the starchy Harvard professor who helped to launch American

Transcendentalism as a self-conscious movement by trying to squelch Ralph Waldo Emerson and his fellow idealist, George Ripley. Consequently, Norton's doctrines and reputation have fallen mostly into the hands of scholars devoted to Transcendentalism. These men and women, though as a body admirable historians and critics, have naturally inclined to somewhat partisan enthusiasm for Emerson, Ripley, and company, and to short shrift for Norton. Historians of Unitarianism, in which Norton played a formative role, have been kinder.[7] Still, it is not far from the mark to say that Norton usually comes off as something of a reactionary, learned, to be sure, but notable for the dryness of his erudition and the blinkers on his vision. And, to be fair, Norton's irrepressible urges to priggery and pedantry give considerable leeway for caricature.

Yet it ought to be, at least, surprising that a man regarded in his own time as the leading light among Unitarian intellectuals—a cosmopolitan, indeed advanced, thinker—proved so blind and narrow, so authoritarian and repressive when challenged by Emerson. Did Norton have nothing to say beyond the predictable conservative anxieties recorded in the standard histories of the Transcendentalist controversy? Was there nothing in his attack on Emerson and Ripley that might still repay attention?

Indeed there was. Norton saw quite clearly some deeply troubling implications of Transcendentalism. Because of, specifically, his own studies of language, he saw these more clearly than anyone else involved. And there may be matters of larger import lurking in his concerns. Exploration of Norton's linguistic and epistemological charges against the Transcendentalists may even help to open a vein of inquiry in nineteenth-century American intellectual history that has until now rarely been worked.

First, however, a few biographical facts are in order, since Andrews Norton is hardly a household name. Norton was born in 1786 in the village of Hingham, south of Boston. His father was a substantial shopkeeper, a man of some consequence in the town, his mother a woman from a family of similar local stature. He entered Harvard College in 1801 as a sophomore, the youngest member of his class, graduating in 1804. At college Norton developed marked scholarly and literary tastes, at one time nursing the ambition to become a great translator of Italian literature who would introduce Americans to the glories of Dante and Ariosto. He was also a pious boy from a pious Unitarian family, so his literary inclinations seemed to point him toward a ministerial career in one of Boston's elegant pulpits.⁸

This ambition, like many others, was to be frustrated. After the usual couple of years of informal postgraduate theological study—in his case at Harvard, with Henry Ware, the most prominent Unitarian divine—Norton began to seek a pulpit. But Norton did not shine as a preacher, and his sometimes acerb intellectualism did not strike everyone as pastoral. Five years after graduating from Harvard, he still had not found a church. Finally, a new congregation in the rude outreaches of Augusta, Maine, invited him to serve a six-month candidacy. Norton sighed and headed for the frontier. But the pioneer spirit was not in him, and after a few weeks he gratefully seized the chance of a tutorship at the young Bowdoin College, on the Maine coast. The year at Bowdoin he spent longing for the intellectual comradeship of Boston and Cambridge.

In the spring of 1810 he returned—still dependent on his father's income. In 1811–12 he served as tutor of mathematics (of all things) at Harvard, but resigned after a year to start a magazine, the *General Repository and Review*. The *Repository* provided an important forum for the emerging Unitarian movement but not a living for Norton: its combative style alienated readers, and its abstract theological articles bored them. But Norton's acuity and theological interests paid off. When the magazine went under in 1813, Harvard appointed him college librarian and Dexter Lecturer on the Criticism and Interpretation of the Scripture. His career had fairly begun.⁹

It was to be a career filled with frustration. His earliest disciple and closest friend, Charles Eliot, died in 1813 at the dawn of brilliant promise. The only other student in whom Norton invested enormously of his hopes, George Bancroft, turned away from Norton's principles and became a bitter mockery. Norton's Harvard superiors stymied his academic ambitions at pregnant moments. He expected, in 1814, to get the Greek professorship endowed by Charles Eliot's father Samuel; it went instead to the slick Edward Everett. When Harvard Divinity School was organized in 1819, Norton had every right to assume that he would be elevated to the new professorship of Scripture; but the Harvard Corporation, worried by the bluntness of Norton's theological polemics, tried to shift him into the college's professorship of rhetoric. Only frantic backstage maneuvering got Norton appointed to a faculty in which everyone knew that he was the preeminent scholar. In the early 1820s he led an attempt to reform the governance of Harvard; the Corporation blocked him. He continued to clash with the authorities for the rest of the decade.

All the while, Norton was trying to complete his masterwork, *The Genuineness of the Gospels*, a project that he had expected to occupy six months when he began it in 1819 but that eventually filled twenty-five years and three fat volumes. In 1821 Norton married Catharine Eliot, sister of his dead friend, Charles. Their father, Samuel Eliot, had recently died, leaving what was at that point the largest estate in Boston's history. By this marriage Norton achieved at a stroke assured social position and much, much money. This fortune enabled him to retire from Harvard in 1830, owing in part to worsening health but as much to frustration with the university. For the rest of his sixty-seven years he pursued the life of an independent scholar on his Shady Hill estate in Cambridge, where he continued to dominate the intellectual horizon of Unitarianism.[10]

It was from his retreat at Shady Hill that Andrews Norton burst, furious, into the Boston press in the fall of 1836. The *casus belli* was a review in the Unitarian *Christian Examiner* by the Reverend George Ripley of James Martineau's *Rationale of Religious Enquiry*.[11] Ripley used the review as an occasion to put forward the intuitionist doctrines of religious knowledge that he and other Transcendentalists had borrowed from German idealism, principally via Samuel Taylor Coleridge and Victor Cousin. In this intuitionist spirit, Ripley attacked the use of external evidences to support Christianity, especially the necessity of miracles to attest the authority of Jesus' divine commission. Ripley thus traduced the central dogma, not only of Unitarian defenses of Christianity in general, but of Andrews Norton's *Genuineness of the Gospels* in particular. Worse, he had done so in the closest thing the Unitarians had to an official journal, a magazine brought to birth and nurtured by, among others, Andrews Norton.

Norton had a reputation for "strong but rigidly chastened passions." This time they escaped discipline. A biting letter to the editor of the *Examiner* declared Norton "much astonished and I may add shocked" at Ripley's doctrines. He asked the editor to announce that Norton had severed his ties with the magazine, lest he be taken as countenancing teachings that "sap the very foundations of religion." The editor, however, apparently declined to pour salt into the wounds that Unitarians were inflicting on each other. When the Unitarian weekly newspaper, the *Christian Register*, also refused to publish Norton's protest, he turned to the secular newspapers. The *Boston Daily Advertiser* of 5 November carried a strongly worded letter dissociating Norton from the *Examiner*'s review and calling Ripley's opinions "vitally injurious to the cause of religion, because tending to destroy faith in the only evidence on which the truth of Christianity *as a revelation* must ultimately rest." Ripley replied four days later, and what Norton had long expected—a "great controversy respecting the truth of Christianity itself"—had now begun.[12]

The next eruption occurred two years later. The senior class of the Harvard Divinity School invited the Reverend Ralph Waldo Emerson, late pastor of the Second Church, Boston—now occasionally supplying pulpits from his home in Concord—to deliver the annual graduation address. On Sunday, 15 July 1838, Emerson preached his celebrated Divinity School address.[13] He rehearsed the themes sketched by Ripley, at greater length and with greater eloquence and with still greater offense to Norton. Emerson praised intuitive knowledge of God, attacked the use of miracles as evidence of Jesus' divine authority, heaped scorn on historical and institutional Christianity—and he pronounced these heresies in the sanctum of New England Unitarianism, as advice to the rising generation of ministers. Norton was livid.

This time he turned immediately to the *Daily Advertiser*, inserting in the 27 August issue a sarcastic attack on what he called the "New School in Literature and Religion." In the succeeding weeks the *Advertiser* carried several articles by Norton and by various adversaries, including a heated exchange with the editor of the *Christian Register*, who resisted Norton's effort to read Emerson publicly out of Christianity. Finally, Norton's brother-in-law, Samuel A. Eliot, a leading Unitarian layman, intervened to cool tempers and at least keep the denomination's civil war out of the newspapers.[14] However, Eliot and much of the Unitarian clergy vigorously applauded Norton's calmer, full-length riposte to Emerson: "A Discourse on the Latest Form of Infidelity," delivered to a newly formed association of Divinity School alumni on 19 July 1839.[15]

The pamphlet war raged on, but its further convulsions need not detain us. It is the reasons for Norton's fury that are of real interest. His combative temper played a role. It had very nearly cost him his professorship in

1819, and he had early adopted as his motto against Trinitarian Congregationalists "*Babylon* est delenda." His own mentor, Henry Ware, had in 1822 dressed him down in print for his sharp tongue. Moreover, the fact that Emerson and Ripley had been his own students at the Divinity School must have stung deeply.[16]

But no one has ever believed that personality traits or personal animus mainly fired Norton's wrath. Perry Miller regarded a "division over the nature of man" as central to the controversy: Transcendentalist "glorification" of human nature versus a lingering Calvinist "debasement" that still infected Unitarianism.[17] There is little evidence of this particular Calvinist ghost in the Unitarians' attic; but Norton did worry that Transcendentalism would persuade Americans that Unitarianism was at heart not Christian—a slur that orthodox Trinitarians had been trying to stick onto Unitarians for decades.

He likely feared, too, that the Transcendentalist rebellion, with its contempt for history and institutions, threatened the bases of social authority. There may even have been an element of generational conflict: Norton was fifty years old in 1836; Ripley at thirty-four was the oldest of the Transcendentalist ministers. More specifically—and historians have not explicitly noticed this—Norton spoke up for the claims of academic expertise, of the kind of specialized knowledge possessed only by accomplished scholars. In this respect, strange as it sounds, the Transcendentalist controversy was a minor episode in the process of academic professionalization.

And, of course, there was the question of miracles. Norton, in common even with Unitarians who regretted the acerbity of his attack, believed that Christ's miracles provided the only sure proof of the authority of the Bible. To deny miracles was to corrode faith in Christianity as a revealed religion. Not for nothing is this pamphlet war sometimes called "the miracles controversy." There was no shortage of reasons for Norton to be upset.

But another well-known element in the controversy deserves deeper exploration: the clash between the Transcendentalists' intuitionist view of knowledge and the other Unitarians' commitment to a Lockean sensationalist epistemology, as mediated by the Scottish common-sense philosophers. It was this commitment that was registered in the standard Unitarian insistence on "external evidences" for Christianity, such as historically attested miracles.[18]

Yet Norton shared these principles with Unitarian leaders who were appalled by the vehemence of his campaign against Transcendentalism, leaders who clearly did *not* share his sense of imminent danger. Norton's greater alarm seems to have arisen from a connection in his mind between these epistemological problems and another set of worries: his concerns about the Transcendentalists' use of language.

Students of the miracles controversy have paid little attention to Norton's linguistic concerns. This neglect seems very strange in light of two facts: first, scholars *have* noticed Norton's studies of biblical language as one source of Transcendentalist literary style; and, second, complaints about abuse of language crop up constantly in Norton's polemics.[19] In his first response to Ripley—that unpublished letter to the *Christian Examiner*—Norton decried "the mysticism and unmeaningness of much of [Ripley's] discussion." His first published reply to Emerson's Divinity School address described Transcendentalism as an offshoot of German idealist speculation and immediately attacked the "obscurity" of "the worst German speculatists." The "great truths with which they are laboring," Norton pointed out with his habitual sarcasm, "are unutterable in words to be understood by common minds. To such minds they seem nonsense, oracles as obscure as those of Delphi." Throughout the controversy, Norton accused Emerson of "using words in a new, arbitrary, false sense."[20]

This line of attack does not figure much in Norton's most widely read polemic, the *Discourse on the Latest Form of Infidelity*. Its recession there perhaps helps to explain why scholars have neglected the theme. But the tactics of the *Discourse* fitted its purpose, which was to insist on the anti-Christian character of Emerson's doctrine, not to expound at length why his teachings were dangerous. Norton was, after all, preaching to an audience of pastors, not lecturing to students or scholars.

Yet the long "note" appended to the *Discourse* when published—a tail that ultimately grew longer than the dog—returned emphatically to Norton's larger point. These "Remarks on the Modern German School of Infidelity" treated Transcendentalism and all other varieties of "German infidelity" as a disease of language. The "first stage" on the road away from Christianity toward atheism was, according to Norton, "the stage of religious mysticism and of the abuse of religious language." (Notice the linkage between mysticism and linguistic failure.) Norton identified the "German infidel school of theology" with such writers as

Schleiermacher, Strauss, De Wette, Neander, and Paulus.[21] He discovered their roots in Spinoza and Kant and blamed the spread of such ideas in part on the malign influence of Goethe. Their leading characteristics he traced to a primal "confusion of thought and unmeaning language." Only by misuse of words could they persuade themselves that "Christian faith has its origin in the mind itself, independently of the Christian revelation"; and from that point their slide into infidelity became, Norton thought, virtually inevitable.[22]

Yet Norton was second to none in appreciating the erudition of German theologians. How could such eminent scholars have fallen into linguistic error? In part, Norton blamed the German language itself, in which, he claimed, "the significations of many words are more unsteady and uncertain than in our own, or in the Southern languages of Europe." But he also pointed to the character of the times. The work of Kant had unsettled philosophical and theological ideas in Germany. "Whenever any great revolution takes place in men's opinions," according to Norton, "mysticism flourishes."

> The mind loses its customary landmarks, distrusts its former belief, renounces its former guides, and, leaving the beaten path, becomes the bewildered follower of him who professes most boldly his acquaintance with the unexplored region on which it is entering. It is confused between new and old opinions, and sees nothing distinctly. Words lose their former meanings, and acquire no stable significations instead; old errors and essential truths are abandoned in common, and paradoxical novelties are enunciated in a new language, understood neither by those who use nor by those who listen to it.

Hence arose the "crabbed, obscure, and unintelligible" metaphysics of German scholars, filled with "confusion of thought" and "unintelligible language." "Propositions are so vaguely expressed as to present no meaning on which the mind can rest." Yet the culprits themselves and their disciples remained blissfully aware of their own linguistic crimes. "He whose own conceptions are vague and inconsistent is not sensible of the want of definiteness or meaning in what he reads. He attaches some unformed notions to words that in fact convey no coherent ideas; and may regard himself in consequence as a profound thinker, able to discover a meaning which less wise men cannot see." Emerson, Ripley, and their ilk had only followed these German speculators into the mists.[23]

It is tempting to believe that intellectual and social conservatism, an almost inbred revulsion from novelty, set Norton against the Transcendentalists and led him to fear that they would "become the mystagogues of no one knows how large a portion of the community." Norton *was* a social conservative, and sometimes this explanation sounds about right, as when he lit into William Ellery Channing for using slogans like Freedom of Thought to "cover over and countenance and encourage" Transcendental doctrines "extravagant in language" and "licentious in speculation." But Norton was not, intellectually and religiously, a conservative, despite the image that most historians have made of him. His stinging assaults on orthodoxy earlier in his career ought to have laid that notion to rest. Ripley knew this well. As he reminded Norton, "we are both too deeply laden with [heresies], to make the spectacle of our flinging stones at each other any thing but ludicrous." Nor was it only Trinitarian orthodoxy that Norton showed himself willing to unsettle. He also let fly at Unitarian beliefs. One Unitarian historian wrote that the "first shock" to "the received liberal theology of the day" came from the biblical scholarship of Norton and his disciple, George Noyes.[24]

We have to conclude that Norton's linguistic concerns were substantive in origin, not temperamental or narrowly ideological. They sprang from his basically Lockean theory of knowledge. Norton believed that all knowledge came from the external physical world through the senses. He did not, of course, mean that all knowledge was knowledge *about* the physical world. Revelations from God provided (as did the structure of nature) reliable knowledge of spiritual reality; but we could know that revelations were truly revelations only by external evidence of divine authority: hence the importance of miracles. As Norton wrote in 1837:

> Religion, in any proper sense of the word, is not an intuitive thing. The history of man, to say nothing of the very nature of the human mind, proves the contrary. Nor can it consist in feelings alone. Our feelings, to have any rational origin or foundation, must refer to objects and facts; and of the existence of these objects and facts we must have proof.

Norton recognized no difference in kind between scientific and religious knowledge—a principle for which Ripley took him to task. The Transcendentalists, with a very different view of religious knowledge, tended to regard truth as relative and partial; they habitually asked, not which of two competing doctrines was true and which false, but which contained *more* truth. But Norton took a yes-or-no approach to knowledge, hence insisted on a sharp and clear-cut distinction between truth and falsity—a judgment that could be determined by testing a proposition against external evidence.[25]

Language provided the essential linkage in this rational-empirical connection of proposition and evidence. Words must express precisely the meaning of a proposition, for its correspondence with reality could be examined only insofar as the proposition itself could be dissected, analyzed, inspected. For the same reason, external reality must be cast in unambiguous statement; words must point unequivocally to "objects and facts" in the physical world. Norton never expected human beings to attain perfect knowledge or to rid language of all ambiguity. But he insisted that certainty of knowledge increased directly as language grew more precise, that we drift away from truth as we allow our language to become looser.

Here the Transcendentalists sinned. Germanic "abuse of language" substituted "phantoms" for the "realities of revelation." The Germans (and by implication their American disciples) had given the *name* of Christianity "to multiform and unstable speculations of their own, unconnected with any established facts or principles; and in framing which it seems to have been forgotten, that what is proposed for belief requires some evidence of its truth."[26] Use of Christian terminology grew more and more hollow, lost more and more of its substantive content, its correspondence with knowable reality. Here lay the most insidious danger of the German "infidels"' abuse of language, for it encouraged believers to slide insensibly from Christianity into a vague theism and, finally, into atheism—without at any point before the end realizing what lay ahead.

Hence Norton's primary objections to Transcendentalism depended on his theory of knowledge: a fact long known by historians, though perhaps not enough stressed. Indeed, Transcendentalism threatened not only religion but the bases of all knowledge. In turn, Norton's analysis of *how* Transcendentalism threatened knowledge devolved directly from his theories of language, a fact apparently never before noted.

Yet Norton's theories of language were scarcely new in the 1830s. Discussion of language bulks large in his writings from his opening article in the first issue of the *General Repository and Review* in 1812. This essay, "A Defence of Liberal Christianity," took aim at the orthodox Trinitarian Congregationalists. Norton argued that they misunderstood the Bible because they treated the language of Scripture as if it had a "true meaning" "insulated" from the "peculiarities of expression characteristic of the writer, or of the age or country to which he belonged; they pay but little regard to the circumstances in which he wrote, or to those of the persons whom he addressed." Put more generally, the orthodox distorted the Bible's meaning by detaching words from their concrete, socially conditioned context. The charge Norton leveled against the Transcendentalists twenty-five years later ran in the same vein: they, too, distorted the meaning of words by discarding their common, socially conditioned definitions.[27]

Norton's sensitivity to language possibly owed something to his involvement with poetry. He won a minor reputation as a poet and hymn writer himself, and he also promoted British poets in the United States, notably Felicia Hemans and Joanna Baillie. Authorship of even "a few poems of surpassing beauty" may seem odd in a man whose prose, according to one admirer, had "the same sort of effect upon the mind as a geometrical demonstration." In fact, Norton's poetry, too, had a Euclidean feel. "His poetry, like his prose," said a sympathetic critic, "is characterized by a careful choice of words, a rare purity of diction, and a studied preciseness in the expression of thought."[28] His poems give the impression of a man less interested in conveying a state of mind or feeling than in replicating in the reader's mind a clear sensory image.

Poetry may have raised Norton's consciousness of words, but his ideas about language took form in the matrix of his biblical scholarship. In the first course of his Dexter Lectures on biblical criticism, delivered in 1813, he returned again and again to the theme of language.[29] The nineteenth-century reader, he argued, with his "modern doctrines, prejudices, and associations," faced enormous barriers to understanding the "oriental style" of the New Testament. The writers of biblical times characteristically "embodie[d] intellectual & moral ideas . . . under sensible images." These "expressions . . . will certainly be mistaken by him who judges of them according to the analogy of our common use of language & puts that sense upon the words in which we should ourselves employ them."

But problems of comprehension hardly ceased with the fairly straightforward need to distinguish between metaphorical and literal styles. For a word is rarely, if ever, "the definite expression of one certain idea, or series of ideas, & of this alone." Rather, the "circumstances in which it is used, are often a necessary commentary for defining its signification." Norton meant "circumstances" broadly. The critic must learn not only the characteristic style of the period, but the idiosyncrasies of a given writer, the range of reference permitted by his social position and intellectual background, the conditions and outlook of the people to whom he directed his message, the historical circumstances under which he wrote, the social and economic character of his society, and so forth. In these lectures, and in Norton's 1819 *Inaugural Discourse on the Extent and Relations of Theology*, a reasonably clear picture of the nature of language emerges.[30] Language operates as a web of meaning, integral with the more extensive web of human social existence: each word takes its meaning from its relations both to other words and to specific tangible referents.

This image of language led Norton to a theory of how the mind processes words:

> Amid the varieties of meaning, & shades of meaning, which the same words may often express with equal propriety, there can be nothing in the mere words alone to decide our choice. The mind must decide for itself from other considerations. In a well known language, and upon a subject with which we are familiar, the decision is instantaneous. In a language with which we are imperfectly acquainted, or upon a subject of any difficulty, the successive acts of the mind may be easily recognized. Whenever we read, a continued exercise of reason & judgment is necessary, to place before us that meaning of words & sentences which was intended by the writer, distinct from all others which they are capable of expressing. This process is continually going on in the mind, & whether the motions are so rapid as to be invisible, or so much retarded as to be perceived without difficulty, they are essentially of the same character.

Possibly Norton's own digestion of foreign languages (he eventually learned to read at least six) helped him to arrive independently at this theory. He acknowledged debts to Locke, Dugald Stewart, and Jean

LeClerc. But he alleged that the "necessity of our thus interpreting the greater part of all language" had not previously been "very explicitly stated."[31] His claim to originality, however, is of less interest than the broad context into which Norton pulled these speculations.

For he immediately applied his language theories not only to the operations of mind, but to questions of knowledge and truth. Leaving aside cases where language was meant only "to produce an effect upon the imagination & feelings," Norton argued that all human knowledge, beyond the immediate perceptions of the isolated individual, depended utterly upon language. He may even have believed that an individual's own perceptions qualified as knowledge only when tested communally through the medium of language, though this remains ambiguous.

Knowledge, of course, did not reside in individual words but in the entire socially conditioned linguistic matrix of a proposition. This web is in constant flux, since the "furniture of men's minds" changes from age to age. Ideas develop and truth progresses; hence new words emerge in the course of social development: some peoples have ideas that others can not. It also follows that ideas cannot arise without words to express them. This bald fact put a sharp limit on communication with God. "Incomprehensible truths *cannot be revealed . . . cannot be expressed* in human language, [which] is formed to express human ideas." No wonder, then, that already in his *Inaugural Discourse* in 1819 Norton was lashing out at intuitionism, German idealist theology, and "truths above reason"—"monstrous shadows," he called them, like those Aeneas met when "entering the confines of the dead."[32]

This outburst brings us back full circle to the attacks on Ripley and Emerson two decades later. What is striking about Norton's linguistic thinking is its breadth of reference, the way in which he deployed his language theories as a key to spring the lock of other fundamental problems of how we know reality. He once even described "the adaptation of means to ends . . . in the works of nature" as "symbolic language."[33] And this particular awareness was, in the end, why Norton reacted so much more vigorously to the Transcendentalist threat than other Unitarian leaders, like Channing, who otherwise shared his theological and philosophical commitments. Norton refused to budge on the evidentiary necessity of miracles for the same reason that he excoriated Emerson's "abuse of language." He believed that, in safeguarding language, he was securing knowledge—most importantly, religious knowledge, but ultimately all knowledge. Norton grew angrier than his colleagues at Emerson because he saw further. His studies in language had alerted him to a danger that the rest only half understood.

Attention to these linguistic concerns illuminates the neglected other side in the Transcendentalist controversy, makes a little clearer what was at stake. We will never understand Norton's horror of Transcendentalism until we understand his ideas about language. But is there reason for anyone not specially invested in Transcendentalism or early Unitarianism to notice Norton and his language theories? A return to the philological context sketched at the beginning of this article suggests an answer—hardly a firm one, but perhaps a promising speculation: some thoughts toward a prospectus for research into the green youth of American philology.

To begin, we need to transport Norton from among the companions with whom he usually resides, Unitarians and Transcendentalists, and place him amid a different batch of associates. Norton was by no means the only person writing about language in antebellum America. Emerson's radically different views in *Nature* (1836) are well known. In 1938 the historian of science Stillman Drake "rediscovered" the *Treatise on Language* of Alexander Bryan Johnson, a banker and (in Drake's opinion) solitary genius of Utica, New York.[34] Starting in the 1950s, the writings on language of the Congregationalist theologian Horace Bushnell began to receive renewed attention.[35] Other antebellum linguistic writers have flitted briefly across the scholarly landscape: William S. Cardell, who published an *Essay on Language* in 1825; Charles Kraitsir, a Hungarian refugee who hung out on the fringes of the Boston-Cambridge intelligentsia; and another language-obsessed banker, Rowland Gibson Hazard.[36] Several others—for example, Bushnell's teacher, Josiah Gibbs, of Yale; or Albert Gallatin and the numerous other investigators of Amerindian languages—could easily extend this list.

One begins to feel that Alexander Bryan Johnson, genius or no, was not so solitary, after all. What to make of this hodgepodge is the problem. In present scholarly perspective, Emerson and Bushnell fit neatly enough into an Anglo-German tradition of speculation about language, most influentially transported to America by James Marsh's 1829 edition of Coleridge's *Aids to Reflection*. The other American language theorists, aside from some connections with eighteenth-century British writers, float in a kind of scholarly void. The few scholars who have noticed them at all have approached them with a view either to explicating the development of literary symbolism or tracking the evolution of Protestant modernist theology. No historian of the United States has really taken language theories seriously as a subject of study in their own right. Indeed, anyone relying on the closest thing to a standard history of American philosophy would never learn that any American besides Emerson wrote about language between 1758 and 1873.[37] So no one seems to have put these writers together and realized that perhaps a philological conversation hummed steadily in America during the first half of the nineteenth century.[38]

Yet what seems to surface in this scattered scholarship—though seen at present only through a glass darkly—is the outline of a long submerged American intellectual tradition. This tradition had well-known eighteenth-century antecedents; for example, Jefferson's linguistic hypotheses in *Notes on the State of Virginia*. But it seems really to have established itself in distinctive form only in the first decades of the next century. An early manifestation was the biblical criticism of Andrews Norton and his friendly adversary, the Congregationalist scholar Moses Stuart.[39] They sparred in very public debates over analogical readings of biblical texts; and, in doing so, they foreshadowed future American divisions over the nature of language (though Stuart, like Norton, seems to have held a basically Lockean conception of language). This tradition, however, then seems—the tentative voice is called for—to have extended far beyond theological boundaries, proceeding through celebrated figures like Emerson, Thoreau, and Melville, as well as obscure ones like Johnson, Kraitsir, and Cardell. It conceivably also included a few academics like Josiah Gibbs, maybe even echoed in Edward E. Salisbury and William Dwight Whitney, among the real founders of specialized philological scholarship in the United States.

But why might these diverse writers have constituted a tradition? And why a specifically American one? That is, what features of their work might have united them in a single universe of discourse, while at the same time setting them apart from European philologists? It was certainly not any agreement about the origins of language, its nature, or its relation to knowledge; for they disagreed ferociously about just such questions.

Yet they asked such questions, and that was what distinguished them. During the Enlightenment, linguistic speculation had served as an important tool for thinking about epistemology, psychology, and anthropology. Thinkers as diverse as Condillac and Monboddo had tried to trace through language, considered in the abstract, the origins of human knowledge, the development of the human mind, the progress of civilization. But early in the nineteenth century European students of language chastened these overblown ambitions.[40] Following the lead of Sir William Jones's celebrated investigations in the 1780s of the affinities between Sanskrit and Greek, philologists repudiated the far-reaching questions of their Enlightenment predecessors, which seemed scientifically unanswerable, in favor of a more limited program of concrete research in actual languages. Bopp, Rask, and Grimm, all of whom published their seminal works just before 1820, converted philology into a more modest enterprise analogous, in their eyes, to comparative anatomy or natural history. The new comparative philology promised to throw light on the origin and history of specific peoples, but not on the universalistic questions asked in the previous century. And when European scholars returned to broader questions about language in the second half of the century, they did so in the very different context of established academic disciplines, with controlling research agenda and evidentiary standards.

American philology, in contrast, seems to have remained stuck in the Enlightenment. For almost a half century after European philologists had spurned freewheeling linguistic hypotheses, American writers on language persisted in focusing on universalistic, speculative questions about the limits of knowledge and the nature of mind. The marginality of America to European intellectual life may have contributed to this apparent persistence in old ways. More likely, the powerful influence of the Scottish Enlightenment in their country encouraged Americans to keep writing about language in the Scottish mode. In any case, discourse about language remained for them a way of talking not about actual languages, but about epistemology and theology.

So it seems fitting that a theological writer like Andrews Norton would stand as a founder of this putative American tradition of language theory. Norton owed his ideas about language to Locke and eighteenth-century writers. His thinking about it took shape in the decade just before Bopp, Rask, and Grimm began to impose their hegemony in Europe. Norton continued to write about language long after their revolution had succeeded across the Atlantic. As a dutiful reader of the latest German philology and biblical criticism, he could hardly have remained unaware of what had happened to linguistic scholarship. Yet he refused to accept the narrowing of the field, and his successors in America proved equally stubborn. They continued to cultivate the broad-gauged Enlightenment approach to language as it grew archaic in the Germanic heartland of philology.

Yet the tradition of speculation that their writings represented has been largely lost to view for over a century. And the excavation of it has barely begun. So it is difficult to foresee how its recovery might affect our understanding of the structure of knowledge in America during the nineteenth century: in the nature of the case, one can hardly trace the ramifications of a network of ideas still mostly buried. Thomas Trautmann has uncovered the tracks of Adam Smith's *Dissertation on the Origin of Languages* in the early thinking about kinship of the seminal anthropologist Lewis Henry Morgan.[41] But such digging remains exceptional.

Still, there is reason to suspect powerful lines of influence lying just beneath the surface. Consider an example. Beginning in the 1850s, a remarkable shift occurred within liberal Protestant theology in America, both Evangelical and non-Evangelical. Statements in the traditional Christian creeds came to be regarded not as factual propositions akin to scientific statements of fact, but rather as "symbols of belief." This shift occurred even among theologians with no debt to Horace Bushnell or to relevant European theologians—and it came at a time when most of these same Protestant liberals were still resisting critical biblical scholarship. Did this reassessment of religious language spring from the arguments among American language theorists about language's capacity to express spiritual truths?[42]

Or take a case from the history of science. J. B. Stallo's *Concepts and Theories of Modern Physics*, published in 1881, has long impressed historians and philosophers of science as an important, yet puzzling, book. Important, because it was one of the first challenges to the conceptual foundations of classical physics, in some ways foreshadowing the revolution in space and time carried through in early-twentieth-century physical theory. Puzzling, because Stallo's critique rested on what he called "the modern theory of cognition," which he never adequately described. The Nobel Prize–winning physicist Percy Bridgman, a close student of Stallo, tried to trace the source of this "modern theory of cognition" but finally could only attribute it to Stallo's "wide reading." Stallo himself assigned its rise vaguely to psychology and to "comparative linguistics." Even Stallo's brief and fuzzy reference makes clear that he could not possibly have had in mind comparative philology à la Bopp, Rask, and Grimm. Something much broader in approach lay behind his thinking. Indeed, his account of cognition bears suspicious affinities to some of the speculations of American language theorists—writings that would have been available to him in Cincinnati and New York, where he began thinking about these issues in the 1850s.[43]

Once could continue to speculate along these lines. Did American language theories figure, for instance, in the background of Chauncey Wright's famous 1873 essay, "The Evolution of Self-Consciousness," and its conception of linguistic signs?[44] Wright was, after all, a close friend and companion in endless talk of Andrews Norton's son, Charles Eliot Norton. And did this tradition then in any way play into the thinking of Wright's young admirer, Charles Sanders Peirce, who went on to found the modern philosophical analysis of semiotics?

Such speculations prove nothing—except that philology in its fecund varieties may present more questions to be answered than we have yet imagined.

CHAPTER TWO

Charles Hodge in the Intellectual Weather of the Nineteenth Century

Charles Hodge stood as a giant in mid-nineteenth-century American intellectual life: a public intellectual (we would now call him) of formidable range and wide recognition. Today only historians and theologically conservative Protestants remember him, but in his day Presbyterians regarded him with much the same awe with which Unitarians gazed upon Andrews Norton.

Hodge allied himself with Norton against the Transcendentalists and German idealism, generally admired Norton's biblical scholarship, but fiercely opposed him in other theological disputes. They agreed on a theory of knowledge descended from Locke via the Scottish Enlightenment. They disagreed not only about Norton's anti-Calvinist Unitarianism but also, perhaps even more fundamentally, about the power of history to shape human knowledge. I venture "even more fundamentally" because Norton regarded Hodge's Calvinism precisely as a historical relic. Norton saw Christianity as historically evolving, with Calvinism (a force for good in a more primitive era) now left behind in the progress of Christians toward fuller truth (to wit, and smugly, Norton's Unitarianism). Such evolutionary ways of thinking about historical change themselves evolved in the Enlightenment discourses about development of language alluded to in chapter 1.

History as a process wherein ideas and beliefs develop from generation to generation: this view more or less appealed to Norton, ultimately appalled Hodge. In turning his back on even a limited historicism, Hodge repudiated the idea that human knowledge was shaped and thus

31

limited by its own past. Yet such an epistemology was coming to define his era—and ours. This chapter suggests why so great an influential became a fossil.

To read Charles Hodge is to place oneself under the orders of a captain who pilots his vessel with rare assurance. The tone of voice is commanding. The range of knowledge is daunting. The hand on the tiller is rock steady.

This unwavering certitude belongs to the polemical style of the Victorian age, and few polemicists in Victorian America could trump Hodge. He never hesitated to put an opponent in debate firmly in his place. (Always *his* place; women could not properly take the field.) Reviewing a book by the Congregationalist biblical scholar Moses Stuart, for instance, Hodge declared that Stuart had "signally failed": "misapprehended the subject in debate; misconceived the meaning of the authors whom he quotes; contradicted himself; done violence to his own theoretical rules of interpretation, and gratuitously denounced" essential doctrines of Protestantism elsewhere professed by Stuart himself. How had Stuart fallen into this swamp of error? "Unconscious of the influence of certain works over his mind," the poor dolt had been led by the nose by German metaphysical theologians "and his own prejudices," a hapless victim of the "instability" of his "mental temperament." On our thinner skins words like these would rasp till we bled. This only shows what wimps we have become or, at least, that we play the game by different rules. Far from regarding Stuart as an enemy, Hodge paid him "unfeigned homage as the great American reformer of biblical study" and stood with him on terms of professional amity and private friendship. And Stuart knew better than to take the formalized arrogance of debate personally.[1]

Yet even by the polemical precepts of his day, Hodge behaved extraordinarily like Zeus pronouncing his high judgments and hurling his thunderbolts accordingly on the inferior mortals below. In part this Olympian attitude may have mirrored the elevated status and didactic role of the Presbyterian minister along the northeastern seaboard in the early national period, which Hodge inherited; in larger part it derived from his own remarkable learning. Alone among American theologians and biblical scholars of his generation, he had studied, and studied seriously, in Germany, the great motherland of erudition; even in the next generation probably only the Swiss-born and German-educated Philip Schaff could boast equivalent exposure.² And only Schaff, among Hodge's immediate peers, seems to have been more comfortable in the German language, the native tongue of the most influential theological and biblical scholarship. Hodge also handled Greek, Latin, Hebrew, and of course French competently and had studied Arabic and Persian, while his diverse writings reflect the staggering breadth of his reading in fields as seemingly remote from his professional concerns as craniometry. I, too, bow to his learning; and his more technical work in theology and biblical criticism—areas in which I am utterly incompetent—I have not dared to assess; indeed, even the judgments I do venture leave me feeling uncomfortably like a gnat hectoring an elephant. Hodge could speak with greater authority than most of his interlocutors for the very good reason that he *knew* more than they did.

But not always; and his habit of confident assertion sometimes outran his erudition. He could blandly declare that, during the colonial era of American history, "ninety-nine hundredths of our population came from Great Britain," a claim that any tyro in American history would have recognized as balderdash and that Hodge himself would probably have withdrawn had he bothered to think. Pontification affected more substantial issues. Hodge not uncommonly—and increasingly as the years passed—delivered himself of asseverations such as that both Old and New Testaments *"everywhere"* distinguish "between the soul and the body as two subjects" and teach "the full conscious existence of the soul between death and the resurrection"; or, similarly, that the doctrine of a generic human existence shared by all individual persons (a belief held by Augustine) was novel in the nineteenth century; or, again, that "ninety-nine hundreths of all good men utterly repudiate" the "theory that all sin consists in acts": declarations so at variance with reality, and so at odds with what Hodge himself must at some level have known, as to make the reader blink in astonishment. Such propositions could not plausibly be argued; they could only be asserted.³

Granted, much of what Hodge wrote for his journal, *The Biblical Repertory and Princeton Review,* he wrote at high speed with little chance for revision, and some of his more astounding overstatements probably owe their origin to this circumstance. But the trait was too deeply engrained to be so easily explained away. John W. Stewart has shrewdly suggested that Hodge's "intolerance for ambiguity" did not at all reflect a self-assured personality. Quite the reverse, Hodge's fatherless and impoverished childhood probably left a nagging insecurity at the core of his psyche. The same psychology might account for his chronically hypercertain rhetoric. Hodge, one might well believe, armored his vulnerability with that external confidence, at times amounting almost to arrogance, so evident in his writings and so sharply in contrast with the tenderness and even emotional neediness apparent in his personal relations. I at least find Stewart's scenario highly plausible.[4]

But I would add to this explanation of Hodge's compensatory overconfidence a different order of insecurity, one that helps us to place him not only in his individual psychological world, but in the mental world of the nineteenth century. The intellectual revolutions of that tumultuous century—revolutions to no small degree arising in the Germany that Hodge all his life admired and despised—did not treat him kindly. The winds of change blew with a deadly chill upon the fundamental axioms of his worldview. Perceptive as he was, he early realized that in such heavy weather any variance in course, still more, any tacking to the storm, might well result in shipwreck. Hodge's confident assertions not only denied to himself the possibility that he might err in navigating through the treacherous waters of the nineteenth century; they served to mark clearly for his audience the course that he insisted must be followed to avoid going on the reefs.[5]

The most threatening risks were of three different orders, though often overlapping. The first was the growing individualism underlying phenomena apparently as unrelated as evangelical revivalism, utilitarian liberalism, and political democracy. The second was the subjectivism commonly linked with "romanticism": the stress on inward feelings and intuitions as sources of human knowledge or insight and the related intimation that human beings mediate, or even construct, reality rather than directly perceiving it. The third, and perhaps the most toxic to Hodge, was the new sensitivity to history as a shaping force, evident in areas as diverse as biological evolution and Hodge's own special field of biblical criticism. The perils loomed all the greater because in no case did they offer utter novelty; rather, Hodge believed, these ominous new departures carried obvious truths to grotesque extremes. Out-and-out falsehood would have persuaded almost no one; unbalanced half-truths had a treacherously seductive appeal. Hodge's responses to these dangers cast light not only on his own thinking but on the dilemmas of his era.

With a polymath like Hodge, the question is where to begin. A convenient entry into his thinking is his views of the church, since probably to no subject did Hodge devote more ink. A good Protestant, Hodge insisted on the priority of the individual's relationship with God over any ecclesiastical mediator and of the word of God in Scripture over any church tradition: principles that he believed to have been "taught by Christ and his apostles." The true church comprised all true believers in Christ, the visible church all "professors of the true faith," spiritually united, though institutionally divided by history and by doctrine inessential to salvation. Even the Roman Catholic Church counted as part of the visible church, for it still professed the "essential doctrines of the gospel" despite adulterating them with a welter of false teaching and "idolatrous" practices; and Hodge liked to think that most of its members would be saved. Otherwise, his contempt for the "Romanists," as he preferred to call them, could scarcely be measured. "Popery" was "by far the most dangerous form of delusion and error that has ever arisen in the Christian world"; it inured its members to "habitual commission of crime" and posed a graver danger to America than German infidelity. Hodge dreaded even the "romanizing" tendencies of the Oxford movement and, closer to home, the Mercersburg theology of Schaff and Nevin.[6]

Within these Protestant parameters, however, Hodge took so high a view of the church that other Americans may have suspected him of sympathy with Oxford. The American tendency to schism at the drop of a hat appalled him; in the cauldron of the Civil War he insisted that "the command of Christ" bound Northern and Southern Presbyterians "to hold together as a church" even while the nation disintegrated. (They disobeyed.) He jealously guarded the prerogatives of the officially constituted governing bodies of the church against lay organizations, especially in matters of clerical recruitment and education. "The organization which Christ and his apostles have ordained" was not to be displaced by mere "societies of man's devising." He felt uneasy about the American Protestant "error"—that is, routine practice—of a congregation supplying its pastor's salary: ministers being "ordained to the service of the whole church," the church as a whole ought to guarantee them adequate support. He even dreamed of a parochial school "in connexion with every presbyterian church in our country."[7]

So powerful was Hodge's hankering for a stronger church that it led him briefly into an astonishing intellectual alliance with the protomodernist American theologian Horace Bushnell, a man whom Hodge in later years could approach only with anathemas. In 1847 Bushnell published the first version of his *Christian Nurture*, repudiating revivalism and arguing in essence that, in the usual course of God's dispensation, parents brought their children to saving faith by a proper Christian upbringing within the bosom of the church. Hodge did caution that Bushnell tended to explain "Christian nurture" in almost naturalistic terms of organic law rather than "the covenant and promise of God." But his criticisms were almost swamped in his enthusiasm for Bushnell's leading point: the "great and obvious truth" of "organic, as distinguished from individual life." Despite the little book's doctrinal divagations, Hodge expected "immeasurably more good than evil from its publication."[8]

Like Bushnell, Hodge deprecated revivalism and the corollary image of the lone individual face to face with God. He insisted instead on the raising of children under the tutelage of the church—and, compared to Bushnell, Hodge stressed church more than parents—as "the natural, the normal and ordinary means" of grace. The revivalist regime "easily induced" believers to "become utterly remiss as to all social religious duties of an ordinary character." And here Hodge edged closer to what lay at the center of his own high view of the church. He seized on Bushnell like a dog on a bone, not because he lay awake nights worrying about how parents were raising their youngsters, but because he was appalled by the modern philosophy "that every man has power to determine and to change at will his own character, or to make himself a new heart." This hyperindividualism, "as every one knows," had come to prevail in the United States. "It represents every man as standing by himself"—a denial of core Christian doctrine and an affront to Hodge's understanding of society and polity as well as salvation.[9]

For Hodge perceived as a heresy, deadly in secular as well as eternal affairs, the nineteenth-century notion that every individual stood on his (or, even worse, her) own feet. He adhered to a distinctively American tradition of republican conservatism with a powerful communitarian ethos, a political outlook that flourished between the death of the older Federalist conservatism after the war of 1812 and the rise of laissez-faire economic conservatism after the Civil War. This important tradition of political thought still awaits its historian, but we can see its lineaments in Hodge.[10]

"Radical principles," Hodge reminded the readers of the *Princeton Review* at the end of the Civil War, "are alien to [the *Review*'s] character and spirit"—and they certainly were to its editor's. Like Burke, Hodge developed a strong sense of the salience of particular conditions in making political judgments; what might be "rational under one set of circumstances, is the height of infatuation under another." He likewise had little patience with speculative talk of "inalienable rights"; he called it "a great fallacy to suppose that the abstract rights of men can be enforced at all times and under all circumstances." Though he came to believe that slavery as actually practiced in the American South involved serious sin, he consistently refused to condemn slavery as sinful in principle: the question was how human beings treated others and what sort of treatment a particular system fostered, not the theoretical relation of master to servant.[11]

As all of this suggests, Hodge understood government not in terms of any speculative theory, but as a historically conditioned institution. Although God intended human beings, as social creatures, to live under government, the forms of it had varied through history. A child of the Scottish Enlightenment, Hodge tended to view such development through the lens of the Scottish theory of the progress of civilization.[12] An American Protestant, he breathed a sigh of relief that his own country's history had firmly shaped its institutions "before the floods of [Irish] ignorance and Romanism were opened upon us." History left other peoples (including American slaves) in less happy circumstances; and Hodge felt entirely confortable with the fact that "accident of birth" determined "the relative position of men in society." Not even political despotism was wrong in itself.[13]

Given these historical realities, no individual bore the blame or credit for social or political conditions. Whatever guilt slavery entailed—and Hodge's impression of this did deepen over the decades—the culpability fell not primarily on the slaveholder but on the community as a whole; for slavery was not the creation "of the individual." "The community is responsible for its existence." This strong communitarian sensibility may help to explain the vehemence with which Hodge rejected the individualistic utilitarian liberalism that increasingly captured the American intellectual imagination in the 1840s and 1850s.[14]

Although his sense of history reinforced Hodge's resistance to the rising tide of individualism, he in no way handed over the political realm to historical contingency. Although God had not ordained one type of government for all peoples, the principle remained that "all events depending on human agency are under his control." "The existence of any particular form of government is as much his work, as the rising of the sun or falling of the rain." More directly to the point, the Bible made clear that government was "not optional": "government, whatever its form, is of God. He has ordained it." It followed that government officials, although in one sense representing the people, "in a far higher sense" represented God. One's "civil duties" therefore had a "religious character," and obedience to the law was required "on the authority of God." This did not imply that a citizen must *always* obey the government; the state could not, for instance, legitimately order a citizen to sin. In such rare cases, the citizen had no "right to resist the execution of the law" but, rightly refusing to comply, must submit to its penalty. Only the people collectively had a right of revolution—and even this Hodge derived from the divine command that human beings organize *some* form of government.[15]

Hodge took as high a view of government, then, as of the church. Indeed, just as he believed that the church was morally bound to support its clergy adequately—and, if necessary, pay for their education as a matter of right—so, by exact analogy, "a wise government" would do the same for its civil service.[16] And in both cases it was the welfare of the organic community, not of some impossible collectivity of unconnected individuals, that Hodge had in mind.

These complex commitments left Hodge of two minds regarding American democracy. He valued the republicanism of the United States, not because he believed people to possess any natural right to govern themselves, but because democracy had an "elevating effect upon the mass of the population"; for participation in politics raised the minds of ordinary people from the dulling grind of their "daily labor," requiring them "to think and act in reference to important and general objects." As to the people's actual ability to "think and act," Hodge had pretty low expectations. Like other conservative republicans, he thought a fairly high level of "moral education" sine qua non if popular government were to work without disaster; and he worried that the public's "passions" might overwhelm their "mind" and "conscience." Not surprisingly, then, he was no friend to any version of direct or participatory democracy. To the contrary, he took something like the old Puritan view that, although the people might elect their magistrate, they had no business telling him what to do once elected.[17]

Yet this was not the whole story of democracy. Try as he might to restrain the power of the people and to deny the high claims for the individual conscience advanced by abolitionists, Transcendentalists, and other unsavory types, Hodge kept tripping over his own religious principles. The problem arose from the "vital principle of Protestantism" itself: "that God is now accessible to all men by Jesus Christ" without going "through the church, or through the mediation of other men as priests." From this followed relentlessly the ultimacy of the individual conscience. "It is a primary principle that the right of private judgment extends over all questions of faith and morals. No human power can come between God and the conscience." So, as much as Hodge yearned to tell abolitionists (and, later, seceding slaveholders) that they could not take the law into their own hands, he had in the end to concede that they could. "Who is to determine whether a particular law is unconstitutional or immoral?" he asked in 1851, vis-à-vis the Fugitive Slave Law (which he himself endorsed). With a palpably heavy heart, he answered: "it cannot be denied, and ought not to be concealed, that the ultimate decision must be referred" to each individual's "own judgment." The radical individualism inherent in Protestantism thus made Hodge more of a democrat than he wanted to be.[18]

His Scottish Enlightenment philosophical principles reinforced the effect. The doctrines of common-sense realism—at least as Hodge understood them—suggested that, in reasonably uncomplicated matters, the collective judgment of ordinary people provided a test of truth. This was especially true in moral questions, such as those that slavery raised, because of the "moral sense" that Scottish philosophers from Francis Hutcheson onward had ascribed to every properly functioning human being. "Every great moral truth has," as Hodge pointed out, "a self-evidencing light." This light may not be visible to "the ignorant or depraved," but it can be seen by "the great body of the intelligent and pious men of the country." (Note that the qualification is *not* supernatural regeneration but natural human knowledge and morality.) It followed that ordinary people, if properly educated and well behaved, could be relied upon to participate politically as responsible and perceptive citizens. True, the question of education, particularly moral training, always remained a problematic one for Hodge; but he did not hesitate to invoke the consensus of ordinary American Protestants to refute his enemies. It seemed hard for Hodge intellectually, being Scottish and being Protestant, not to be a democrat, however reluctantly.[19]

In these tensions and even contradictions, we begin to see how radically out of step Hodge was with the leading intellectual trends of his century—as perhaps were most thoughtful Old-School Presbyterians. The key issue was neither mistrust of democracy nor misgivings about individualism (doubts shared by many conservative Americans) but, rather, Hodge's philosophic refusal to accept history as a fundamental force shaping the human condition. This put him at odds with most of the other leading conservatives in the nineteenth-century transatlantic tradition: with Edmund Burke, Alexis de Tocqueville, and Benjamin Disraeli across the water, and with John Randolph of Roanoke, Daniel Webster, and Charles Eliot Norton in the United States. Hodge did, of course, understand that particularities of human existence changed over time, like forms of government and even the church's understanding of Christ's teaching. But for Hodge, despite all his communitarian instincts and almost against his wishes, the ultimate unit of human reality remained the individual; and the individual endured essentially unaltered by history.

It should be emphasized that this denial of the power of history did not follow logically from Hodge's Reformed presuppositions about the *potestas ordinata* of God. Just as human agency was compatible with divine determination (God ordinarily choosing to achieve His ends by human hands), so an orthodox Calvinist could accept God accomplishing His will through the less personalized form of human agency called history. Historicism, then, did not necessarily imply naturalism, as Hodge sometimes seemed to suggest.

But historicism did imply the shaping of the individual by his or her culture and the shaping of that culture by the history that had produced it, and this mediation between the individual and ultimate reality was what Hodge could not swallow. He had grounds both philosophic and religious. Philosophically, his Scottish common-sense realism insisted that each individual perceives reality immediately: this perception conditioned by the unchanging structure of human consciousness, but not by any historical particularity. The atemporal perceiving mind stood, as it were, outside of history, face to face with reality. Religiously, Hodge's "vital principle" of Protestantism likewise put the individual immediately before God, as revealed in Scripture. Neither the essential doctrines of the gospel nor the grasp of these by the regenerate were in any way conditioned by history; nor did any institution existing in history—that is, the church—need to mediate between the individual and the saving grace of God. The atemporal perceiving soul stood outside of history, face to face with eternity. And so, despite considerable cost to the plausibility of his communitarianism, of his Burkean understanding of political institutions, of his high view of the clergy and the church, deeper commitments wedded Hodge to a radically atemporal individualism.

This ahistorical individualism meshed neatly with his sometimes vicious anti-Catholicism. Hodge came by his hostility to the Roman Catholic Church almost subliminally, for antipopery had provided a core element of Anglo-American political ideology since the seventeenth century. Many of his anti-Catholic outbursts, though they may make our more ecumenical skins crawl, need to be put in context as simply reflexes of this culture. However, his more reasoned critiques of Catholicism—and of the catholicizing Oxford movement, which he feared and despised almost as much as Rome itself—serve to flesh out for us his repudiation of history.

For the role and nature of historical development figured crucially in Hodge's polemics against "Romanism." In these attacks, Hodge probably most often assailed "the error of a mediating church or priesthood"; but he also declared that the "whole question between Protestants and Papists" boiled down to "whether there is any unwritten traditionary rule of faith or practice now binding on the church": a formulation that focused precisely on the relation of the church to history. For Hodge, the only norm that could bind the church—and the only criterion by which it was to be judged—was the now timeless, unchanging "authority of scripture." Though Christianity was a historical religion in the sense that Christ revealed its truths and founded the church *in illo tempore*, the faith once delivered to the saints was handed over entire and pure, once and for all, in the Scriptures. And it was imbecile to believe that mere historical continuity testified to verity. "A church may have been originally founded by the apostles, and possess an uninterrupted succession of pastors, and yet be now a synagogue of Satan." The "road of history" *did* lead to Rome: proof that it led astray.[20]

Hodge was far too good a scholar to deny that development had occurred in the church's understanding of doctrine, but this did not imply that history had shaped doctrine itself. In "different ages," "one or more great truths of revelation" became "the subjects of perpetual conflict, until the mind of the Church was brought to a clear and comprehensive view of what was revealed concerning them," as in the Christological controversies of the early church. But Hodge insisted that the Christian "system of doctrine" had been "recorded in the Bible" "distinctly," "fully," and "clearly." Of this system "there can be no *development*," only better grasp. Hodge set himself explicitly against John Henry Newman's theory of doctrinal development—denying that any "doctrine can ever be unfolded or expanded" beyond its biblical statement—as well as against Philip Schaff's teaching of the "organic development" of the church from an embryonic beginning. For Hodge history mediated neither the church nor its beliefs. "The Church of the present does not derive its life by way of transmission from the Church of the past, but immediately from Christ by his word and Spirit, so that while inheriting the results and attainments of former ages to aid her in understanding the Scriptures, her faith always rests immediately on the word of God."[21]

This last phrase suggests the most powerful reason why Hodge was skittish about history. The idea of historical development threatened more than the Presbyterian Church and its creeds; it threatened the Bible itself. And, in gauging Hodge's response to historicist biblical criticism, one must remember that his world pivoted on the Bible. "There can be no solid foundation for theological opinion," he always insisted, "but the original text of Scripture fairly interpreted." His abhorrence of the Oxford movement owed much to the Tractarians' acceptance of tradition as an authority parallel to Scripture: "When men begin to forsake the scriptures for tradition, and dote about fables, they seem to lose the ordinary power of discriminating truth." Whatever was "the doctrine of the Bible" on any subject, that was "also the doctrine of the church"; and Hodge believed all true Christian doctrines to be fully and unambiguously stated in Scripture.[22]

There is more here than the generic Protestant principle of *sola scriptura*. Hodge held firmly the Reformed view that the "universe is not a machine left to go of itself" but rather that God ordains every happening. Therefore he regarded God's revelation of His will in the Bible as the handbook of ultimate authority for questions in politics or science as much as in theology. No matter how overwhelming the arguments supporting some political conclusion, for instance, "they would be driven to the wind by one clear declaration of scripture" to the contrary.[23]

The Bible in its entirety had therefore to be shielded against every imputation of ambiguity or uncertainty. Yet ambiguity and uncertainty were precisely the result of nineteenth-century historical criticism of the Bible.

Hodge was far from contemptuous of the achievements of the German scholars, who dominated the field. After all, he believed, the Scriptures had to be "historically interpreted" in a limited sense, "that is, we are bound to take them in the sense in which they were intended to be understood by the persons to whom they were addressed." And the philological scholarship of "the modern German school of expositors" had immensely benefited "the careful student of the Scriptures, who is desirous of ascertaining with accuracy and certainty, the meaning of the word of God."[24]

But, not content with clarifying the meanings of the words of the biblical text, some of the most influential German scholars had gone on to challenge the received understanding of the nature of the Bible itself. Where Hodge and other traditionally minded Reformed Protestants maintained that the Bible shone with a "self-evidencing light" that proved its truths intuitively (like a mathematical axiom) to a regenerate reader of any time or clime, Germans treated its books as historical products of particular ancient cultures, decisively shaped by those cultural contexts and fully comprehensible only within them. Where Hodge believed the Bible to have an "obvious sense" that only "violent exegesis" could distort, Germans argued that existing knowledge of historical context did not suffice for a good understanding of some books. Where Hodge saw the work of authors led by the plenary inspiration of the Holy Spirit to pen words "as though spoken directly by the lips of God himself," Germans perceived words written by limited men very much of a particular time and place. Where Hodge regarded the Old and New Testaments as "one book," the "product of one mind" (God's), presenting "one grand concatenated system of truth, gradually developed during fifteen hundred years," Germans claimed that the Bible comprised a welter of distinct texts, with their own separate authors and outlooks, each to be understood in terms of its own history.[25]

The most extreme of the German historicist critics, most notoriously David Friedrich Strauss in *Das Leben Jesu*, completely "reject[ed] the gospel history as a history." They claimed that there existed no historical evidence to justify treating the Gospels as narratives of actual events; they represented the New Testament as a very different kind of book, "a mere mythology" or "collection of fables, destitute in almost every case of any foundation in fact." To read the Gospels as an actual record of Jesus Christ's life, teaching, death, and resurrection was simply to misunderstand the nature of the texts. Rather, their "truth must be sought" through "a mytho-symbolical interpretation" of the supposed history. The virus was spreading even in the United States; "even among the orthodox," people began to "talk of a mythology of the Hebrews," while some Unitarians abandoned "not only the miracles of the Old Testament, but those of the New."[26] Hodge dug in his heels.

For, as *Das Leben Jesu* showed, it was one short step from a Bible entangled in history to a Bible unmoored from any permanent meaning. Hodge understood with remarkable clarity what was at stake. His recognition of the fissile tendencies within American society and American Protestant churches perhaps made him more sensitive to the hyper-individualist, antitraditional threats to religious belief, and vice versa. (He lamented the advantage that their solidarity gave "Romanists" in the struggle for America's soul.)[27] Horace Bushnell certainly saw more lucidly than Hodge that no theological formula could escape having a culture-bound, contingent character; even for a Victorian Hodge was unusually blind to the salience of cultural diversity. But Hodge realized, as Bushnell did not, the crucial importance of stable orthodox definitions as guideposts and anchors for meaning, without which beliefs tended to dissolve into vapor.

And vapor was rising. The corrosion of "the objective form of truth as presented in the Scriptures" by historicist criticism made it easy to regard Christianity as merely "a feeling, or inward life," more or less "independent of a system of doctrines revealed by God and obligatory on men as objects of faith." Thus the way was opened for the pantheistic philosophy rooted in Hegel and broadcast in more popular terms by Cousin, which Hodge regarded as the animating principle of German "infidelity," namely, "that God is the only real existence of which the universe of mind and nature is the phenomenon." In his earlier years Hodge did not worry that German aberrations would ever prevail in England or the United States, Anglo-Americans having too much "sanity of intellect" and being too deeply steeped in the Bible. And he continued to think German idealist doctrine relatively harmless to ordinary Christians in the impenetrable prose of Hegel, but far more dangerous in the "popularized Germanism of Cousin"—which, "we understand," was even "taught to girls." He also grew more alarmed after American Reformed theologians like Horace Bushnell and Edwards Amasa Park began to publish their German-influenced protomodernist works around 1850, and he thereafter dedicated his pen to warning his fellow citizens against German theology. He certainly thought that Americans like Bushnell, Park, and John Nevin were spreading destruction, even if they remained unaware of the true causticity of their still timid importations of German teaching.[28]

"In all its forms" the "new philosophy" undermined the orthodox conception of Christianity as an unchanging and eternally true "system of doctrine." It rejected "the fundamental doctrine of a God who is the real Creator and Governor of the world, distinct from it, though everywhere present in it, who is not bound to a process of development, and to act according to fixed laws, but may act how and when he pleases." Instead, "the world and history" became "a process, a development of God." Hodge presciently identified such immanentism as the most salient religious consequence of historicism and as the bridge that would carry many Protestants away from traditional orthodox Christianity.[29]

This radical theological historicism opened the way, Hodge judged, to an equally radical and destructive religious individualism. In the developmental theory religion was no longer a "form of knowledge" nor a "mode of action," but "a life, a peculiar state of feeling": Christianity specifically being a "form of the religious consciousness produced by Christ, or in some way due to him, and derived from him." The "intuitions of the religious consciousness" by their nature could have no fixed and permanent forms, but varied from time to time and from individual to individual. And if "the facts and doctrines of the Bible are the mere forms of the spirit of Christianity," then the interpretation of both the Bible and the creeds became labile and individual, subject to "the opinion and prejudices of the reader": every man his own interpreter. Language itself lost its limpidity. The "fixed rules of interpretation" fell into confusion; "Christian language" was twisted into unheard-of and "anti-christian" meanings. The "divine character of Christ" might mean only that he was an extraordinarily good man. "Let philosophers and errorists," Hodge cried, "find words for themselves, and not profane the words of God by making them a vehicle for the denial of his truth."[30]

Hodge's rhetoric could grow overheated, formulations lean to caricature, but in substance his complaints came tolerably close to what Horace Bushnell was writing, allowing for Bushnell's own animus against individualism. "Dr. Bushnell could sign any creed by help of that chemistry of thought which makes all creeds alike." "Nothing can be more opposed to Scripture," Hodge believed, than such "depreciation of the importance of doctrine." Bushnell, to be sure, did not think that he was depreciating doctrine, only appreciating it in a different way.[31]

For Bushnell had fallen under the spell of history, learned to admire her formative power, whereas Hodge had not succumbed to this new siren of the nineteenth century. Bushnell's epistemological watchword was *growth*, Hodge's *fact*. Hodge believed of course that human knowledge accumulated over time, so that Victorians collectively knew more than ancient Romans; he accepted that the *expressions* of knowledge would reflect the idioms peculiar to a given society, but he did not think knowledge itself in any fundamental way *conditioned* by historical context. A fact recognized by Plato would (assuming a normally functioning mind) be recognized in the same way by Charlemagne, Ignatius of Loyola, and Charles Hodge.

This radically atemporal character of knowledge followed from Hodge's adherence to the "common-sense" realism of the Scottish Enlightenment, especially as formulated by Thomas Reid. The human mind functions in the same way in all peoples, providing self-evident truths (or "facts of consciousness" or "laws of belief impressed upon our nature"), which make knowledge possible and the truth of which no one can prove or can deny without absurdity. "A man undertakes a desperate task who attempts to argue against the intuitive judgments of the mind or conscience," wrote Hodge, self-evidently. Equipped with "instinctive beliefs" such as causation and duration, we can make coherent the relations of the various objects that we perceive directly (as we also intuitively believe) through the senses. And thus we produce facts, which we assemble into larger bodies of knowledge. The Bible is a special case, because only persons "under the influence of the Spirit of God" can reliably recognize its self-evidencing truths. But not entirely special, since in the end we can only trust that the Creator has not played a nasty trick on us and "impressed upon our nature" false and misleading "laws of belief." "The ultimate ground of knowledge," Hodge made clear, "is confidence in the veracity of God." Just as God did not change, just as human nature did not change, neither did facts change.[32]

Although imagination certainly had a place in human life, that place was nowhere near knowledge. Hodge distinguished sharply between "the logical understanding" and "the imagination," and he regarded as respectable but unreliable "sentimental religionists, whose devotion must be kindled through the imagination." Bushnell, Hodge fumed, tried "to seduce us from cleaving to the letter of the scriptures" by appealing to the imagination; Hodge's own appeal in matters of doctrine was to "clear and decisive proof." To his common-sense realism Hodge added a robust "Baconian" distinction between "fact" and "theory," a suspicion of premature theorizing (at least by others), and an insistence on staying close to the facts.[33]

This "Baconianism" provided his self-described theological method. Hodge defined "Christian theology" as "nothing but the facts and truths of the Bible arranged in their natural order and exhibited in their mutual relations." The apparent distinction between "facts" and "truths" seems only apparent, for it immediately disappeared; nor did Hodge try to answer the questions begged in "natural order" and "mutual relations." But he did expatiate on this definition in a passage worth quoting *in extenso:*

> Such being the nature of theology, the duty of the theologian is first to ascertain and authenticate the facts of Scripture, that is, make it clear that they are indeed contained in the word of God. This induction of facts must, as far as possible, be exhaustive. All must be collected, and each must be allowed its due value. No one is to be ignored or modified. Then secondly, the theologian, having obtained his facts, is to present them in their natural order; that is, the order determined by their nature.
>
> The philosophy of the facts is in the facts; underlies, and arranges them, and determines their mutual relation. The theologian has no more right to explain the facts by his own philosophy, than he has to manufacture the facts for his philosophy. His business

is simply to exhibit the contents of the Bible in a scientific form. His relation to the Scriptures is analogous to that of the man of science to nature.

The same fact was always the same fact. The Bible belonged to the realm of eternal truth, not to that of history.[34]

And, as Hodge's last analogy suggests, it also belonged to the realm of science. Scientists and theologians tended to investigate different orders of questions and properly worked "independently yet harmoniously." However, as Hodge rightly pointed out, they often "overlap each other." Both, for instance, inquired into the "origin, nature, prerogatives, and powers" of human beings; and, the field being "common to both," neither had a right to warn the other off his ground. But Hodge went further. Facts being facts, the facts of the Bible, such as "sin and redemption"—"just as certain, and infinitely more important, than the truths of science"—ought to weigh in scientific theorizing with facts derived from other sources. "It is not only unwise but unphilosophical for the man of science to conduct his investigations on the assumption that nothing more than scientific facts can legitimately be taken into view." Hodge did not apply a simple-minded or one-sided criterion to the relation of science and the Bible. Biblical critics also needed to take scientific conclusions into account, and modern astronomical and geological theories had changed the church's understanding of some passages. But facts, from whatever source, were timelessly true and universally applicable across all domains of knowledge. Nothing could make clearer how the nineteenth century was distancing itself from Hodge.[35]

An inevitable air of melancholy hangs about Hodge's career. Only a handful of Americans of his day commanded the erudition he did; perhaps still fewer intellectuals of his generation exerted an influence as broad. Yet in the end neither his learning nor his ascendance could protect his worldview from being swept under the tide of historicism. At Princeton itself a remnant of loyalists did continue Hodge's work, but in the twentieth century even they were forced to abandon ship and ended marooned on the margins of American culture.

Hodge remains for us today a remarkable figure. He was among the last, and in many ways one of the most admirable and clearsighted, of the thinkers who lived "before history"—that is, who lived in a world of stable laws and stable essences, before historicism and its offspring (such as the concept of cultures) had transformed the way in which we understand our world and how it came to be. One might even venture the claim that Charles Hodge was the last major American intellectual who was fully a citizen of Enlightenment, immune to the ravages that the nineteenth century worked on the axioms of the eighteenth.

One might further argue that had Hodge not been so lovingly wedded to the atemporal common-sense realism of the Scottish Enlightenment and the antitheoretical conception of science that went with it, had he instead been willing to adapt to his own apologetic purposes the hermeneutic conception of knowledge that historicism fostered and even to weld historicism to his strong conviction of divine providence, he might have fared better, and so might the Christian worldview he defended. But to propose this is itself profoundly ahistorical. It is hard even now to imagine what an *orthodox* Protestant historicism might have looked like in the nineteenth century. Certainly, the protomodernist theologians like Bushnell who followed the historicist course found themselves in the end with a version of Christianity that would have appalled Hodge.

No, Hodge does not merit becoming one more victim of the enormous condescension of posterity. He deserves our respect. The Old-School ship of traditional Presbyterianism could not have enlisted an abler captain in his time and place. It was not his fault that he found himself sailing on a strange new sea, with no adequate charts to guide him. Charles Hodge's career stands as a synecdoche for the intellectual history of orthodox Christianity in the nineteenth century.

CHAPTER THREE

Secularization and Sacralization

Some Religious Origins of the Secular Humanities Curriculum, 1850–1900

Just as knowledge assumed a new face when it came to be seen as a product of history, so, too, did visions of knowledge alter when its religious framework weakened. Both of these mutations really took hold only in the nineteenth century, and they influenced each other. Both have attracted the attention of historians, but neither is thoroughly understood, particularly the fallout from faltering theistic axioms. In their different ways, Norton and Hodge were unsettled by early tremors from these earthquakes.

The following essay examines a piece of the second problem: What happened to the knowledge embedded in the curriculum of American colleges and universities when its explicitly Protestant setting faded in the second half of the nineteenth century?[1] More precisely, I look at two seemingly distinct, though roughly contemporaneous, developments: the rapid rise of the humanities in college education and the retreat of a Protestant philosophy that had once given the curriculum at least a veneer of coherence. These two events, I suggest, were linked by more than time, though neither can be explained entirely in terms of the other. The specter of language study, so often sighted near shape-shifting knowledge during the nineteenth century, creeps in again, this time in the form of textual philology as a model for renovated humanities. Fittingly, the specter of Andrews Norton also makes an appearance, in the person of his son, Charles Eliot Norton.

American college teachers are familiar with a curious puzzle. Step outside of a college, and you cannot fail to see that scientific and technical knowledge orders our lives and shapes our futures. Yet talk to the professors on a college curriculum committee, and you generally find the humanities vaguely regarded as less dispensable, more primordial, than the natural sciences. Even chemists incline to concede that literature and philosophy somehow lie closer to the heart of liberal education than what goes on in laboratories.

Why should this be so? No single answer will suffice. But some of the answers may be found in the transition from old religious conceptions of higher education to new, apparently secular ones. This motion had already begun, spare and sluggish, in the seventeenth century, when American collegiate learning still meant only Harvard. The pace quickened after 1850: by 1900 it had become a grand march. Sketching a few of the moves in that dance of secularization may help to resolve the riddle with which this chapter began. This venture in intellectual choreography will possibly clarify an obscure meaning of the modern liberal arts — one widely sensed, I believe, but not clearly seen. More modestly, it should at least shed a little light on the complex relation between religion and secularization in American higher learning.

Historians of higher education broadly agree when and how curriculum changed as the old classical college evolved into the modern undergraduate college.[2] Before the mid–nineteenth century, colleges shared virtually a single curriculum, with local variations. The American colonies had inherited the basis of this course of study from the English Renaissance and Reformation. In it, learning centered on ancient languages, but instruction took place in English. Colonial colleges also taught rhetoric and elocution, mathematics, logic, divinity, and natural philosophy.[3] This curriculum really cohered around nothing but tradition. But it did assume, almost subliminally, the unity of knowledge: all truth flowing, as was supposed, from God. We may assume that the fifteen-year-old boys who infested Harvard or the College of William and Mary rarely questioned the axiom.

In the later–eighteenth century, Scottish common-sense philosophy threw a new light onto American intellectual life: illumination extended even into its darker penumbrae, such as the colleges. The invading Scots brought with them a cogent doctrine in support of this hitherto fuzzy epistemological faith. Invasion came not only in the form of the works of Thomas Reid and Adam Smith but more literally in the persons of Scottish and Scotch-Irish academic parsons, such as Francis Alison (College of Philadelphia) and John Witherspoon (College of New Jersey). In colleges the chief curricular fallout from the Scottish assault was a senior course in moral philosophy.[4]

Between the Revolution and the Civil War, this moral philosophy course became the capstone of the curriculum almost everywhere. It gave students an explicit, articulated explanation of the unity of God's truth—and hence of the unity of the curriculum. Indeed, like a black hole pulling in all the interstellar debris in its neighborhood, the moral philosophy course sucked in a hodgepodge of intellectual flotsam and jetsam that would boggle a modern professor: topics ranging from political economy to the origin of language to animals' rights. The lecturer, generally the college president, posed large questions, gave large answers. He showed how solutions to problems in ethics, political theory, law, psychology, religion all flowed from the divine constitution of nature. All this fitted together in a grand schema derived loosely from Protestant theological doctrine, more tightly from Scottish philosophical teaching.[5]

This is not to say that actual course work formed an interconnected whole. Far from it. For one thing, elementary drill in languages and mathematics blighted vast stretches of the day. A virtuoso of moral philosophy could not have persuaded a bunch of eighteen-year-olds swotting Greek verbs that these conjugations led inexorably to Newtonian celestial mechanics and thence to the perfections of the Deity.

Anyway, that was not the point. When knowledge seemed in principle tied together—the study of a single unified divine creation—a professor scarcely needed to explain *how* particular bits of learning connected in order to convince himself and his students that somehow they all *did*. In fact, the college president did just that. He not only exemplified to the senior class that particular bits of learning linked up—the ethical principle of chastity followed from the sociological facts of demography—but also provided the philosophical framework within which knowledge formed a seamless whole.[6] It was not some palpable connection between individual courses that unified antebellum college curricula. It was the conviction, felt and taught, of coherence ultimately stemming from the Creator.

Yet in the decades after 1860 this sense of coherence grew thinner and thinner, finally vanishing like smoke. Increasing specialization and fragmentation of knowledge contributed to its disappearance: the *pedagogical* map of knowledge, implicit in the curriculum, gradually converged with the ever more detailed *general* map of knowledge, implicit in intellectual work outside colleges.[7] Also disintegrative was the weakening of consensus on the existence of God, especially fragile in academic circles. When the creator began to appear dubious, the unity of creation no longer appeared axiomatic.[8] But the centrifugal forces—and there were others—are not the point here.

The outcome is. Particularly in the emerging universities, a jumble of new undergraduate curricula hived off from the old unitary course of study. Most of these aimed at vocational training, loosely defined: architecture, engineering, agriculture, pedagogy, pharmacy, business, science, music, and more.[9] To be sure, amid this collegiate Babel, the traditional classical curriculum retained pride of place. Yet the confusion of tongues infected even it. Within the liberal arts course, subjects of study multiplied, and the tide flowing toward the elective system pulled them apart from each other. Students shared less and less of a common education. Most tellingly, the old moral philosophy course itself disintegrated, giving birth in its death to several of our present academic specialities: economics, philosophy, sociology, political science, and, less directly, anthropology.

The pace of fragmentation varied. The emerging universities moved fastest. Many smaller colleges kept their old curriculum, or at least its religious framework, well into the twentieth century. And colleges that retained an explicitly and specifically religious identity may well have postponed or mitigated this process of fissioning (as Catholic colleges appear to have done through the first half of the twentieth century).[10] Yet, by 1900, at the institutions recognized even then as leading change, any claim to an integrated curriculum—much less, unified knowledge—appeared dubious if not downright fraudulent. The firmament, however, did not ring with lamentation. In bald fact, the undergraduate's experience had taken a sharp turn for the better. Teaching methods were less boring, professors less ignorant, students themselves less childish. Even college food improved.

At the same time faculty members in the colleges moving into this brighter future had good reason to worry about the larger meaning of their curriculum. Not that many of them wasted hours fretting. Cheering the innovations that, incidentally, undermined coherence was understandably more popular. Indeed, the abolition of compulsory chapel provoked louder howls, inside and out of academia, than the demise of moral philosophy. But the implicit secularization of curriculum struck much closer to the heart of the college. And some professors did grow anxious about the larger meaning of their work. Yet the coincident secularization of academic knowledge made absurd any thought of restoring curricular coherence on the old basis of shared religious beliefs. Where moral philosophy had once stood, a great void now gaped.

And, if nature no longer abhorred a vacuum, professors did. Attempts to fill this one account for many of the innovations in general education in the twentieth century. Columbia's Contemporary Civilization course in 1919; Robert Maynard Hutchins's reorganization of the Chicago curriculum around the "Great Books" in the 1930s; the General Education program outlined in Harvard's "Redbook" in 1945; the Great Awakening in core curricula that began around 1980—the intellectual history of the modern American college could be written as the Quest for Coherence. Put too simply, the advocates of a robust "core" are seeking a replacement for the senior course in moral philosophy—but looking in a secularized academy that cannot admit the God who made the moral philosophy course work.

For readers acquainted with the history of American higher education, the foregoing narrative holds no surprises, so far as it goes. But it does not go very far in one direction. Briefly, we know that in many schools (in the long run, all) the putatively coherent antebellum curriculum fell apart, and we know in general the sorts of courses and requirements that replaced it. But we do not know how—or even whether—the new curriculum was meant to remedy the intellectual incoherence resulting from the breakup of the old one. This neglected question needs answering: How did these changing colleges, in reconstructing the liberal arts, respond to their crisis of coherence in the decades after 1860?

Answering it is not easy. Historians of higher education in this period, fascinated by the emergence of universities and graduate schools, have neglected undergraduate curricula, still more, undergraduate teaching.[11] Even histories of expressly liberal arts colleges slight the development, ideologies, and justifications of curriculum in favor of institutional growth and student life. And the content of course work, in particular, is rarely examined. Everyone knows that colleges introduced many new subjects in the last half of the century. What professors actually taught under these rubrics is almost terra incognita. To guess at the substance of courses, even their rationales, usually requires inference from anecdotes, from textbooks, or, still more remotely, from monographs about scholarship in the discipline. What professors actually told students, what students heard professors say (rarely the same thing), what purposes professors believed their courses to serve, what methods they used to achieve these goals—the data bearing on such questions remain as pristine as if the archives were in Albania.[12]

A foray into this territory is the aim of this chapter. The particular terrain will be the undergraduate arts-and-sciences colleges of universities, with a special eye on probably the two most influential instances of the type: Harvard University and the University of Michigan.[13] This focus results partly from the fact that the emerging universities led the transformation of curriculum, partly from idiosyncratic practical reasons.[14] Harvard was a private university self-consciously striving to educate an elite, Michigan a public university with democratic aspirations. Harvard under Charles W. Eliot was a standard setter for late-nineteenth-century higher education, Michigan under Henry P. Tappan and James B. Angell the foremost model for Cornell and for the great midwestern state universities. Finally, both Michigan and Harvard, being among the largest universities in the period when modern American higher education took shape as well as among the more innovative, faced more rapidly and more urgently the breakup of the old classical course of study than did small colleges, some of which kept the old curriculum and the old convictions associated with it virtually intact into the twentieth century.

Yet, whatever its justification, the fact remains that my discussion of liberal arts education here never scrutinizes a traditional liberal arts college like Amherst or Grinnell. Hugh Hawkins has aptly remarked the perverseness of looking mainly at the two largest American universities: "One can argue that universities set the pattern, but I rather suspect a collegiate ethos developed in smaller colleges which universities came to envy and to imitate."[15] There is much truth in this view. Yet necessity dictates that choices be made, and Michigan and Harvard serve here chiefly to highlight patterns detectable elsewhere in the historiography of higher education. Moreover, the collegiate ethos to which Hawkins properly calls attention perhaps had more to do in the long run with pedagogical method than intellectual content.

Intellectually the most visible change in the liberal arts curriculum was diversification. This multiplication of subjects itself had multiple causes. Modern foreign languages, along with more serious instruction in English composition and rhetoric, began to invade the classical curriculum shortly after 1800, advancing under the banner of "utility." The division of the natural sciences into more specialized disciplines required the old natural philosophy and natural history courses to subdivide likewise into physics, chemistry, geology, zoology, and so forth. Sometimes the introduction of new subjects, or demand for greater attention to old ones, induced fission in the curriculum, such as the "scientific" [i.e., nonclassical] course" introduced by President Eliphalet Nott at Union in the 1820s or the founding in the 1840s of the Sheffield School of science at Yale. Then the old moral philosophy course gave birth in its death throes to economics, sociology, psychology, and other courses in the "social sciences." History, although spinning off from the study of classical languages, often took its ideology from the social sciences as well. So various did subjects of study become that the curriculum spun out of control. For half a century colleges experimented with versions of the elective system before finally settling—most of them—on the present method of concentration in a "major" and distribution of other courses outside it, to bring order to the welter of entries in their course catalogues.[16]

The catalogue entries most relevant here were those in philosophy, literature, and the fine arts. For the new buzzword of undergraduate general education was "liberal culture," and these three subjects, especially the last two, were most often invoked to exemplify it. (This is by no means to deny the centrality of the social sciences in curricular thinking, carrying often more prestige than the humanities. But, as their label suggests, the social sciences expressed more the scientific than the cultural aspirations of higher education.) The old shibboleths of the classical curriculum—that it ensured the "discipline" and the "furniture" of "the mind"—had by no means vanished. Indeed, as secularization advanced, "mental discipline" (the student learning "how to think rather than what to think") possibly "became an even stronger justification for liberal education" than in antebellum curricular rationales.[17] Nor, for that matter, did "liberal culture" itself thrive only where education had lost its religious foundation; for instance, a specifically Christian version of it flourished at Yale.[18] Liberal education has never suffered lack of variety in its rationales.

Yet, when a new one shoots into prominence, it merits a close look. By 1880 college presidents intoned the words "liberal culture" like the ritual incantation of some new cult. And rightly so. To be sure, "liberal culture" was far from the only ideal percolating through undergraduate curricula in the late–nineteenth century: the cachet of "science" possibly had greater appeal to most faculty, perhaps most students as well. Nor should liberal culture be confused with the liberal arts *tout court*. Psychology and economics, for instance—not to mention the natural sciences—did not mesh well with liberal culture. Yet, so far as the secular liberal arts curriculum had any substantive *unifying* principle to replace the divine order outlined in moral philosophy, the protean notion of liberal culture was it.

Protean it was. Defining "liberal culture" would drive a lexicographer to despair. It certainly involved enthusiasm for breadth of learning, as opposed to narrow specialization. It favored the cultivation of imagination over the sharpening of intellect or the acquisition of information. Cynicism further suggests that it produced the kind of social polish later requisite at cocktail parties. Beyond this, the fog sets in. Whatever liberal culture was, students seem to have caught it by exposure to the "best" works of literature and art, famously Homer, Dante, and Shakespeare, Raphael and Rembrandt. Music seldom figured largely, probably because the phonograph did not come along quickly enough.

Like most large ideals, liberal culture wrapped up in a single package a complicated bundle of desires. These ranged from craving for social cachet to yearning for spiritual enlightenment. A week at Harvard circa 1890 would certainly have impressed one with the former, but it is the latter, the "spiritual" face of liberal culture, that now requires attention. For this aspect proved most salient in the specific roles that philosophy, literature, and the fine arts came to play in the emerging liberal arts curriculum in secular-minded universities.

Of this triumvirate, philosophy had by far the oldest career in American education. Colleges had insisted on it, in some form or another, from colonial days. But the throne from which philosophy reigned over the antebellum college, the senior moral philosophy course, had collapsed. Once the monarch governing the hierarchy of knowledge, philosophy was demoted to ordinary citizen in the democracy of the elective system. Stripped of the great mélange of knowledge integrated into the moral philosophy course, philosophy now meant the remnants left behind when economics, sociology, psychology, and even theology departed.

This remainder fragmented into a collection of technical subspecialities, ranging from logic to metaphysics.[19] Michigan in 1886–87 provides an example of the change. It had then an exceptionally strong department, comprising G. S. Morris and John Dewey. This polymathic pair offered an astonishing range of courses on the history of philosophy, logic, political philosophy, aesthetics, ethics, and metaphysics, as well as on individual philosophers from Plato to Herbert Spencer.[20] Students had vastly more philosophical training available than in any antebellum college. But it now lay chopped up into scattered pieces, the consumption of any of them left to individual discretion. Philosophy no longer exercised even the shadow of an integrating force.

Yet this observation, while strictly correct, probably does not accurately represent philosophy's place in the new liberal arts curriculum around 1880 or 1900. Apparently many philosophy professors came to their discipline in search of answers to religious doubts, not a few of them being ministers or ministers *manqués*.[21] It seems a fair inference that these concerns shaped their teaching. Certainly the premier philosophical work written by college professors in this era—that of James, Royce, and Dewey—had much to do with epistemological and moral problems inherited from the wreckage of traditional Christian beliefs.[22]

Probably few college philosophers were trying literally to rebuild the old moral philosophy course. And, in general, they seem to have taught their subject in the late–nineteenth century more as analysis, less as inspiration, than in earlier decades. But it does not take a sharp eye to ferret out thinly disguised religious concerns in the philosophy classroom. These may explain the prominence of idealist metaphysics in philosophy departments around the turn of the century: a bulwark against the threat of materialist scientism.[23] In any case, it was philosophy teachers of an ethical, even explicitly religious, stripe to whom students flocked: men like Charles E. Garman at Amherst and George Herbert Palmer at Harvard. Garman's legendary course sought deliberately to shore up the Christian beliefs of his students, so it seems apt that they spoke of him "with perfect reverence."[24] This suspiciously religious phrase provides a clue worth following in other areas of the curriculum.

The teaching of literature lacked philosophy's long pedigree. True, students had traditionally encountered classical literature as part of learning Greek and Latin. And, more recently, English poetry and oratory had entered college teaching as an aid to the study of rhetoric. Michigan in 1854–55 offered a "cursory" survey of English literature "designed chiefly to establish fundamental principles of [stylistic] criticism, and to cultivate correctness and propriety of style."[25] But such uses were purely ancillary. Apparently no American college taught English literature as an independent subject before 1857, when Francis A. March introduced it at Lafayette College. Despite its late start, literature rose rapidly to curricular stardom. For example, Yale had no truck with the stuff until 1870, when Thomas R. Lounsbury, a professor at Yale's Sheffield Scientific School, sneaked English literature in (as it were) through the back door. Yet by 1900 English had "replaced classics as the backbone of the humanities at Yale."[26]

Both Harvard and Michigan had a long head start on Yale. They introduced English literature in 1858–59, the year after March taught the first course. James Russell Lowell taught the initial course at Harvard (a senior elective), Andrew Dickson White at Michigan.[27] During the 1870s, the subject sank deep into the curriculum at both schools. The men chiefly responsible stand among the giants of American scholarship. At Harvard the key figure was Francis J. Child, known to generations of undergraduates as "Stubby" and still known to scholars and folk singers for the massive collation of traditional British songs universally called "Child's Ballads"—the towering monument of nineteenth-century American textual philology. (Child produced as well an important edition of Spenser and a seminal essay in Chaucer studies; it is a scandal to scholarship that he lacks a full biography.) His counterpart at Michigan was Moses Coit Tyler, whose background as popular lecturer and health reformer gave no clue that his achievements would almost rival Child's. With his two great works on early American writing—*The History of American Literature, 1607–1765* and *The Literary History of the American Revolution*—Tyler founded practically single-handedly two academic subdisciplines: American literature and American intellectual history.[28]

Both Child and Tyler began their professorial careers as instructors of rhetoric—Child in 1851, Tyler in 1867. Both chafed under the burden of correcting student compositions, and both from the beginning eased the pain with small doses of literature teaching.[29] In the early 1870s both struck out more boldly to fix a large and permanent place for English literature. Child began to offer a course covering Chaucer, Shakespeare, Bacon, Milton, and Dryden; in 1876 he split Shakespeare off into a separate course. He tacked on a couple more courses during the next few years, and in the 1880s Harvard's English department began to add more members, and with them, more literature. Meanwhile, Tyler at Michigan in 1874–75 introduced a senior elective in English literature and in the following year—startlingly—one in American literature. American literature proved episodic, but by the end of the decade Michigan students chose annually from a range of English literature courses, open not just to seniors but to all undergraduates. In 1878–79 the Michigan list comprised "Introductory" (offered in both terms), "Chaucer," "Shakespeare," and "Study of Masterpieces."[30]

Yet simply to say that Child and Tyler "taught literature" can mislead. For they approached their subject from a direction now alien to undergraduates and distasteful to most of their professors: by way of philology. The traditional center of gravity of humanistic scholarship, philology provided a powerful paradigm of knowledge well into the second half of the nineteenth century. (It is important to keep in mind the distinction between philology understood as the study of old texts—including classical philology and biblical criticism—and other varieties of language study, such as comparative philology, historical linguistics, and so forth. In the nineteenth century "philology" labeled all these enterprises.[31] But principally textual philology is relevant here.) Only when a very different model of knowledge, one drawn from the nomothetic natural sciences, elbowed philology onto the sidelines in the late–nineteenth century, did it acquire the seedy air of pedantic fact grubbing that has ever since made the discipline seem as dreary as November in Michigan. In its cheerful heyday, philology produced a distinctive mode of college teaching, belonging neither to the antebellum classical curriculum nor the twentieth-century liberal arts.

Philological teachers aimed not to interpret a text but to supply the lost general lore from an author's culture needed to read it comprehendingly. At Lafayette College, Francis March's students approached *Paradise Lost* "as if it were Homer," with March supplying grammatical, etymological, mythological, biographical, "and other illustrative matter" to help students understand what they were reading. Likewise, Child's Shakespeare class entailed close reading of eight or ten plays, with "much thumbing of Schmidt's *Shakespeare Lexicon*." Direct evidence of

Tyler's teaching is hard to come by, but the occasional knowing allusion to *Quellen* suggests no less philological an approach than Child's.[32]

Given these principles, it made no sense to teach recent literature. Philologists assumed that reading literature required no special techniques: students could read Chaucer in the same way as George Eliot or, for that matter, the *New York Times*. Nor did the text harbor latent or unintended meanings: Chaucer and George Eliot were, at bottom, no more mysterious than the *Times*. True, literature often contained symbolic or allegorical levels of meaning rarely found in the newspapers; and early literature courses doted on works laden with such meanings—*The Faerie Queene, The Divine Comedy*. But such symbolism was neither mysterious, unintended, nor hidden. The reader simply needed to learn the definitions of the symbolic apparatus that the author had chosen to deploy. It was a matter of knowledge, not insight, of fact, not interpretation. The similarity of these views to Protestant biblical literalism is probably not entirely coincidental.

In any case, to concentrate on Spenser and Chaucer was ordinary, to go beyond the seventeenth century striking. The Urcourse in literature, March's at Lafayette, apparently halted in the seventeenth century. Johns Hopkins's first regular instructor in English, appointed in 1879, "touch[ed] nothing later than Shakespeare." Until the 1880s Dryden was the latest author taught at Harvard. (And one wonders whether the course would have stretched to include him, were Dryden not chock-full of obscure allusions to the political and literary life of his epoch.) Tyler, at Michigan, was unusual in bringing authors as modern as Burke, Wordsworth, and DeQuincey into the curriculum and in allowing American literature any place. But even in Ann Arbor the stress fell strongly on fourteenth- through early-seventeenth-century writers; and the American literature was not anything that today's undergraduate would recognize, except perhaps from history courses, for it seems to have included a high concentration of Puritan ministers and to have stopped at the Revolution. As late as 1890, with the Michigan English department expanded to five members, instruction remained heavily concentrated on Shakespeare and earlier writers. Common knowledge gave students the information needed to understand a novel or poem of the last century or two: what was there to teach?[33]

At times the philological teachers can sound stultifyingly narrow, especially when described by the professors who pushed them aside.[34]

But the relevant distinction was not between generalist and specialist, humanist and Gradgrind.³⁵ To cover the span of English literature from Chaucer to Dryden in one semester, as Child did, does not imply obsession with minutiae. And James Russell Lowell's casual, not to say lackadaisical, teaching style hardly suggested a nit-picking fussbudget:

> A student would trudge blunderingly along some passage [of Dante], and Lowell would break in, taking up the translation himself very likely, and quickly find some suggestion for criticism, for elaboration or incidental and remote comment. Toward the close of the hour, question and answer, or free discussion yielded to the stream of personal reminiscence or abundant reflection upon which Lowell would by this time be launched. Especially would he recall scenes in Florence, sketch in words the effects of the Arno, Giotto's Tower, the church in which Dante was baptized, where he himself had seen children held at the same font; and so Lowell gave out of his treasures. . . .³⁶

This is the genial man of letters lounging on Parnassus; but it is also the philologist laboring in the classroom, providing students with a detailed commentary to explain individual references in the text, giving them the sort of information that (Lowell assumed) Dante's original readers would have had.³⁷

Yet Lowell was more than a philologist. He was a moralist. He believed that imaginative writers were in essence moral teachers, that therefore immersion in great literature made readers more ethical.³⁸ Lowell had experienced as a Harvard student the moral didacticism of the antebellum college; it was second nature for him to carry it into the classroom when he himself became a professor. But his moralism had a special sheen. He had imbibed something of the Emersonian idea of the poet as seer and of the Carlylean idea of the poet as prophet. So Lowell translated the poetic function of moral illumination onto an almost transcendental, quasi-religious plane. He spoke as readily of the "mysterious and pervasive essence always in itself beautiful" as he did of the etymology of a Provençal noun.³⁹

This strain in Lowell—the note of mysticism and reverence sounding amid his hardheaded common sense—echoed in more and more literature classes as the century neared its end. George Woodberry, at

Columbia, was said to have infused a spirit of "natural piety" into the teaching of literature, while at Yale "words of enchantment" issued from the lips of Charlton Miner Lewis. Arthur Marsh, America's first professor of comparative literature, wrote in 1888 that he wished his work to subserve "the imaginative and spiritual life of man." Cornell's Hiram Corson tried to specify these elusive "aims of literary study." The "acquisition of knowledge" was, he conceded, "a good thing." So was "sharpening of the intellect" and "the cultivation of science and philosophy." But "there is something of infinitely more importance than all these—it is, the rectification, the adjustment, through that mysterious operation we call sympathy, of the unconscious personality, the hidden soul, which coöperates with the active powers, with the conscious intellect, for righteousness or unrighteousness."[40] This sounds like a mélange of Matthew Arnold and Rosicrucianism.[41]

The belief shared by Rosicrucians with the new breed of English professors was that human beings worked out their salvation by establishing relations with spiritual truths embodied in sacred texts. Philology was pushed aside. Mere elucidation of phrases and contexts no longer illuminated a poem, for its significance lay deeper than its signification. The professor's task became inspiration, not information. Antebellum teachers had also sometimes sought to inspire students: at Harvard Longfellow seems to have approached literature in that mood.[42] Moral philosophy courses commonly tried to improve the seniors as well as inform them. Yet inspiration becoming the central aim of literary study was a new thing.

And any great work of literature, not just the archaic ones philologists favored, could uplift the properly disposed student. Hence, as the teaching of literature took an inspirational turn in secular universities in the 1880s and 1890s, modern poetry and novels appeared in courses. The goal of literary education became to saturate students with the deep truths revealed in great literature. And to do so the teacher needed to induce in the student a receptive mood of due reverence. In the new version of liberal education, a whiff of incense perfumed not only literature courses, but all treatment of the high-cultural heritage.

Indeed, the third key subject in "liberal culture," art history, entered the college curriculum only when secular universities began to feel the need to inject a dose of the vaguely spiritual—as distinct from the specifically Christian. Art was not entirely a curricular novelty. Antebellum colleges had occasionally offered drawing courses; and Michigan had made inconclusive gestures in the direction of something larger in the early 1850s. Yale in 1869 created a School of Fine Arts, independent of the college, to teach painting and drawing. Syracuse in 1872 introduced courses in "drawing and the history of art," leading to the establishment in the following year of an art school separate, as at Yale, from the college and focused on practice. None of this touched the liberal arts curriculum except glancingly.[43]

Art history—or "appreciation"—went far deeper. The founder of college teaching in that subject was Charles Eliot Norton. Hired at Harvard in 1874 for one year on a frankly experimental basis as "Lecturer on the History of the Fine Arts as connected with Literature," Norton was the next year promoted to "Professor of the History of Art," the position he adorned until his retirement in 1898 at the age of seventy. By 1895 William Dean Howells could write that Norton "stand[s] for Harvard in the humanities." Howells perhaps went overboard in asserting that no "fact of our higher civilization" was "more signal, more interesting" than Norton's influence. But it would be hard to overestimate his resonance in the 1890s as spokesman for and icon of "liberal culture" and liberal arts education.[44]

Undergraduates being undergraduates, not all took Norton so seriously. In the old man's last years, escape from his occasionally sententious lectures via fire escape was apparently not unknown to dapper youth. Even then, such blithe disregard was far from the norm. And many spoke of his courses in (metaphorically at least) hushed tones. Students kept recurring to the word "inspiration." Norton was supposed to have led young men "to a truer conception of beauty, and a higher ideal of character and purpose."[45]

This note—that the study of beauty benefited character and purpose—sounded again and again in assessments of his teaching. William Lloyd Garrison Jr. thanked Norton for offering his sons "high ideals, noble ambitions, and the indescribable qualities that constitute character." A student (later editor of the *Atlantic Monthly*) recalled that in Norton's courses, "Beauty became not aesthetic satisfaction merely but took her place high among Moralities." We are back with James Russell Lowell or Hiram Corson, with art somehow giving birth to the ideal, which somehow builds character, infuses ethics. Norton's son used to joke that his father taught modern morals as illustrated by the art of the ancients.[46]

Such notions hovered in the near vicinity of religion, at least as conceived by liberal moralists. George Woodberry, himself an influential teacher of literature at Columbia around the turn of the century, said expressly that Norton's teaching had given him "a perception of spirituality." Another Norton student, the Harvard English professor Charles T. Copeland, described Norton as "a preacher to his students"—though, Copeland added, an "urbane" one (an agnostic Phillips Brooks?). Albert Bushnell Hart, yet another Norton student who ended as a Harvard professor, wrote to him on his retirement: "Yours has been the chapel which students have loved to frequent."[47]

Norton himself had struggled hard enough to legitimate his agnosticism that he was in no danger of confusing his classroom with a chapel. But he did believe that "every generation of youth needs inspirers among the elders," and he intended his teaching to meet this need. Literature served as well as art history for inspiration. Indeed, "the true conception of the Department of Fine Arts," he wrote, "might be expressed by giving to it the name of the Department of Poetry,—using the word 'poetry' in its widest sense as including all works of the creative or poetic imagination." Thus the study of Dante (which Norton taught after Lowell's retirement) became, in Norton's hands, "a study of literature, of poetry, of religion, of morals."[48]

But why did the study of poems and paintings entail religion and morals? Norton impressed on his students that "there cannot be good poetry, or good painting or sculpture, or architecture, unless men have something to express which is the result of long training of soul & sense in the ways of high living & true thought." Art was more than paintings and buildings. It was "an instrument of expression of the higher faculties & emotions of man." "The study of the history of the Fine Arts," therefore, became "the study of the attempts to realize in form the ideals of the mind." Acquainting students with the greatest works of literature and art brought them into contact with the highest human ideals, with "the noblest men the world has known."[49]

In this way, systematic exposure to "poetry in its widest sense" cultivated and disciplined the imagination. And for Norton the imagination was central to the moral life. It brought students into sympathetic relations at once with their fellow human beings and with the highest ideals of the race. It was this profound moral, almost spiritual, effect—this stretching up to the ideal and out to other persons—that made education in the fine arts "a mode of culture without which all other education but imperfectly develops human character."[50]

It followed that Norton treated "Art for art's sake" as "folly" and delusion. He recognized that the artist could, and often did—Norton was no naïf—pervert his talent and skills to create "what is not beautiful." After all, "expression" depended on "character"; and the artist was no more immune to moral infections than anyone else. But truly great works of art were by definition beautiful and, *ipso facto*, comprised a course in ideal morality; for "The beautiful is the good made perfect." If beauty was the "good made perfect," it was the highest purely human ideal. And, for an agnostic like Norton, any ideals transcending the human were illusions. Hence, beauty became for Norton "the highest aim of life." Insofar as Norton had a religion, beauty was it:

> The poets, clearing our vision, help us to see the fair ideals which they create, veiled by the mists of common life, beckon us onward to the heights that lie in the light above the exhalations of the earth. We follow, and tho' we never overtake, the pursuit is not in vain. With each upward step our imaginations breathe a purer eye, and see with clearer vision.

This effusion perhaps did not match the rigor of Thomas Aquinas, but it was what Norton and other teachers of his stripe had to give.[51]

And it worked. Students flocked to the "preaching" in Norton's "chapel" (as Copeland and Hart had it) at the historical moment when Harvard's real chapel became voluntary—and drew a much smaller congregation than Norton's secular substitute. For the infusion of moral or spiritual meaning into poems and paintings became necessary only at that symbolic divide: when the secularization of Harvard's curriculum deprived learning of the coherence previously given it by shared religious beliefs. The problem was not to find a replacement for belief—Norton remained exceptional in giving it up—but to replace its lost unifying expression in the curriculum of secularizing universities and colleges. Norton had invented a partial, but compelling, substitute for the moral philosophy course that had once spelled out these shared convictions. Inheriting the moral didacticism of the old college curriculum, Norton grafted it onto the new subjects that lay at the core of liberal culture and somewhere near the core of liberal education. When education lost the *intellectual unity* certified by moral philosophy, Norton replaced it by infusing "liberal culture" with a common *moral purpose*. Having secularized the sacred, he proceeded to sacralize the secular.

The thinness of this surrogate for religiously founded instruction was not chance. The extreme vagueness of its "spiritual" claims was the key to its success. Only so attenuated a religiosity could creep back into Harvard's now secular curriculum, appealing to both traditional Christians and newfangled agnostics.[52] Norton's agnosticism, common knowledge around Boston, had gotten him into hot water at the outset of his teaching career. His unbelief was still atypical of professors at its end. But by the 1890s he and his teaching had come to be seen as essentially religious. Wrote one former student, himself a minister, "He had no use for the outward forms of religion but he understood and emphasized and illustrated the spiritual values, and he revealed [a revealing word] to us that there may be as much true religion in the spirit in which one doubts as in the most exact formulas of belief." Some of the professed guardians of the exact formulas agreed. An orthodox Protestant magazine published its obituary of Norton under the headline "A Christian Gentleman": despite belonging to no church, he was "none the less a follower of Christ."[53]

In retrospect, Norton's doctrine seems feeble: idealistic moralism puffed up with a vague spirituality. But his reputation as educator among his contemporaries strongly suggests that he was not alone in promoting it as quintessential to the liberal arts. And recall the shift from philology to inspiration in the study of literature. By the turn of the century, a lot of English professors aimed to reveal to the student those meanings in a work of art that (to adopt Hiram Corson's critical vocabulary) would "adjust" the student's "hidden soul" to "righteousness." No wonder that professors expected students to react with "reverence" to Homer, Dante, Shakespeare, and Milton. It seemed fitting and just to call such works the "canon" of great literature, exactly as one spoke of the books of the Bible.[54]

Was the new "liberal culture" the old moral philosophy retuned in an inspirational, rather than analytic, key? Did philosophy, literature, and art history come to be taught as a way of reinfusing purpose into a college curriculum that had lost its intellectual meaning?[55] Did the humanities provide a unifying goal for education that the social and natural sciences could not (despite their greater methodological coherence, their more evident utility, and their superior contemporary élan)? And are the humanities still seen as central in liberal arts education, because they filled the moral vacuum left when explicitly theistic instruction departed the college? Does, then, a form of religion lie at the buried foundations of the humanities, even constitute a hidden agenda? And is their affinity to religion one reason for the curricular primacy, still presumed, of the humanities over the sciences?

If Charles Eliot Norton stood for Harvard, as Howells claimed, and if Harvard stood for all liberal arts colleges, the answers would seem to be yes. But Harvard is not the world (though the contrary dogma is held in some quarters), so these questions remain questions.

CHAPTER FOUR

The "German Model" and the Graduate School

The University of Michigan and the Origin Myth of the American University (written with Paul Bernard)

While chapter 3 involved what we now call "undergraduate education," the present one examines the tortuous path that led in the United States to "graduate education." This, like the mechanical reaper, was a nineteenth-century American invention; though tardier in its adoption by other lands than McCormick's brainchild, it eventually exerted worldwide influence.

The problem of curricular incoherence, central to chapter 3, appears briefly near the end of this one, but as outcome rather than instigator of change. Neither religion nor philology plays an explicit role in this essay, though it is worth noting that the secularization of higher education provides the silent background of this drama and that the principal actors in the later scenes are a classicist and a historian.

The main target here is the simplistic notion, endemic among professors, that Americans created their research universities by copying "the German model." One still frequently hears learned men and women, including historians, who ought to know better, repeating the mantra. Contrary to this academic myth, German example was protean, not univocal, and American practice inventive, not apish.

The origin of the American university, the graduate school in particular, has a kaleidoscopic quality. The pieces are all familar—the early-nineteenth-century colleges with their tiny faculties, small student bodies, and limited curricula; the catalytic example of the great German universities; the takeoff of research; the emergence of graduate training; the professionalization of academic disciplines; the expansion of curriculum; the growth in numbers and infrastructure. Put these bits together, and there appears Cornell or Chicago, Michigan or Notre Dame. But how to fit them together? Where, especially, to put the German example, the piece around which others often appear to coalesce?

Something like a standard pattern has taken shape in university history—one not so much wrong as overly simple. It can be briefly summarized.[1] Before the Civil War, American colleges devoted their energies mostly to controlling unruly students, their curricula to rote learning of classical languages, rhetoric, and simple mathematics. In today's terms, they resembled high schools more than colleges—and certainly not universities, for the best of them aimed only to transmit the existing culture; the expansion of knowledge lay utterly outside their purpose. But the very defects of antebellum colleges provoked reform. Deepening discontent with their intellectual decrepitude inspired efforts to breathe new life into these dry bones; college reform became a persistent issue from the beginning of the nineteenth century.[2] It finally achieved success in the decades after the Civil War.

The key innovations came from a cadre of academics who looked at colleges from a common point of view deriving from a shared educational experience. Since early in the century, aspiring young Americans had embarked for Germany to pursue studies unavailable in their own country.[3] Returning, they imported more than *Wissenschaft*; they brought back a new idea of higher education. These German-trained professors were at first voices crying in the wilderness. But their influence expanded after midcentury when leading college presidents went on pilgrimage to study European education, especially the celebrated German universities.[4] These lessons were swiftly applied. From the failed attempts of the 1820s to pull Harvard out of its slumbers to the invention of the modern American university at Cornell and Johns Hopkins in the 1860s and 1870s, it was the example and personal experience of German universities that commonly inspired reformers and shaped their vision.[5]

Americans saw four principal elements in the German model. First, the Germans clearly distinguished preparatory studies, appropriate to the *Gymnasium*, from the higher learning, proper to the university. Second, German universities assumed as their mission the advancement of knowledge (that is, production of and training in original research). Third, the universities gave both professors and students the independence needed to pursue knowledge (*Lehrfreiheit* and *Lernfreiheit*). Fourth, this research ideal took flesh in distinctive institutional arrangements—notably the seminar, to train researchers, and the Ph.D. degree, to certify their competence. American reformers seldom wished to duplicate exactly the German university in the United States, and German influence ultimately had little direct effect on undergraduate colleges. But these four principles shaped advanced studies. More specifically, the German research ideal and the institutions linked with it led directly to that American invention, the graduate school.

No one believes that German influence tells the whole story. For instance, many scholars see professionalization as an independent force driving the move toward research universities.[6] And, as historians have long pointed out, American university reformers borrowed selectively from Germany.[7] For example, *Lehrfreiheit* translated fairly well into the American practice of academic freedom; but *Lernfreiheit*—the German custom by which a qualified student could enroll at any university, in any course[8]—never habilitated itself in the United States. And what Americans did borrow, they reworked. The Ph.D. degree functioned quite differently in the two countries. In American universities the Ph.D., from the beginning, usually entailed much more substantial research than in Germany. And in America the degree served well into the twentieth century almost exclusively as gateway into the professoriate, in Germany chiefly as a ticket into the civil service or secondary-school teaching. (Indeed, most German students never even took a university degree but used their university studies as preparation for a *Staatsexamen*.) Most strikingly, the Americans concocted a novelty never imagined in Germany: the distinction between undergraduate and graduate studies.

Yet, if the German example does not explain everything, it explains a lot. If native social changes fed the deepest roots of the American research university, Germany still provided the "research ideal." If the German university had little to offer the American undergraduate college, it still was the main influence on advanced training. If Americans picked and chose among German practices, they still got from Germany the characteristic concepts and institutions of graduate education. So the story goes, and it is a plausible one.

Yet, on closer reading, the tale begins to unravel. To begin with, by no means every university reformer waxed lyrical over Germany. Indeed, invocations of German example are in some cases peculiarly sparse. President Charles W. Eliot, the architect of modern Harvard, in his inaugural address in 1869 gave one fleeting mention to Germany in almost thirty printed pages (France got more attention).[9]

The story grows still more tattered. German influence accounts clumsily even for the changes it is supposed to explain in American higher education between 1850 and 1900—even in graduate education. There are too many ill-fitting connections, too many outright gaps. Why did the requirements for and uses of the Ph.D. change so drastically in the United States? Why did the seminar, a semiautonomous institute in Germany, become a one- or two-semester class in America? Where did Americans get the unheard-of notion of distinguishing "undergraduate" from "graduate" schools? The glaring disparity between Teutonic example and American practice may explain why historians put so much emphasis on Johns Hopkins, the one well-studied American university that demonstrably did try to emulate the Germans.[10]

How often did reformers actually follow German patterns? Perhaps even more to the point, *how* did they follow them?

An adequate reply to that question requires the writing of a very large book. But the starting point is easy to find. It lies in recognizing that the German model came in many versions. Different Americans impressed with German education drew differing lessons from its achievements. Their responses varied, less because of ignorance of German practices (as some historians suggest) than because of awareness of American problems.

True, the role of ignorance should never be discounted. Inadequate preparation in the language, brevity of time, the distractions of exotic sights and tastes prevented many American students, possibly most, from knowing well the German universities they attended. Andrew Dickson White seems to have got mostly language practice out of his dilatory term at Berlin, and he was no slouch.[11]

Yet not every Yankee in Göttingen was an innocent abroad, and doltishness goes only so far to explain why each returning scholar recited his own distinctive list of Teutonic virtues and vices. Americans naturally picked out as the salient features of German universities not what a German academic might have chosen, but what rubbed hardest against their own discontents with American higher education. Joseph Cogswell, for instance, was particularly struck by the specialization and diligence of Göttingen's scholars, George Ticknor by the size and currency of its library, John Lothrop Motley by its library—and the absence of dormitories![12] This last impression (which also figured in Henry P. Tappan's specifically Prussian ideal) comes alive when one recalls how much energy antebellum American professors had to pour into merely custodial supervision of the youngsters in their charge. And this peculiarly American reaction makes the point. The motive of reformers was not to emulate Germany, but to improve their own colleges. And thus the origin of the *research university*—Germanic influence and all—only comes into focus when viewed as one outcome of a century-long struggle to redefine the American *college*.

This effort began not long after 1800. From their seventeenth-century beginnings, American colleges had offered an education inherited from the English Renaissance. In early-nineteenth-century colleges, teaching still centered on Greek and Latin, rhetoric, natural philosophy, and mathematics of a fairly practical sort. This was a training nicely suited to prepare teenage boys for life as seventeenth-century gentlemen or even for further study of theology or medicine in seventeenth-century universities.

Its relevance to nineteenth-century America came increasingly into doubt. The celebrated Yale Report of 1828 defended the classical curriculum as providing "the *discipline* and the *furniture* of the mind."[13] But other studies seemed equally able to discipline the mind, while furnishing it to more modern purposes. Ultimately two new paradigms came to compete for control of the colleges. Clear distinction of these two patterns oversimplifies a very confused situation and is possible only in retrospect, though contemporaries were certainly aware of tugs in both directions. One model (appearing in some institutions as early as the 1820s) stressed modern languages, mathematics, and the sciences and claimed to offer an education somehow useful in a modern commercial and technological world. The other developed more gradually out of the old classical education, often claiming the classical mantle. It continued to emphasize Latin and Greek, adding history, literature, and the fine arts; it prized the formation of character and intellect rather than usefulness and by the 1880s had evolved into what we now call the liberal arts ideal.[14]

The "utilitarian" paradigm moved toward specialization of knowledge. The example of increasingly arcane scientific expertise, of newly insistent professional claims to authority, of greater division of labor in the economy all pulled in this direction. Inside and outside the college, division of *intellectual* labor promised efficiency and progress. Indeed, utilitarian reforms were thought to link the college or university with the "real" world outside it. In this sense they belonged with contemporary innovations like the agricultural experiment station and the teaching hospital; they anticipated such early-twentieth-century phenomena as the "Wisconsin Idea" and the industrial research laboratory.

The liberal arts paradigm resisted specialization, insisting on broad grasp and integration of knowledge rather than expertise. It drew strength from the pervasive integrating influence of Scottish common-sense philosophy in antebellum colleges and, later in the century, from idealist philosophy infiltrating from Germany. The liberal arts movement also gained salience from the Victorian crisis of religious faith, which encouraged the search for new sources of cultural unity and spiritual vision to replace the loosening glue of belief in God. In 1895 Charles Eliot Norton summed up the animus of the liberal arts paradigm: "The highest end of the highest education is not anything which can be directly taught, but is the consummation of all studies. It is the final result of intellectual culture in the development of the breadth, serenity, and solidity of mind, and in the attainment of that complete self-possession which finds expression in character."[15] The analogy with the German *Bildung* ideal appears strong, but in fact advocates of the liberal arts looked more to Matthew Arnold than to Wilhelm von Humboldt.

No one drew neat lines between the utilitarian and liberal arts paradigms. The same college president often urged both ideals in a single speech; advocates of each never hesitated to borrow notions native to the other. These labels identify the two major directions of reform, not two warring camps. If these clusters of ideas rested ultimately on incompatible principles, consistency has never been the hobgoblin of academic minds. The baffled offspring of this mixed marriage still bless our campuses today. But to understand the uses of German example, one must realize that college reformers felt pulled toward these two distinguishable, if seldom clearly distinguished, goals.

Amid this swirl of conflicts over the shape of American higher education, the University of Michigan took form. Michigan's young life powerfully influenced the evolution of the research university—and not merely because by the 1870s it had become the largest American university. Henry P. Tappan's much-discussed innovations at Michigan in the 1850s and early 1860s provided the first American model of a modern university. Andrew Dickson White, "perhaps the most significant of the university builders in the United States," spent a decade at Michigan absorbing Tappan's ideas before becoming the first president of Cornell.[16]

Such trailblazing was not much evident in the university's beginnings. At its start Michigan had combined some organizational innovation with a very traditional curriculum. The effective history of the university began with its founding in Ann Arbor in 1837. Lacking any clear American precedent for the role of a state university, the state's constitution writers turned to the French philosopher Victor Cousin's celebrated 1832 report on Prussian education—the most systematically developed and, thanks in large part to Cousin, the most admired of the German educational systems. Following Cousin, Michigan's lawgivers declared the university the capstone of a unified system of public instruction—a capstone, to be sure, with only dreams under it. The example of the Prussian rectorial system (reinforced possibly by sheer parsimony) also apparently suggested a rotating chancellorship, taken each year in turn by one of the professors.[17]

Prussian influence went no further. The university's internal workings, leaving aside its revolving chancellorship, mimicked faithfully the old-fashioned American collegiate model. Lacking any distinctive idea of what curriculum ought to be, the university's regents copied the traditional classical pattern. The faculty even adopted the language of the 1828 Yale Report, though insisting that "mental discipline" was more important than "mental furniture."[18]

Tradition did not bring stability. Cramping poverty disfigured the university's first several years, domestic bickering its next few. The state's political leaders soon felt the need for a steadier hand at the helm than a one-year chancellor's, and the new constitution of 1850 mandated a permanent president. The regents finally hired one in August of 1852.

The man they got—having failed to lure more prominent candidates—was Henry Philip Tappan.[19] A Congregational minister, sometime professor at New York University, writer on philosophic subjects, and great fan of Victor Cousin, Tappan offered as his chief recommendation for the Michigan job that he had recently stamped himself an authority on higher education. In 1851 he published a book called *University Education*, devoted largely to praising the Prussian system à la Cousin, "acknowledged to be the most perfect in the world." Indeed, Michigan's halfhearted visions of building a New Berlin in Washtenaw County's green and pleasant land probably helped to persuade this New Yorker to come west.[20]

For Tappan wanted "a University worthy of the name," by which he meant a Prussian one. He, like the Michigan constitution, imagined the university as capping a unified state system of public instruction. However, Tappan regarded the existing curriculum at American colleges, including Michigan, to be like "that of the Prussian Gymnasia." Ultimately he wanted college work to hive off into the state's secondary schools, which would then assume the current role of American colleges; that is, become Gymnasia. This shift would eliminate the solecism of "a University Faculty giving instruction in a College or Gymnasium."[21]

Tappan realized, however, that for the present the university must continue to give collegiate instruction; so he set as his "first object... to perfect this gymnasium." Tappan wished to make the "correspondence" between college and Gymnasium "as complete as possible." (The "German ideal" before 1860 was characteristically invoked more to support elevation of academic standards and relegation of rote learning to secondary schools than to advance any scheme resembling a research university: the identification by Americans of the German university with the *discovery* of knowledge seems mostly a postbellum development.) To this end Tappan immediately instituted within the Department of Literature, Science, and the Arts "a scientific course parallel to the classical course," with English, history, and additional mathematics displacing Greek and Latin. Tappan stretched the Prussian analogy pretty far here, for the Gymnasium was resolutely classical. Yet he felt the appeal of the utilitarian paradigm, especially in a frontier state (and so did the state legislature: it had mandated some such instruction in the Reorganization Act of 1851). Tappan was quite likely also influenced by the similar curricular reform set in place by Francis Wayland at Brown two years before Tappan reached Ann Arbor. There was to his mind nothing auxiliary or second-rate about utilitarian studies at the "Gymnastic" level.[22]

These reforms expanded the German ideal into what Tappan called "the comprehensive idea of a University." Here a student was supposed to find any instruction desired, including schools of agriculture, fine arts, industrial arts, and pedagogy (though the questing student would have looked in vain for these at Tappan's Michigan). This comprehensive ideal would later resurface in the founding of Cornell by Tappan's disciple, Andrew Dickson White. It would exercise decisive influence on the structure of American universities, especially state universities. Yet Tappan insisted that such schools could not form part of the university "properly speaking." This august entity by definition comprised only the faculties of theology, law, medicine, and philosophy.[23] Adding various subuniversity studies simply patched up deficiencies of American colleges, considered in their role as quasi-Gymnasia. And, "after all that can be done to perfect it," the "Undergraduate course" or "Gymnastic department" is "still limited to a certain term of years, and, necessarily, embraces only a limited range of studies."[24]

These limits seemed to Tappan a crippling defect, for "a system of Public Instruction can never be complete without the highest form of education." Tappan was scarcely alone in recognizing the essentially propaedeutic nature of American colleges. Even the 1828 Yale Report declared as the purpose of collegiate training *"to lay the foundation of a superior education."* Tappan's distinction lay not in recognizing the need, but in trying to meet it—and in invoking a particular version of the German model to do so. A real university must, like Prussian ones, offer "those more extended studies in science, literature, and the arts, which alone can lead to profound and finished scholarship." Following "Prussian principles of education," Tappan regarded such advanced study not as an ornament of the university's work, but as "the culmination of the whole."[25]

He proposed, therefore, "to open courses of lectures" in which college graduates and others prepared "by previous study" could pursue "the highest knowledge." He intended this "University Course," as he called it, to "form the proper development of the University, in distinction from the College or Gymnasium now in operation." All this, he assured his readers, was "in accordance with the educational systems of Germany and France." The course included twenty subjects of study, ranging from "Systematic Philosophy" through "Ethics and Evidences of Christianity," "Chemistry," and "Philology" to "The Arts of Design."[26]

In keeping with its character as true university work, the University Course discarded altogether the method of instruction by class recitation, then still common to all American colleges. Teaching was instead to "be conducted exclusively by lectures." The student would also have "full opportunity" to use "the library and all other means that can aid him in literary cultivation and scientific researches."[27] These "researches" probably did not mean what we now call original research (though that was not excluded) but something closer to looking up information independently, as an undergraduate is now said to "do research" for a term paper. Study in the University Course, unbounded by specified time limits, aimed at the achievement of erudition rather than the fulfillment of requirements. Otherwise, in method and level of teaching, the closest analogy in our present universities is probably to upper-level undergraduate lecture courses.

More to the point, the University Course resembled instruction in German universities. "This Course," Tappan wrote, "when completely furnished with able professors and the material of learning, will correspond to that pursued in the Universities of France and Germany." Despite his pretensions, Tappan was at this date hardly an authority on the "German system." Yet he had learned its broad structure and absorbed his own version of its ideals. Independent learning based on lectures and reading, rather than recitation tested by regular examinations; pursuing the latest knowledge, rather than imbibing traditional learning; concentrating on a few chosen fields, rather than following a standard and rigid curriculum—in all these respects Tappan's program borrowed heavily and self-consciously from the German universities of his day.[28]

Yet Tappan did *not* borrow the elements that loom so large in the received history of German influence and the rise of graduate education. He shied away from narrow specialization, avoiding even the German pattern of examination in one major subject and two minors. He ignored the German Ph.D. degree. Increasingly aware of the prominence of re-

The "German Model" and the Graduate School | 79

search in German universities, he never incorporated it into the University Course. Far from hostile to research, Tappan urged it on his faculty. But discovery of new knowledge never figured as a substantial *educational* ideal in his programmatic statements. Tappan believed lectures and independent reading entirely adequate to convey the "highest learning" and apparently never mentioned the seminar, already the symbol of erudition in Germany.[29]

The most persuasive explanation for this pattern of selective adaptation is the simplest. Tappan's immersion in the problems of American collegiate education had decisively shaped his understanding and uses of the German university. This is not to deny his genuine and uncolored admiration for German education. But his Prussian enthusiasms inevitably filtered through his concerns about the inadequacies of American colleges. And the filtered remains made up his program for the advanced education of college graduates.

Thus, Tappan's "German" system at Michigan was very much part of the confused struggles to reshape the American college. Like Wayland at Brown, whom he much admired, Tappan had considerable sympathy with the "utilitarian paradigm." He worried not so much that the old classical course had grown irrelevant, but that its relevance had grown too limited. With the increasing importance and complexity of science and technology, colleges—especially those responsible to the public at large—needed to add such useful training to their curricula. These concerns led Tappan to the "scientific course" in the "Gymnastic department" and, more generally, to his astonishingly broad construction of the Prussian Gymnasium and his refashioning of the Prussian system into a "comprehensive university."

Yet Tappan's deepest educational loyalties lay with the "liberal-arts paradigm." This informed both his view of the German model and his "University proper" in Ann Arbor.[30] For Tappan, the culmination of education was the integrative culture that he associated with "the highest learning." Hence he quite naturally placed ideals like independent minds, thirst for knowledge, and breadth of learning at the intellectual core of the German university. (How much Tappan's notions actually owed to Humboldt's *Bildung* ideal is not clear.) And he isolated as the key institutions of the German university those arrangements that appeared to him to support such ideals, such as the lecture system. By the same token, Tappan's preoccupations blinded him to the salience of other features of German universities—including the careerism and narrow specialization that had smothered Humboldt's dream in its cradle.

German influence on Tappan was authentic. The pedagogical structure of the University Course and, to some extent, even the liberal arts ideals underlying it really *were* borrowed from Germany—but from a Germany itself seen through the lens of the liberal arts paradigm. *Tappan's* Prussian university, just as his University Course, aimed to produce erudition grounded broadly in "truth, knowledge, beauty, and culture." Indeed, Tappan had a strong sense of the interconnectedness of all knowledge, utterly remote from caricatured notions of German professors, but fairly close to the *Bildung* ideal associated with Humboldt's name.[31]

Yet the University Course was not a direct ancestor of the liberal arts college any more than of the graduate school. It offered education at a much higher level than any mid-nineteenth-century college, in terms of both what it taught and how it taught it. Tappan despaired of the youngsters then entering college mastering such a curriculum. Those who wished *either* the preparatory classical studies of the Gymnasium *or* a simply utilitarian education would find it in college. True liberal education awaited those who had made it through college. Yet, though postgraduate, the University Course was hardly graduate school in the later sense: it lacked both narrow specialization and focus on research training. Although Tappan's University of Michigan was the most celebrated German-model university in midcentury America, it resembled no mature form in the American university. German influence in American higher education followed a more tortuous path than historians have generally allowed.

Tappan's vision of university studies amounted to little more than a pipe dream when he left Ann Arbor. Why he failed is a matter of conjecture: perhaps chiefly for lack of clientele. Michigan did institute several "postgraduate" lecture courses toward the end of his tenure, but who populated them is a mystery, since there were never more than two or three resident graduates in arts and sciences.[32] Still, in proposing to turn college graduates into learned Germans, Tappan began the serpentine movement that eventually led to graduate training at Michigan. In the process, he also stepped on too many toes. The wonder is that he survived for over ten years. In 1863 the Board of Regents, unjustly, foolishly, inevitably, fired him.

The "German Model" and the Graduate School

Tappan's successor was Erastus O. Haven, who spent his six years in office scowling at innovation.[33] In his haste to restore the good old days Haven immediately expunged from the catalogue the self-consciously Prussian statement on the "Organization of the University" that had appeared throughout Tappan's term; eventually he even dropped the word "undergraduates." Nevertheless, Tappan's University Course had taken on a life of its own, even if a feeble one, as the route by which aspirants to the master's degree prepared for their examinations. On average, about six graduate students seem to have attended each year during the Haven interregnum—actually an increase over the Tappan years.[34]

When Haven resigned in 1869 to become president of Northwestern, it took the regents two years to find a replacement. In the meantime Henry Simmons Frieze, professor of Latin, served as acting president. Frieze had come to Ann Arbor in 1854 and immediately caught Tappan's Germanophilia. The next year he traveled in Europe, apparently attending lectures at Berlin during the winter term. "What he saw with his own eyes more than confirmed his previous impressions of the great excellence of the German gymnasial and university training, and after his return he never ceased to commend the application of German methods" to American schools and universities.[35]

It was therefore no surprise that Frieze revived Tappan's project of turning the state's high schools into Gymnasia. He even looked forward to replacing ultimately the bachelor's degree with a certificate of proficiency, to be granted by the high-schools-become-Gymnasia. This would have amounted to an American version of the Prussian *Abitur,* though apparently minus the standardized examination required of Gymnasium graduates in Prussia. (The *Abitur* not only certified successful completion of the Gymnasium course but *ipso facto* qualified a student for university admission.) Frieze actually did inaugurate a scheme of admission-by-diploma for graduates of high schools inspected and approved by University of Michigan faculty, eventually including schools as far away as New York and New England.[36] This idea evolved into the now universal American practice in which high-school transcripts replace the old, widely varying entrance examinations given by every college. But outside the university Frieze's ambitions seemed never quite understood. The high schools never became Gymnasia. College studies remained in college.

Serious development of graduate education took place after James B. Angell arrived in Ann Arbor in 1871.[37] Angell held the presidency until 1909. During his first two decades, all the distinguishing marks of today's graduate school appeared at the university: the distinction from both undergraduate education and postgraduate professional studies; the focus on training in original research; the entrenchment of the seminar as the characteristic method of such training; the awarding of the Ph.D. as the research degree; and finally, in 1891–92, the formal organization of the graduate school.

James B. Angell was the chief architect of the modern state university, a giant of the founding era of the research university. But he was almost entirely marginal in the story of graduate education. Unlike Tappan or Frieze, he cherished no broad vision of the future. Though fond of uttering appropriate pieties on public occasions, Angell really operated as promoter, fund-raiser, manager. In exercising these skills extraordinarily well, Angell carved out the niche that university presidents fill today. His diverse interests, humane sympathies, and genius for compromise made him effective and popular. He had a good eye for talent: hired it, nurtured it, gave it a free hand. He often welcomed innovation but usually let others do the innovating, particularly in graduate education, for his heart lay with the college. The graduate school evolved less under Angell's direction than under his benign smile—and under the long shadow of Henry Philip Tappan.[38]

The key players were Henry Frieze and Charles Kendall Adams. Frieze was not only Tappan's most ardent disciple; he also enjoyed a friendship with Angell stretching back over twenty-five years. This long-standing amity, together with his own experience in running the university, gave Frieze probably more leverage than any other member of the faculty. After stepping down as acting president in 1871, Frieze embarked on his second European journey, this one of two years' duration. He renewed his admiration for the German university during a term at the University of Tübingen "diligently studying Sanskrit under that great scholar, Professor Roth."[39]

The other major actor, Charles K. Adams, imbibed Tappan's ideas direct from the source as a Michigan undergraduate. A second critical influence was his professor of history, Andrew Dickson White. White had arrived in Ann Arbor in 1857, Adams's freshman year, and immediately proved a rousing teacher. He "sent a sort of historical glow through all the veins and arteries of the University," Adams later recalled. White introduced a vaguely German mode of instruction (possibly inspired by his own brief attendance at Berlin), replacing recitations with lectures and encouraging students to read beyond the textbook. His reliance on lectures soon spread to other professors—an enduring and substantial innovation. White also proposed somehow to "exercise" students in "original investigation," though this ambition vanished from the catalogue after his first year.[40]

Adams, graduating in 1861, continued his study of history under White, receiving in 1862 one of the first earned master's degrees. In that same year Tappan appointed him a junior faculty member. When White became president of Cornell in 1867, Adams replaced his mentor as professor of history. Upon appointment, Adams immediately took a year's leave to travel and study in France, Italy, and Germany. This *Wanderjahr* evidently stoked an already warm enthusiasm, inherited from Tappan and White, for the German university. Adams returned fired with the idea of extending, along German lines, White's reform of college history teaching.[41]

This urge vented itself in a new course for seniors in 1871–72: "something akin to the *Historische Gesellschoft* [sic] of the German universities." That is to say, a seminar, by some definitions the first taught in the United States. Adams sent his students off to write papers, armed with lists of assigned topics and of "the best authorities in the University library"; and each week class discussion centered on one of these student essays.[42] The seminar method struck a chord among students.[43] It soon popped up in a few other fields. It is hard to know exactly what Adams's imitators assumed they were imitating, but occasional hints suggest self-conscious discipleship to Germany.[44]

Yet were Adams and his colleagues really teaching seminars properly called? In terms of the received history of graduate education, the answer is no. The Michigan seminars catered mainly to advanced undergraduates, not graduates. Nor did the students in them pursue original research as now understood in American Ph.D. programs (that is, the discovery of information, or implications of information, not previously recognized: the effort to advance knowledge). Adams's seminar—evidence is lacking for the others—centered on carefully directed exercises in the use of sources. Students wrote fairly short papers, typically using printed collections of excerpts from original sources and following a "pamphlet of 'questions' with references" prepared for them by Adams. Far from pursuing independent projects, each week all students in the seminar studied the same subject. To be sure, the seminar involved "a higher grade of historical investigation" than lectures, but Adams never hinted that it looked toward original research or even preparation for it (though presumably a student who intended a career as historian would have enrolled in the seminar). Not any desire to train professional researchers, but dissatisfaction with the rote learning, recitations, and elementary instruction of the old college curriculum pushed the university's faculty toward the seminar.[45]

Yet these Urseminars probably resembled more closely than their descendants the practice of mid-nineteenth-century German universities. German universities, after all, had no "graduate" students, simply students. Seminars provided advanced training for those who intended to make a career in the field of the seminar, but not usually a career of original scholarship. Most students probably aimed to become Gymnasium teachers.[46] Indeed, until well after midcentury, training for pedagogy seems explicitly to have dominated the purposes of seminars.[47] German seminars did train students in research techniques, on the assumption that in this way a student achieved a sophisticated grasp of the subject matter. But something like Adams's small-scale exercises in using documents was probably much commoner than the original research projects on which American seminars soon came to center.[48] If the early Michigan seminars now look more like undergraduate than graduate study, it was not because they were unfaithful to their German models.

The seminar was only one of a batch of changes at Michigan in the 1870s meant to raise the level of college work. The lecture method continued gradually to infiltrate instruction; the credit-hour system was introduced; and, in the late 1870s, the university expanded the number of electives permitted in undergraduate programs. Unlike the seminar, none of these had German associations (the lecture method having been around long enough at Michigan to lose its Teutonic coloration).

Yet, like the seminar, they had the unintended consequence of laying a firmer basis for postgraduate education. They freed faculty to teach more sophisticated and specialized courses and to devote more attention to advanced students. This upgrading of undergraduate education thus made realistic two changes in higher degrees introduced in the midseventies: the toughening of requirements for the master's and the awarding of the Ph.D. degree. By 1880, twenty-one candidates for advanced degrees were enrolled in Ann Arbor. Not all were postgraduates—a reminder that "graduate education" had not yet jelled.[49]

The university followed the German model in its Ph.D. requirements: awarding it "on examination" for "special proficiency in some one branch of study, and good attainments in two other branches." A first degree and two years' residence were prerequisites. Research was probably from the beginning associated with the new degree in many cases, if not most. In 1879 the university formally declared that "faithful and industrious work" did not suffice; the candidate must also evince "power of original research and of independent investigation."[50] But it is not at all clear that the Ph.D. was primarily meant for researchers or even specialists; nor does research (as distinct from independent reading) seem always to have bulked large in Ph.D. work, especially outside the natural sciences. It does seem that natural scientists typically regarded the Ph.D. as a research degree from the outset.[51]

Frieze and Adams warmly supported all these innovations. Frieze hoped that they would lift Michigan "out of the narrow ruts" of the local college, make it "a national University." But such scattershot changes did not create a true university. "It is manifestly difficult, if not impossible," Frieze wrote in 1880, "to change the Gymnasium into a University by merely building up a system of post-graduate courses, as a sort of annex to the old established curriculum of four years; for the post-graduate work will thus continue to be a mere subsidiary appendage, and the so-called Collegiate Department will still be the central and characteristic part of the institution."[52]

Frieze had long hungered for the day when Tappan's dream might take flesh in Ann Arbor. He wanted collegiate studies, pending their relegation to the high schools, pushed back into the first year or two of the Michigan course, leaving three years for university studies proper— explicitly on the model of the German universities.[53] Frieze found a zealous second in Adams. Angell, while not hostile to such ideas, was hardly the man to transform Michigan into Tappan's notion of Berlin. But in 1880 Angell left Ann Arbor on a diplomatic assignment, and Frieze once again became acting president.

Acting presidents are not supposed to revolutionize their institutions. They do, however, have to respond to emergencies. In the spring of 1881 Frieze discovered a convenient pair of them. Judge Thomas M.

Cooley, the star of the Law School, threatened to quit unless he could shift his teaching to constitutional law and history. Frieze agreed, even proposed that Cooley lecture in the arts faculty as well as the Law School. Cooley replied that his courses might then be grouped with kindred subjects in a complete program. Frieze saw in this suggestion the means to douse another fire. Charles K. Adams's old teacher, Andrew D. White, was wooing Adams for Cornell, promising to let him organize a school embracing historical and political studies. Frieze offered to make Adams dean of a similar new outfit at Michigan and trumped White by putting the celebrated Cooley on Adams's faculty. Thus was hatched the School of Political Science.[54]

Its presiding deity was Henry Philip Tappan. Adams, presumably in consultation with Frieze, designed the program to correspond to Tappan's vision of the true university, hitherto found only east of the Rhine. Students would enter the School of Political Science after completing their "secondary or gymnasial training" in the ordinary "required studies" of the first two years of college (at Michigan or elsewhere). Once admitted to the school, students learned through the methods proper to a university: lectures and seminars. After a minimum of three years' study, they became eligible to present a thesis and take oral examinations. The thesis had to show "elaborate study of the subject considered" and "so far as is practicable . . . original research." The orals tested "special proficiency" in one branch of knowledge and "good attainments" in two others. A sufficient degree of "excellence" on both thesis and examinations earned the Ph.D. The three-year term, the lectures and seminars, the thesis and examination, the major field with two minors, the Ph.D. as the ordinary university degree were all familiar features to German students. The School of Political Science was as close a replica of a German university as anything that had ever existed in America—or ever would.[55]

So close that it puzzled most of the university's faculty. The School of Political Science as such roused no notable opposition, but the awarding of the Ph.D. to its graduates ignited an explosion. Angell's son reported to his father a "quite warm" dispute pitting "Frieze & Adams vs the crowd." The crowd feared that awarding the Ph.D. after only five years of study "would cheapen the degree." Frieze called them old fogeys, simply afraid to do anything differently from Harvard. In any case, the faculty established a committee to report on the question: a committee that included Frieze and Adams among its five members.[56]

Both men conceived the School of Political Science in the larger context of reforming the traditional American college. Two months before Cooley suggested the new program, Adams had written to Angell about allowing students more freedom of choice, even permitting the better of them to finish in three years or proceed to a master's degree in four. Frieze, in reporting to the regents in June 1881, had suggested extending the principle of the new school to the entire faculty of the Department of Literature, Science, and the Arts.[57]

Frieze and Adams now used the faculty committee as a vehicle to do just that. Its report recommended including the rest of the arts-and-sciences faculty in this "true University." A few modifications reassured the "old fogeys." Ultimately, the faculty further insisted that the Ph.D. thesis "evince power of research and of independent investigation"—the standard adopted in 1879—and that doctoral candidates learn enough French and German "for purposes of study." To assuage faculty concerns that students would fritter away their time, each student had a three-member faculty committee to supervise her or his program: the putative ancestor of the dissertation committee. But with these concessions (and with the support of Angell, who returned at midyear) Frieze and Adams at last pushed through the faculty in the spring of 1882 an idea of university education dramatically new for America. Its name echoed Tappan: the University System.[58]

Conventional college and postgraduate programs remained in place alongside the University System. At the end of the sophomore year, having completed what Frieze thought of as Gymnasium work, students elected either the ordinary credit system (itself a recent innovation) or the University System. Credit-system students took courses for two more years, accumulated credits, and earned a bachelor's degree, as American undergraduates still do. Students who opted to enter the "true University" attended lectures, took seminars, and pursued independent work, all focused in groups of studies. (An attempt by Frieze and Adams actually to divide the arts-and-sciences faculty into four subfaculties—professedly following German practice, though not in fact very closely—had failed of adoption.) At the end of two years, the student took examinations in one major field and two minors. Students who merely passed received a bachelor's degree. Students who passed with distinction and presented an acceptable thesis received a master's degree. At the end of the third year came another examination in the three fields and another thesis. Students awarded the bachelor's degree at the previous examination now had a chance to present a thesis along with the examination and earn a master's. For those students who had earned the master's a year previously, leaping this final hurdle brought a Ph.D.[59]

This seemed very like Tappan's German program of advanced education. And both structure and inspiration were indeed similar. Yet much had transpired in the nearly two decades since Tappan's ouster. Graduate education had become a reality, if not exactly a numerically overwhelmingly one, both at Michigan and elsewhere. The two or three "resident graduates" of the Tappan years had grown to a couple of dozen. Tappan's University Course took its rather airy form in a college populated by teenagers; Frieze and Adams could not help but take into account a critical mass of career-minded twenty-five-year-olds. Moreover, Michigan faculty now could measure the Frieze-Adams proposals against competing American programs of advanced education, not just foggily understood German ones. In the debate over the University System, professors drew comparisons to the Harvard Ph.D. as often as the German one.[60]

And the example of Harvard, Yale, or Hopkins weighed on the side of greater specialization, heavier stress on research. Research and publication, and with them specialization, had by this time worked their way into the normative conception of the university professor, though not yet the college professor. Professors engaged in research expected their advanced students to work with them; students, for their part, began to expect training in research as part of normal preparation for the life of professor.

Both professors and students began also to look upon the Ph.D. as certifying this sort of training. The degree was a foreign transplant brought in, repotted, watered, and beloved only by professors; it appealed, at first, to no other occupational group. Not surprisingly, those who hoped to become professors made up most of the candidates for it. Thus the degree itself became linked to professorial training, especially training in the specific skill that distinguished the high-powered, new-model professor from the tattered older version: research. This linkage was reinforced by the centrality of specialized research in the careers of German professors, even though the educational program of German universities did not focus on research. The Ph.D. was, in Germany, the ordinary arts degree. But as the professor's degree in America, it acquired the character of the German professor rather than that of the program in which he lectured.

Adams and Frieze's version of the German model had thus evolved some distance from Tappan's. As Tappan's disciples they kept alive a conception of German university education as culturally formative and broadly integrative. Yet, with its focus on three limited fields and its specialized thesis, their University System was more cramped than Tappan's University Course, even if closer to the realities of German education. They had diluted Tappan's understanding of the German system, informed by the incipient liberal arts ideal, with a substantial admixture of utilitarian motives. The compromises forced on them by skeptical colleagues pushed them further in this direction.

Thus, research held a secure place in the University System. Both Frieze and Adams believed that university professors bore an obligation to expand knowledge. The flexible rubrics of the University System allowed students to train for a specialized academic research career; a few of them, particularly in the natural sciences, seem to have done so. (At every stage of the development of advanced degrees at Michigan, training in the natural sciences seems to have been more research-oriented than in other fields.) President Angell went overboard in claiming that "original research of real worth will be expected in every case." In fact, the requirements only mandated research "so far as the resources of the University permit"—not a stiff standard for students writing theses in, for example, American colonial history. Adams and Frieze would probably not have gone even this far, for they did not regard the Ph.D. as quintessentially a research degree. But their colleagues did and insisted that every thesis demonstrate the *capacity* for research.[61]

Yet the University System did not chiefly mean to train researchers or specialists. Lecture courses, independent reading, the occasional seminar were expected to dominate workloads—as one might suppose when students began after the sophomore year. The typical thesis probably amounted to nothing more ambitious than today's undergraduate senior honors thesis. Nor did the curriculum focus effort on one discipline—in contrast to the graduate programs then developing at Hopkins and elsewhere.[62] Whether the major and minor fields bore any relationship to each other depended on the inclinations of particular students and professors, as indeed it had for graduate students in the 1870s. The fields chosen under the University System often fell, not surprisingly, into either scientific or nonscientific triads—like history, political economy, and German, or zoology, geology, and physiology. But combinations like Greek, philosophy, and physics were not unheard of. The University System fostered more concentration than the credit system, but it aimed no more at specialization than at the production of scholars.

The real intention was to produce effectively educated citizens. Frieze hoped to give students "a large and thorough preparation for the duties that will devolve upon them as citizens and members of society," to "fit them for those public duties to which every citizen is liable to be called." Adams shared this outlook. And on this point both were in harmony with Angell—which provides another reason for his support of the University System. In stressing the usefulness of such training— "preparation for duties" as distinct from formation of character—all three were leaning toward the utilitarian paradigm of college reform.[63]

Finally, though, the University System subordinated utility and special training to wider ideals. An advanced education was here not tightly focused but integrative. In the view of Frieze and Adams, even students training as specialists should learn to put their advanced training in the service of the commonweal. Even students intending a research career should learn to fit their research into broader advances in knowledge. And, conversely, even students seeking a general education should learn to handle some special field with technical sophistication. Advanced education was still to be liberal education, though less fullblooded than in Tappan's version. As a later advocate of the University System explained, "The argument for a certain degree of specialization does not rest upon the demand for specialists but upon the claim that some practice in specialization is necessary to complete a liberal education. An educated man ought to be able to pass just criticism on the intellectual products of his own time." It was this sort of advanced, but liberal, education that Tappan believed German universities to supply. It was to provide this education that Frieze and Adams tried to reform the college—and simultaneously channel the emerging demand for graduate training—into the University System.[64]

There is little point in rehearsing the actual deficiencies of the University System in supplying the article in question, which were considerable. There is even less reason to speculate on whether the University System could have realized this perhaps utopian vision. For the System sputtered and wheezed little past wishful thinking.

Few faculty or students seemed to know what to do with it. Frieze and Adams could persuade their colleagues to approve the institutional changes constituting the University System; they could not implant in their minds the larger vision of the German university that infused these arrangements with appealing meaning. Only a handful of students entered the program. At first the majority proceeded directly to master's degrees; but by 1886 the old notion had decisively reasserted itself that the bachelor's was the proper undergraduate degree; and the University System became simply an alternative to the credit system as *preparation* for an advanced education. No undergraduate ever proceeded to a Ph.D. on the University System. When Adams left for Cornell in 1885, only Frieze remained to speak for Tappan's idea of advanced education. He died in 1890. In effect, the University System had predeceased him.[65]

Its demise in no way cramped the growth of other species of advanced education. Indeed, what became the conventional form of graduate education flourished in impudent good health—and without, it seems, deliberate feeding. Graduates showed up to work for an advanced degree, and faculty dealt with them catch as catch can. The number of graduate students quintupled in the decade after 1881; by its end Angell was handing out three or four doctorates annually.[66] The students finally grew so numerous, their training so confused, that in 1891 the college set up a graduate school to manage the operation.[67]

The infant graduate school was swaddled in repeated invocations, almost ritual incantations, of its German pedigree. Professors and students alike seem to have looked to Germany as their intellectual homeland. But their Germany was not Tappan's, Frieze's, or Adams's. It was the land of the German *professor*, not of German *education*. The operative image of the German university now refracted the Berlin of the research ideal, not of the *Bildung* ideal. The Ph.D. became linked exclusively to specialized training in original research. Descriptions of graduate courses stressed their technical nature and highlighted the distinction between graduate and undergraduate work. Beginning in 1894, Ph.D. candidates had to choose as their two minor studies "cognate[s] to the major"; one of them could be simply "a more thorough treatment" of the major. The language requirement insisted on French and German "sufficient for purposes of research," as opposed to the earlier "purposes of study." The Ph.D. thesis now *had* to be "an original contribution to scholarship or scientific knowledge" that was "confined within narrow bounds," requiring at least "the greater part of one academic year" to prepare.[68]

The graduate student's virtue, one Michigan professor wrote in 1892, "is an independent scholarly grasp of one or two subjects." This man conceded that imparting a "general education" is "an honorable calling"—may even be good for the researcher in small doses—but "it is not the proper function of a university professor."[69] So much for Tappan. General education belonged in the preparatory years of the college. Advanced education meant specialized research training. Just when the liberal arts paradigm was finding a permanent home in the liberal arts college, the utilitarian paradigm was settling down for a long winter's nap in (among other places) the graduate school.

These sharp distinctions between undergraduate and graduate education did not force themselves on the university. To the contrary, the *inability* to find any real difference between the supposed two levels embarrassed Michigan professors time and again in the early years of graduate education.[70] They drew the line not to map an existing divide, but to create one. An increasingly specialized and research-minded professoriate believed that mature knowledge should belong in specialized divisions, separate from general culture, and they acted so as to give life to their belief. By doing so they brought to birth the graduate school and killed the University System.

Tappan's vision of the American college transformed into a true university starved in an environment that gave it no sustenance. For by the 1880s the American college had reconstructed itself in forms that left no place for any scheme like the University System. On the one hand, the liberal arts paradigm had defined the *college* as a place where students absorbed general culture before going on to advanced training. The turn-of-the-century college might voice the Mr. Chips ideal of the Amhersts and Williamses; it might fly the flag of maturity-through-independence, like the Harvards and Michigans with their elective systems. But general education, understood as the province of the college, was inevitably understood as preparatory.

On the other hand, the utilitarian paradigm increasingly expressed itself in specialized training, with knowledge cut up into segments related only instrumentally. To the traditional law schools, medical schools, and (more recent) divinity schools were added engineering schools, business schools, education schools, and the like. The new graduate schools of arts and sciences resembled these, with the crucial difference that the graduate school did not define its subject (its equivalent of engineering or divinity) as an applied skill but as "pure knowledge."[71] This knowledge meant not the general culture of the college, but specialized disciplines only marginally related to the discourse of other specialized disciplines. And advanced education meant training in research in one of these specialized disciplines. A student who moved from the preparatory education of the college to the advanced education of the graduate school left general culture behind.

And this increasingly clear division of labor brought with it a change in the meaning of "the German model." If Michigan is typical, German influence neither increased nor diminished between the 1850s and the 1890s. (And the histories of other major universities do suggest, mutatis mutandis, a similar pattern.)[72] But what German example was held to teach varied enormously from time to time and place to place. Broadly and very tentatively speaking, in the 1850s (and probably earlier), the university-Gymnasium distinction, the lecture system, and perhaps the *Bildung* ideal suggested ways to upgrade college education, but probably nothing like the professional graduate school. Yet by the 1880s the German research ideal suggested, or at least legitimated, just the sort of undergraduate-graduate distinction institutionalized in the graduate school. To be sure, German universities had changed over these years; most to the point, by the 1880s seminars and laboratories had developed into highly visible institutions dedicated to research. But more important were changes in the American context, notably in the character of the professoriate, that encouraged American academics to read the German evidence differently.

Out of the cocoon of the old-fashioned American college, then, emerged that strangely divided personality native to the New World, the American university. The graduate school and the new-model college evolved as distinct, largely unconnected entities. In them the same faculty often taught, students moved from one to the other; but, in each, different educations and different conceptions of knowledge prevailed.

For a while in the 1850s and 1860s, it looked as if the Prussian road would lead Americans to something rather like a supercharged liberal arts college, drawing students from a souped-up high school. But, around the 1870s, most American academics began interpreting the highway markers differently; so the road veered sharply. More precisely, Americans discarded the *educational* program of German universities. (Rejection was not necessarily deliberate; how well Americans, even those who studied in Germany, understood the German system is still very much an open question.) They then took the German invention of highly specialized *professorial* research—not, properly speaking, a part of German university education at all—and built on it the advanced segment of American university education. Precisely because specialized research training made no sense for most university students, such advanced education had to be split off from the ordinary university course. This division compounded the irony of stealing the ordinary German degree for the use of the graduate school.

This transmogrification of German practice was the really substantial American contribution to the research university. The Germans invented the research ideal. The Americans invented an institution to house and perpetuate it. By throwing this distinction into sharper relief—and by clearing away the underbrush that has obscured some roads not taken—Michigan's story helps to clarify the knotty problem of German influence in American university history. It also reminds us that the founding principles of the graduate school defined graduate training in self-conscious opposition to general education and common culture. The ever narrowing gyre of specialization was no accidental spinoff from the modern fragmentation of knowledge, but the flight plan of the graduate school from its launching.

CHAPTER FIVE

The Forgotten History of the Research Ideal

The "research ideal" is another hoary origin myth of the American university. That some such ideal did gain power between 1850 and 1900 lies beyond dispute. That it appeared only in one edition or that it always closely resembled what professors later thought of as "research" are highly doubtful propositions. This chapter suggests that at least two "research ideals" competed in the last decades of the nineteenth century. And, once more, language study looms large, for one of these, I claim, had roots in philology.

The creation in the late–nineteenth century of the American university, powered at its core by a new ideal of professorial research, may well be the most visible success story in the history of education in the United States. By the turn of the twenty-first century American elementary and secondary schools seemed creaky compared to those in other economically advanced societies, but American research universities drew students from all over the world. It is no wonder that the rise of the university is celebrated in what we may regard as not so much history in the usual sense, but a great origin myth. In it, doughty champions of research smite doddering defenders of old ways and found gleaming new cities of scholarship.

Historians of higher education know that the story is more complicated. They stand in relation to other academics rather as biblical critics stand in relation to unsophisticated Christians. And, like biblical critics, they have learned that cherished myths prove impervious to unwelcome facts. One still hears erudite men and women relate with childlike enthusiasm the old tale of the German university transported to the American strand.

The central motif in the origin myth is the triumph of the research ideal. And there is no doubt that professors in the later–nineteenth century poured out gallons of ink arguing about research. Oddly, historians of higher education, while universally registering the importance of "research" in the new universities, have not examined very closely what was actually said about it. Yet when one begins to dissect the arguments over the place of research in the first American universities—and over the very nature of academic research—ghosts of very strange visage arise from those musty pages.

To understand these arguments, to begin to make the acquaintance of these lost ancestral spirits, we need first to recall that universities did not spring up ex nihilo in the United States. Rather, they grew from efforts to correct perceived deficiencies in American undergraduate colleges.[1] To understand the ideas prevailing in the new universities, we first have to remember a few things about the colleges that preceded them: two of particular salience to the meanings of "research."

First, although college curricula were pretty disjointed, the senior course in moral philosophy laid a veneer of intellectual coherence over these studies and, indeed, over knowledge in general. The presuppositions of the moral philosophy course reflected, in turn, the basic axiom of knowledge in what was still a religiously based culture; to wit, all knowledge formed a coherent whole because reality itself was coherent: the universe was purpose-built by a divine Creator. The conclusion logically followed that, with enough effort and erudition, any piece of knowledge could be related to any other piece.[2]

The second thing to remember about the colleges is that the professors who taught in them were usually "generalists." They taught a wide variety of courses and rarely had detailed knowledge of any particular subject. In modern American terms, most of them resembled high-school teachers more closely than college professors. If they wrote books or articles—which most did not—they characteristically wrote for a general, educated audience, not for specialists.

This situation changed dramatically between 1850 and 1900. During those decades college reformers invented the modern American university. (They also invented the modern liberal arts college, but that does not concern us now.) In the last half century, historians of higher education have cobbled together a comprehensive story of how this happened.[3] The story is far from perfect, in large part because scholarly attention has in recent decades shifted away from the origin of the university to its twentieth-century development; away from the institutional and intellectual shape of higher education to its social role; away from the history of emergent universities to that of what used to be called "the old-time colleges."

In consequence, the emergence of the university is still a half-built narrative. For instance, at its center remains a still too simplistic reading of the influence of German universities in America.[4] For another instance, it completely overlooks two key domestic influences on thinking about universities: the model presented by theological seminaries, the first American institutions to provide academic graduate training, and the example of biblical criticism, the first sophisticated learned discourse in America. This defective historiography limps along, for lack of anything sturdier to replace it.

One piece of the story, in particular, has so far gone largely uncontested. In the emerging universities, it is said, the old generalist professors were increasingly challenged by newfangled specialists: disciples and apostles of a new ideal of academic research. Often trained in German universities, some even had a German Ph.D. degree. They taught (or at least wished to teach) only one subject—chemistry, not the gamut of natural history; Greek, not ancient languages; economics, not history and the social sciences. They had detailed learning in this particular discipline. They pursued serious original research on specialized aspects of their subject. They organized themselves into professional associations comprised of specialists in a single discipline: the American Philological Association (1869), the American Chemical Society (1876), the Archaeological Institute of America (1879), the American Historical Association (1884), and so forth. These societies in turn spawned learned journals, in which specialists shared their research with each other.

Gerald Graff draws an exemplary contrast between two Harvard professors of the late–nineteenth century, James Russell Lowell and Francis James Child, which illustrates this supposed academic revolution. They were friends; but Lowell was the dilettantish generalist, roaming largely and lightly over literature, concerned to inspire his students rather than to train them, himself disdaining real research. He used his 1889 presidential address to the Modern Language Association to urge the association "to shift the emphasis from [research-oriented] philology to literature." Child was the specialized philologist, equipped with a German doctorate, "recognized as a far greater scholar" than Lowell; he taught Shakespeare as "the distinctions of quartos and folios, sources, stage conditions."[5] Specialists like Child, inspired by the Germanic research ideal, withdrew from the garden of general lore to cultivate intensively their own private plots.

As a result, erudition became unprecedently deep in individual fields of knowledge, but the connections *between* fields inevitably broke down. By 1900 or shortly thereafter, in American universities research (and graduate studies, which had come to mean training for research) consisted of investigations in a hodgepodge of unrelated academic specialties. A specific example of this transition, indeed an apt symbol for it, is the fate of the traditional moral philosophy course. Once the authoritative demonstration of the unity of knowledge, the moral philosophy course fissioned in the decades after the Civil War. From its breakdown emerged separate disciplines never before taught as independent subjects in American colleges: political science, economics, sociology, anthropology. Its moralistic purpose hobbled off into the new philosophy departments as ethics, where it was soon drained of any moral aim. The old unity of knowledge yielded to a babel of mutually incomprehensible disciplinary discourses. The ever louder calls for "interdisciplinary" research, heard since the 1930s, reflect, in this scenario, Sisyphean efforts to atone for this academic fall from grace.

So the story goes, and it is a plausible one. It is probably also wrong. Or, to be more precise, it represses lost alternatives—represses them so thoroughly as to hide the arguments that actually went on in the new universities. This is history written by the victors, even if the victors now feel a little guilty about their triumph. And, like other cases of victors' history, the story's very structure incorporates and perpetuates the defeat of the losers.

Yet, as soon as one steps outside of the story, as soon as one frees oneself from its assumptions and closures, the texts left behind from the 1870s, 1880s, and 1890s make room for a very different tale. The reader is warned that what follows is a sketch map of terrain still mostly terra incognita. Yet sketch maps, for all their defects, are an invaluable tool for explorers.

Insofar as I can see into this particular wilderness, the crucial struggle in early American universities did not take place between "generalists" and "specialists." It brought into conflict, rather, advocates of two different research ideals, two opposing models of erudition; the war was not between old and new, but between two new versions of scholarship. Neither was "generalist" in the usual sense of limited or dilettantish learning. Both insisted that professors in the new universities should exhibit deep erudition and real expertise. But where one group saw little or no connection between specialized areas of knowledge, the other continued to regard all knowledge as composing a unified whole, accessible, moreover, to a generally educated public. The struggle over the research ideal did not pit ignorant "generalist" against erudite "specialist," but what we might call "specialized" or "disciplinary" erudition, on the one hand, against a kind of "common" erudition on the other.

The first, or "specialized-disciplinary" research ideal derived most probably from the natural sciences—or, to be more precise, from the fields of astronomy and physics, increasingly mathematicized and increasingly inaccessible to ordinary educated people. This is not surprising, for the growing prestige of the natural sciences in nineteenth-century America is a truism. What *may* be surprising is the extent to which nineteenth-century research in the biological and earth sciences (the old field of "natural history") found its intellectual bearings elsewhere, outside of the natural sciences—but this is not an issue we can pursue now.

The second, or "common erudition," research ideal derived most probably from the other great nineteenth-century model of scholarship, philology. The enormous resonance of philology as a paradigm for knowledge is much less well known than the parallel influence of physical science, especially for America, and thus requires some elaboration.

The term "philology" was used broadly in the nineteenth century to denote three quite different enterprises. The first was theoretical discussion of general principles of language and speculation on its origin: what developed into "linguistics." The second was comparative historical philology, which traced the evolution of particular languages and language groups and resulted most spectacularly in the recovery of the previously unsuspected Urlanguage, Indo-European. The third was the historical study of texts, initially Greek and Latin authors and the Bible, eventually generating studies of more modern literatures. Of these three divisions of philology, the largest influences on the "common erudition" ideal of research emerged from classical philology and biblical criticism. These two subjects were the pride of the first great modern universities, in Germany in the later–eighteenth and earlier–nineteenth centuries, and were also, not coincidentally, the most highly developed academic discourses in the United States before 1850.

A certain conception of knowledge was built into the very method of textual philologies such as classical and biblical criticism. In order to grasp the meaning of words and phrases in an ancient document, the scholar had to know a great deal about the institutions, mores, religions, domestic practices, laws, festivals, agriculture, and so forth of the society in which the author wrote. So apparently straightforward a term as "father" might have very different meanings in a strongly patriarchal society than in one with matrifocal households. Put succinctly, philologists believed that a text could only be understood properly within the context of the culture that had produced it.[6] Moreover, because cultures changed over time, the critic had to place a text in its moment in time. The ideas and practices shaping a document written in Rome in 100 B.C.E. differed from those forming a Roman text in 250 C.E. To say that every text was a product of a particular culture was also to say that it was a product of history. We would call this idea of knowledge "historicist" and perhaps "organic." These notions fitted neatly with Scottish Enlightenment ideas dominant in America, especially in American colleges. The notion of the "progress of civilization," central to Scottish social theory, easily suggested that human knowledge was best understood, in broad gauge, as a product of historical evolution. Individual pieces of knowledge naturally bore a genetic relationship to each other.

Given its axioms and American context, philology spawned an ideal of research quite different from that in physics or astronomy. Rather than subdividing the map of knowledge into specialized territories, it encouraged efforts to situate information within the broad boundaries of entire civilizations or cultures. Rather than erecting methodological barriers that made it hard for nonspecialists to pursue learning, it tended to push all sorts of diverse knowledge together into a common arena, accessible to any curious inquirer.

With these two competing ideals of research in mind, the alleged warfare in which forward-looking specialists battle backward-looking generalists begins to look different. The sharp contrast that Gerald Graff draws between James Lowell and Francis Child grows blurry. The supposedly specialized, German-trained scholar ranged in his published research from Chaucer to Spenser to popular ballads (which does not argue for cramped narrowness of focus) and in his teaching over as many centuries as Lowell. And the supposed foe of philology not only never criticized philological research as a method, but loudly applauded it in other scholars and abetted it directly in the Dante researches of Henry Wadsworth Longfellow and Charles Eliot Norton.

Why did such a man exhort the Modern Language Association to turn away from philology and stress literature instead? The answer is simple. He never did any such thing. Lowell's presidential address to the MLA did not denigrate philology. It merely vindicated (and in mild tones) the teaching of *modern* languages and literatures to go along with the classical studies that had traditionally ruled the educational roost. Toward the end of his talk, Lowell did briefly discuss the relation in college teaching of modern languages and modern literature. He pleaded at this point for the study of literature *as well as* language and for the study of language as a doorway to literature. Gerald Graff oddly interprets Lowell's attitude here as antiphilological. This makes sense only if one assumes that philology amounted to nothing more than the narrowly construed study of language, opposed to the study of literature (rather than that philology was an approach to the study of both literature and language). The former assumption was Graff's, but certainly not Lowell's. In fact, in the passage Graff cites, Lowell was referring specifically to courses in "comparative philology," not to a philological approach to literature. Moreover, so far as I know, Lowell never breathed a hint of skepticism about Child's teaching, and Lowell was not a notably reticent man in his letters.[7]

Or consider a passage describing Lowell in the classroom, quoted by Graff from Horace Scudder's biography of Lowell: "Especially would he recall scenes in Florence, sketch in words the effects of the Arno, Giotto's Tower, the church in which Dante was baptized, where he himself had seen children held at the same front [*sic:* "font" in original]."[8] Graff takes this description as exemplifying the generalist, in contrast to research-oriented philologists like Child. Informal this pedagogy certainly was (Lowell sometimes taught his Dante classes at home). But it exemplifies just what Child also was up to: the philologist's practice of filling in the background needed to understand a text. And it shows how such practices could lead to an extraordinarily broad and holistic conception of the knowledge required.

In his MLA presidential address Lowell gave his own example of his teaching:

> Thirty years ago I brought home with me from Nuremburg photographs of Peter Fischer's statuettes of the twelve apostles. These I used to show to my pupils and ask for a guess at their size. The invariable answer was "larger than life." They were really about eighteen inches high, and this grandiose effect was wrought by simplicity of treatment, dignity of pose, a large unfretted sweep of drapery. This object-lesson I found more telling than much argument and exhortation.[9]

Lowell was not merely using an example from art to illuminate literature. He was treating techniques of writing and those of sculpture as subject to a common analysis, as belonging, in other words, to a single framework of knowledge.

Another example from the Lowell-Child circle shows the inadequacy of the generalist-specialist dichotomy. Charles Eliot Norton was the first professor of art history in the United States; that is, he played a very large role in founding a new, specialized discipline (and is seen today by members of that discipline as one of their Urfigures). In the new spirit of the research ideal he pursued heavy-duty investigations in the archives. The material published in his "Urkunden zur Geschichte des Doms von Siena" in the Leipzig scholarly journal *Jahrbücher für Kunstwissenschaft* in 1872 appears to have been the first significant archive-based contribution by an American to German research in art history. Norton published monographs based on this research, notably *Historical Studies of Church-Building in the Middle Ages* (1880). So far he seems the model of the new breed of specialist.[10]

But only so far. Norton wrote almost all of his publications for a general audience, not for other scholars. And he never wished to organize a professional association for art historians. (The learned society for art historians in the United States, the College Art Association, was founded only in 1912, four years after Norton's death removed a major block to specialization in the discipline.) He also published important original research in entirely different fields: most notably Dante studies, which he founded as an academic subject in America, and English Renaissance literature, to which he contributed a seminal essay in modern Donne scholarship. Art history itself he saw as fully integrated into the general study of what we might now call the human sciences:

> In a complete scheme of University studies the history of the Fine Arts in their relation to social progress, to general culture, and to literature, should find a place, not only because architecture, sculpture and painting have been, next to literature, the most important modes of expression of the sentiments, beliefs, and opinions of men, but also because they afford evidence, often in a more striking and direct manner than literature itself, of the moral temper and intellectual culture of the various races by whom they have been practised, and thus become the most effective aids to the proper understanding of history.[11]

Norton grouped the visual arts under what he called "the arts of expression," a category extending to literature and music. Not surprisingly, Norton's students ranged from the great art historian Bernard Berenson to the influential literary critic Irving Babbitt, to the important Dante scholar Charles Grandgent, to the first professor of comparative literature in America, Arthur Richmond Marsh. But Norton never supervised a Ph.D. dissertation, and as research took firmer hold in American universities he increasingly often expressed contempt for what he saw as Germanic pedantry.

Norton did start one professional association—but in the wrong field. In 1879 he organized in Boston the Archaeological Institute of America to promote research by Americans in both classical and Americanist archaeology. He already had more in mind: two years later, under Norton's prodding, the AIA created the American School of Classical Studies at Athens to train young Americans. Norton served as AIA president for over a decade; he is well remembered, both in the AIA and at the American School, as the Founder. The AIA quickly became the disciplinary organization for American archaeologists (at least, classical archaeologists), like the American Historical Association for historians or the Modern Language Association for scholars of literature. Indeed, the AIA seems actually to have assumed its role as the essential disciplinary center more quickly and more completely than the other two groups.

But its membership never comprised experts alone; it also included—and by design—a large number of generally educated, interested amateurs. This was also true of the AHA in its early days (and perhaps of the MLA as well); in the AIA the tradition to some extent endures, long after nonprofessionals deserted other disciplinary learned societies.

Too many things in Norton's career do not compute. Charles Eliot Norton makes hash of the accepted story of the research ideal. There is a delicious irony in a wide-ranging essay by Laurence Veysey on the organization of knowledge in the humanities. At one point Veysey enlists Norton in the camp of "cultivated generalism," in opposition to the advocates of "advanced research." Thirty-some pages later, he invokes again the "genteel amateurism of Charles Eliot Norton." On the next page, in the course of discussing institutions created to foster the research ideal abhorrent to these generalists, Veysey cites the American School of Classical Studies in Athens as the first humanistic research institute independent of a university—apparently unaware that it was founded by the genteel amateur Norton.[12]

Nor was Norton the only "genteel generalist" in late-nineteenth-century America given to serious research in more than one "discipline." There were the physician and geologist Joseph LeConte, the psychologist and philosopher William James, the zoologist and historian Elliott Coues, the marine biologist and ethnologist William Dall, the ornithologist and archaeologist Charles Abbott, the historian and political theorist John William Burgess, the anthropologist and ornithologist Henry Henshaw, the geologist and archaeologist Newton H. Winchell, the theologian and experimental psychologist George Ladd, the astronomer and economist Simon Newcomb, the bacteriologist and archaeologist Theophil Prudden, the economist and sociologist William Graham Sumner. There were too many scholars like these, active in two or three academic fields, to leave credible the myth of disciplinary specialization as the leitmotif of "research" in the new universities. Such polymathic researchers were key contributors to the founding, as research-based academic studies in the United States, of anthropology, archaeology, art history, economics, English literature, French literature, history, Italian literature, comparative literature, palaeontology, philosophy, psychology, and sociology. Maybe more.

Nevertheless, professors today rarely remember these polymaths as disciplinary progenitors. The art historians who recall Norton as the first of their kind in the United States seldom realize that he also started serious scholarship on John Donne; the Dantists who venerate him as founder of the Dante Society are generally unaware that he also began the Archaeological Institute and the American School of Classical Studies.

There is a reason for this amnesia. The research ideal of people like Norton and William James was from the earliest days of American universities in competition with the "specialist" research ideal. Even Charles Eliot Norton's beloved philology often fell under the sway of a more "scientific" model of research. The great classical philologist Basil Gildersleeve of Johns Hopkins University gravitated toward such an ideal of disciplinary specialization—and always kept a certain distance between himself and Norton's projects to promote classical studies, despite being perhaps America's most eminent practitioner in the field. By 1920 or so the ideal of "common erudition" had been pretty well squashed in favor of disciplinary specialization, and the William Jameses and Charles Eliot Nortons then came to be memorialized merely as great mavericks or extinct gentlemen of letters.

Why did they lose? Without much more, yes, research, it is impossible to say. One factor does present itself as a reasonable speculation: for all their insistence on the unity of knowledge, people like Lowell and Norton had no plausible framework for it. Moral philosophy had provided such a matrix, but it was closely associated with the dominance of Protestant Christianity in American colleges. When academic knowledge grew secular, academics backed away from a Protestant worldview and *ergo* rejected the philosophy that expressed it. The Nortons and Jameses and LeContes—often freethinkers, even agnostics—were not about to fall back on a supposed divine unity of creation. Yet nothing else remained to provide a coherent framework for knowledge. The advocates of "common erudition" never generalized into an framework equivalent to moral philosophy the philological principles from which in practice many of them worked, probably because they never recognized a need to replace moral philosophy. That things hung together was an inherited assumption that seemed self-evident.

The contrasting example of France is instructive. When Victor Cousin began lecturing on the history of philosophy at the just reopened École Normale in 1828, he used this history to create a coherent conspectus of philosophic knowledge.[13] (Cousin had earlier in his career been much impressed with Scottish common-sense philosophy, which lay at the foundation of the moral philosophy course in American colleges. One wonders about possible filiations.) Cousin not only dominated French philosophy for the next two decades; he also drafted Guizot's landmark school reform and later served as minister of public instruction. His magisterial version of the history of philosophy—which functioned as a *laïciste*, or secularized, parallel to moral philosophy—was incorporated into the highly centralized French educational system as the capstone course in the final year of *lycée*. Every French teenager bound for university absorbed, or at least endured, Cousin's legacy. This foundation remained intact into the twentieth century.[14]

As a result, French work in human sciences had both a larger theoretical framework and a tradition of relating specialized research to larger contexts of meaning. This perhaps helps to explain why French academic culture nurtured Durkheim, Mauss, Lévi-Strauss, and Foucault. And why the columns of *Le Monde* are regularly filled by professors, a breed who rather infrequently soil even the op-ed page of the *New York Times*.

The lesson of all this is not that Americans had a chance at Eden in 1885 and lost it. The restaurants of Paris do sustain a remarkably high average of cuisine, but even that city is not paradise. No historian can plausibly claim that the model provided by Charles Eliot Norton and his kind should have triumphed or even could have survived.

The conclusion is more modest but important enough: our present notions of "research" and what it implies are not self-evident, not "natural." They have a history, from which "research," as we use the word, gets its meaning. And unless we recover that history as best we can, we will never understand very well just what it is we all are ultimately about when we do "research." Nor will we be able to wrestle effectively with the uses and limits of research in our contemporary "research universities."

PART TWO

Contemporary Interventions

CHAPTER SIX

Catholicism and Modern Scholarship

A Historical Sketch

This chapter bridges the historical essays in part 1 and the prescriptive ones in part 2. It assembles most of the historical themes broached in earlier chapters—religion, academic knowledge, philology, and historicism—and exemplifies how they entangled each other. Uniquely in this book, however, it focuses on Europe rather than the United States. It also paints with a very broad brush. The occasion demanded a wide view, and standing back from the canvas can help us to return with greater accuracy to visualize the finer-grained historical problems we usually sketch.

In particular, the linkage between the historicizing effect of philology and the secularization of knowledge is perhaps clearer here than in any of the other essays. Some European historians have begun to nod in this direction, but by and large few scholars have noted the connection, perhaps because philological scholarship after 1800 has attracted little attention of any sort.[1] Yet few academic practices have had stronger, if usually unintended, force in making religion intellectually implausible—and thus in creating the problems to which subsequent chapters address themselves.

Few, if any, historical developments are more complex than the long evolution that historians and sociologists commonly and too loosely label "secularization." Originally secularization meant the transfer of ecclesiastical institutions, properties, or persons to lay control. But it has come to resemble the dormitive virtue once attributed to opium: misleading because it purports to be an explanatory term while all it really does is name a phenomenon in more elevated language. "Secularization" is misleading also (when applied outside its original and specific context) because it suggests a *disjuncture* between religion and something else when often what actually happened was a *recasting* of the relationship in question, not a severing of it. Nonetheless, lacking any better general term, we seem to be stuck with "secularization" for the nonce, and in this chapter I reluctantly continue to use it, but hedged with the qualifications stated above.

"Secularization" encompasses a bewildering variety of ways in which, over the span of centuries, religion and religious institutions lost much of their importance and power in western European and American culture and society. There were also a bewildering variety of *reasons* why religion in so many different ways found itself more and more on the cultural margins.

Yet, however long and intricate the unfolding of these developments, however many the reasons, and however deeply marked Europe may still be by its Christian past, the outcome is clear. No one could plausibly describe western European culture at the present time as pervasively or profoundly religious. True, in the United States religious faith still moves a majority of the population, and some churches prosper. But the constitution excludes by law religion from state-sponsored activities; and the informal, extralegal exclusion of religion is almost as rigorous in other American centers of intellectual influence and cultural power. In most universities, in the television industry, in Hollywood, in major newspapers and magazines, in the boardrooms of giant corporations, Christianity has no more grip than it does in corresponding European institutions.

This situation is not necessarily reason for grief. After all, during the long centuries when Christians did hold power, they did not always use it well, to say the least. If Lord Acton was right in saying that power tends to corrupt, his dictum applies to church as well as state. Indeed, Acton was thinking of the church when he coined the phrase.[2] Christians may be more faithful to Christ if they speak to power from a position of weakness, rather than trying to wield power themselves. But neither weeping nor rejoicing over the present status of Christianity has much point. As western Europeans and North Americans, we live in a largely post-Christian world, and the question is, How shall we live?

Catholicism and Modern Scholarship | 111

Scholars need to ask this question about their work as much as other people do about theirs. As a historian, I do not pretend to philosophize, only to provide some historical context in which the question can begin to be fruitfully considered. More specifically, I shall sketch briefly the process by which universities and scholarship became alienated from the Christian framework within which they once flourished. This is a daunting task, one that requires a large book rather than a short chapter. Inevitably, I pass over many things of importance, oversimplify many others. I cheer myself by reflecting that I am offering the reader an opportunity to exercise the virtue of charity and and to take my sketch for no more than it is: an effort not to provide solid answers but to raise important questions.

As is well known, the church gave birth to the university. Like other mothers, she early and often found reason to be unhappy with her children. Some scholars liked intellectual adventuring. The church usually did not, especially when the scholars in question dabbled too deeply in pagan wisdom or otherwise sailed too close to heresy. A professor published; a bishop condemned. It was an often repeated sequence. But it was not the usual one, and despite more or less regular tension between ecclesiastical authorities and university scholars, the scholars shared the basic intellectual axiom of the church: "The belief," as Walter Rüegg puts it, "in a world order, created by God, rational, accessible to human reason, to be explained by human reason and to be mastered by it; this belief [underlay] scientific and scholarly research as the attempt to understand the rational order of God's creation."[3] It followed—though the conclusion was not always articulated and did not need to be—that knowledge formed a coherent whole: that all parts of knowledge ultimately could be connected because every area of knowledge focused on an aspect of one single divine creation.

These unquestioned monotheistic assumptions, usually cast in specifically Christian form, still framed academic knowledge in Europe and America long after the Reformation shattered the medieval unity of the church. Tendencies toward the secularization of knowledge stemmed from sources quite different from any breakdown of this Christian framework of knowledge, and the breakdown occurred only after these secularizing currents were well advanced. For clarity of analysis, we can divide these tendencies into two types, so long as we recognize that the division is artificial and that in reality each interacted with and reinforced the other. One category is institutional secularization: a gradual divorce of the church from the institutions of knowledge, most importantly universities. The other is intellectual secularization: a growing distance between the practices of learning and the axiom of a creator God as the foundation of knowledge.

The story of institutional secularization is well known and need only be summarized briefly. It begins almost with the founding of the earliest universities. The growth of universities involved a transition from a small, quasi-familial community of learners, in which a patriarchal teacher personally supervised the spiritual as well as intellectual life of his students, toward an increasingly depersonalized institution, whose members were more able to go their own ways. This transition was itself a step toward the slackening of ecclesiastical control, already apparent during the Middle Ages. By the end of the medieval period, moreover, probably only a minority of university students was still untonsured clerics, while "the salaries of the professors were increasingly paid by secular authorities and the universities were ever more subjected to the supervision of the municipal or princely authorities."[4] We should not think of institutional secularization as a radical change that began in the modern period.

Yet the distance between churches and institutions of learning did increase far more rapidly in the wake of the Reformation, as a result not of religious reform but of the growing coherence and power of monarchical states. These newly energetic governments intruded into traditional domains of the church, including the universities. Princes also began to promote competing centers of learning. The Collège des lecteurs royaux (later called the Collège de France), founded by François Ier in 1530, and the Royal Society of London, on which Charles II bestowed his royal blessing in 1662, are only the most celebrated of many such foundations. By the eighteenth century ministers like Pombal in Portugal and Van Swieten in Austria were diverting the universities themselves to state purposes. The most influential new foundation of that century, the University of Göttingen, was created expressly to serve the principality of Hanover, to which end it helped to bring into being a new field of knowledge, *Staatswissenschaft*.[5] Against this background, it is no surprise that most faculties were laicized well before 1800; indeed, the University of Paris had secularized all its faculties except theology before 1600.[6]

These early-modern developments should not be exaggerated. It was precisely in this period that the Jesuits rose to vast influence in higher education on the continent, and some important universities remained clerical monopolies well into the nineteenth century, including Oxford and Cambridge. Even Göttingen was officially a Lutheran institution, and almost every university required religious orthodoxy of professors.[7]

The sharp breaking point came with the French Revolution and its Napoleonic aftermath. In France itself and in territory under its direct rule, the old universities were suppressed, to be replaced (if at all) by entirely secular state institutions. They remained secular when reconstructed after 1815. Even where Napoleon's writ did not run, the principle of state secularism increasingly guided university development in western and central Europe after 1800. Within decades of its founding in 1809 the University of Berlin became the great model of higher education for both Europe and America, and Berlin rested on the principle that no creed would be required of teacher or student.

When in 1834 the bishops of newly independent Belgium resurrected the ancient university in Leuven, which Napoleon had quashed in 1797, they founded an old type of institution in a new historical situation. A consciously Catholic university under clerical leadership now had to be set in pugnacious defense against the secular liberalism that dominated the state universities and much of intellectual life outside them.[8] True, secularization moved at a different tempo in Spain and Italy, and England also trod more slowly than the continent. But secular principles achieved their first great victory in England with the founding of London University in 1828, and the final citadel fell in 1871 when Parliament abolished the remaining religious tests and the clerical monopoly of fellowships at Oxford and Cambridge.[9]

This institutional transformation, well on the way to completion throughout western and central Europe by the time Parliament voted in 1871, deprived explicitly Christian scholarship of most of the institutional bases it had held two or three centuries earlier, although of course many of the researchers at work in secular universities were in their personal lives Christians. Catholic scholarship, in particular, henceforth found its home almost exclusively in the relatively few Catholic universities and the more numerous theological faculties. In these locations, however, it flourished in a kind of artificial isolation, almost an institutional ghetto, cut off from the larger universe of European universities.

This history of institutional secularization is fairly well understood, at least among historians of higher education. The process of intellectual secularization is not nearly so familiar, in large part because historians of European education have paid more attention to the institutional than the intellectual dimensions of university history. And when they *have* investigated the intellectual history of higher education, they have usually construed it narrowly as the history of curriculum or of academic disciplines.[10] Yet intellectual secularization may well be more important than its institutional counterpart, because it was more fundamental in setting the parameters within which scholars work today.

To be sure, with the leading institutions of scholarship in Europe moving toward secularization, it is no great surprise that intellectual secularization also occurred. But the latter was by no means a simple result of the former. Intellectual secularization followed its own distinctive path, with important consequences for academic life in the Catholic world.

Granted, there is a sense in which one can say, as one can in the case of institutions, that the impetus toward intellectual secularization is as old as the university. After all, the university embodied from the beginning an approach to knowledge that favored human reasoning over direct engagement with Scripture. Bologna aroused papal suspicion even before it developed fully into a university because of its focus on a secular study, the civil law; and the hostility of some church leaders in the thirteenth century to the study of that notorious pagan Aristotle has passed into legend. But to recite such stories is merely to rehash the truism that Christians, like adherents of every complex religion, have always argued over where the boundary fell between the pure and the impure. The ascendancy of theology as queen of the sciences never came seriously into question in medieval universities, nor did the axiom that all scholars sought knowledge of a divinely created order.

A more credible secularizing tendency appeared in the fifteenth and sixteenth centuries in the form of humanistic philology. The problem was not so much that humanists promoted an alternative educational program oriented toward rhetoric rather than theology and philosophy. To replace philosophy or even theology with other studies does not necessarily increase the distance between scholarship and religion. The great humanist and philologist Erasmus (1469–1536) indeed regarded a critical-philological approach to the Bible as a way of bringing students back to the living founts of Christian faith from what he saw as the arid desert of Scholasticism. Erasmus may not have been entirely fair to Scholasticism, but that is not the point: academic polemicists in the sixteenth century were rarely fair to each other. The point is that Renaissance humanists were not by the nature of their trade any more secular-minded than medieval Scholastics.

Rather, the reason why humanistic philology represented a genuine step toward intellectual secularization appears in its methods, specifically in implications of its methods that were not fully realized until the nineteenth century.[11] If a scholar wished to understand a document from another time and place, he needed to know the background that clarified the meanings of the writer's words. What political institutions or religious rituals or marriage customs or farming practices cast light on the shades of meaning? Erasmus himself "constantly" asked "who was writing a particular document, whom he was addressing, what he was really saying, and what were the surrounding circumstances that help explain what he said." Students of Scripture he advised not merely to learn languages but to "study the history and geography of the Hebrew and Roman worlds."[12]

As I have described earlier in this book, from this philological practice an intellectual axiom eventually followed: historicism. All cultures are in flux; the careful scholar can discern patterns of change over time in every one. Already in the seventeenth century the leap was made from Renaissance philology to the idea that "historical facts" are not "self-evident" but "obtain significance only from the context in which they are embedded." From this grew historicism: the "tendency to view all knowledge and all forms of experience in a context of historical change."[13] Laws of nature might be timeless, but products of human beings—writings, paintings, buildings, mores, ways of making love and making war—were time-bound. Really to understand them, one needed to situate them in the flow of the history that shaped them.

This idea eventually proved corrosive to the Christian conception of knowledge as a unified whole, which had been taken for granted from the earliest universities into the eighteenth century. For in its founding axiom historicism contested any cogent epistemological holism. Knowledge, even of nature, was a product of human culture. And if all human cultural products were determined by unique and contingent histories of particular societies, without any general law of progress or development to tie them together, then no larger pattern could link all cultural histories, and knowledge of them, into a whole. To be sure, one might in an act of faith posit the unity of all human history and thus rescue a Christian conception of knowledge. But historicism hardly encouraged the making of axioms at war with its principle that unique cultural circumstances determined all human systems of belief. The historicism that slowly evolved from the pious philology of men like Erasmus in the end devoured their assumption that all knowledge cohered because it was all knowledge of one divine creation.

Indeed, historicism threatened to gobble up Christianity itself and, for that matter, any conviction of objective truth transcending human beings. If our beliefs are inescapably shaped by the historical circumstances under which we happen to live, how can they claim either objective reality or transcendent validity? Making everything depend on its historical setting makes everything relative. Ernst Troeltsch first fully explained this "crisis of historicism," as early as 1922, in his celebrated *Der Historismus und seine Probleme*. Why, specifically, does belief in the Christian God or religious doctrines remain plausible—especially if one assumes, as nineteenth-century biblical scholars did, that "the scriptures, both Jewish and Christian, are to be understood only through the same means of elucidation, as are applied to all other writings of similar or great antiquity"?[14] Why does Christian belief have any better claim to eternal validity than belief in the gods of Olympus or the Hindu pantheon?

Even the nascent historicism of the later–eighteenth and early–nineteenth centuries hit dangerously close to Christian belief. By the turn of the twentieth, full-blown historicism had become commonplace. The most influential American humanistic scholar of the later Victorian era described morality as "the result and expression of the secular experience of mankind." Another eminent professor told students in 1906 that religion, like any other "historical phenomenon," "can only be explained by its history."[15] Historicism thereby helped to explain why around 1900 scholars and scientists came to distinguish "truth" more clearly from "knowledge" and to define "value-free knowledge" as the aim of the university.[16] Ironically, the corrosive force of historicism then went on in the later–twentieth century to help in sapping the foundations of "value-free knowledge" as well.

In its slow workings historicism eroded the axioms on which Catholic scholarship had operated since the founding of the first universities: the once seemingly evident truths that God had created a single universe, knowable by human reason; that knowledge therefore ultimately constituted a single whole, however diverse the methods used to obtain it; and that all knowledge pointed to God, however indirectly, because it was knowledge of a universe created according to His design and governed by His laws. In scholarship grounded on historicist principles, in contrast, all knowledge was knowledge formed within a specific culture and proper to that culture and therefore not ultimately congruent with the knowledge produced in other cultures; and all knowledge was determined by human historical experiences and therefore could not give reliable information about God's designs. The axiom of a creator God, essential to Catholic thought, no longer made sense in historicized intellectual life. By the later years of the nineteenth century, this development had decisively transformed scholarship in Europe and was well on the way to overtaking American scholarship as well.

By then, however, another key development within the academic world had joined with historicism to destroy the old axiom of the unity of knowledge. This was the rise of disciplinary specialization, alluded to in chapter 5 with respect to the United States. The newness of disciplinary specialization was obscured for English speakers by the fact that "discipline" is an old academic term that acquired a new meaning after 1850.[17] Yet novel it was. Increasingly, in nineteenth-century universities throughout the West, academic knowledge came to seem subdivided into specialized domains, each with its unique methods barring entrance to scholars from other disciplines. This brand of specialization went far beyond simple expertise, which implies only familiarity with many details of one or more sites on the map of knowledge.

What was changing was whether a scholar could move from one site to another far away. In the Anglophone world, as late as the 1870s and 1880s, researchers in most areas could use any techniques and pursue researches across whatever fields they wished. In Germany they had already lost this flexibility by the 1820s and 1830s, if not before. Indeed, the transformation began in the new-model German universities, varying in speed in different national cultures. But whether in Germany or Britain or elsewhere, scholarly competence began to require restricting oneself to one's "discipline."

Disciplinary specialists thus drew new borders on the previously undivided map of knowledge, marking out separate territories. They fortified these frontiers between "disciplines" with methodological fences that kept out nonspecialists. They declared, though at first uncertainly and confusedly, that knowledge does not form a whole but divides itself into distinct cultures, each governed by its own methodological principles and scholarly traditions. The implication, seen only dimly by many academics as late as 1900, was that a specialist in any discipline could work satisfactorily in another only by a strenuous feat of reacculturation.

The immediate effect on academic research was to redouble the effect of historicism in shattering the axiom of Christian epistemological holism on which Catholic scholarship had rested, thus weakening also the underlying assumption of divine creation. When John Henry Newman declared in 1852 that "Religious Truth is not only a portion, but a condition of general knowledge" and that "to blot it out is nothing short . . . of unravelling the web of University Teaching," he was already fighting a rear-guard action, and a losing one.[18]

Both the rise of historicism and the emergence of disciplinary specialization occurred in a broader climate of growing doubt about whether God even existed. This chapter is not the place to trace the reasons for the growth of atheism and agnosticism in the nineteenth century.[19] The fact itself is sufficiently well known. While probably a majority of Europeans, and certainly of Americans, continued to believe in God well into the twentieth century, the existence of God was no longer an unspoken axiom of the culture, especially not in the increasingly secular-minded universities. In these circumstances, the theistic presuppositions underlying Catholic scholarship stopped commanding acceptability in the larger world of academic research. Work by Catholic scholars would be taken seriously only if stripped of the scholar's own most basic beliefs about reality.

Adding to their problems was the growing assumption of the primacy of individual judgment as the ultimate test of truth. This was a characteristic of the secular liberalism that formed the ideology broadly framing most professorial research in the nineteenth century, an ideology that, mutatis mutandis, has persisted in universities into our own time. Goldwin Smith, arguing in 1864 against religious tests for degrees at Oxford University, built his case largely on the claim that "tyrannizing over conscience" threatened the very nature of a university.[20] Catholic scholars labored under the burden of loyalty to a church that proclaimed itself exactly what Smith denounced: a corporate guardian of truth to which individuals must submit. The accusation has dogged Catholic scholars ever since that they cannot pursue the truth freely if dogma fetters their thought. This is the basis of George Bernard Shaw's mot that a Catholic university is an oxymoron. This attitude is not so much a substantive barrier to the integration of Catholic scholarship into general scholarship as it is a cloud of suspicion that makes Catholic scholarship (as distinct from scholars who happen to be Catholic) appear dubious to potential non-Catholic collaborators.

These converging historical developments have pushed to the side, in the modern university, not only Catholic intellectual traditions but also those of other Christian confessions and of Judaism.[21] This marginalization has taken a toll on learning. The distinguished Yale critic Geoffrey Hartman has lamented (with specific reference to literary studies) that only the tip of "the iceberg of interpretations is visible in the contemporary, secular era. The greater part, linked to religious sermons, law-finding, and mystical brooding, remains neglected or deliberately ignored by the predominance of an unreflective Enlightenment paradigm." And while Hartman accepts that "it was salutary for literary criticism to separate from theological exegesis," criticism nonetheless "impoverished itself by rejecting so large a tradition of textual response."[22] Blaming this situation on eighteen-century Enlightenment, as Hartman implicitly does, is a mistake, as I hope I have made clear. But his larger point holds true.

In the academic world that matured in the nineteenth century—which is still by and large our academic world—Catholic scholars have, it appears to me, three choices. They can abandon any belief that their religion is relevant to their scholarship and work just as if they were secular scholars. (This is probably the commonest response, at least in the United States.) They can pursue their scholarship in a kind of Catholic ghetto isolated from the scholarly mainstream, a choice that both weakens their research and sacrifices any influence that Catholic intellectual traditions might have in the larger world of research. Or they can find a new way of relating their Catholic traditions to the academy at large.

Any such new path would have to begin with the concession that the decidedly nontheistic, secular understanding of knowledge characteristic of modern universities will not accommodate belief in God as a working principle. But human beings, however deeply flawed, remain capable of partial communication across cultural frontiers. There is no reason why secular researchers cannot learn to value a great deal that is embodied in Catholic intellectual traditions, so long as Catholic scholars do not insist that they accept the whole package, God and all—and so long as Catholic scholars rid themselves of smugness about the superiority of their own traditions. Both Catholic and non-Catholic scholars may have a great deal to gain from opening a bridge between Catholic intellectual traditions and the secular university. To start thinking about how to construct that bridge is the point of the essays in part 2 of this book.

CHAPTER SEVEN

The Evangelical Intellectual Revival

A bit of autobiography clarifies this chapter and to some extent the next two. In 1985 I published a book exploring how the option of not believing in God became a serious possibility in American intellectual culture. Although I approached the question purely as a problem of intellectual history, the book interested historians of American religion. They began to invite me to their professional parleys, where I came to know several scholars whom their colleagues good-naturedly called "the Evangelical mafia": Nathan Hatch, George Marsden, Mark Noll, Grant Wacker, and other more or less Evangelical Protestants. These "mafiosi" have had an impact on the historical understanding of religion in America all out of proportion to their numbers.[1] Though not enticed by the distinctives of their theology, I came to admire as well as like them.

As a result of my travels in these new circles, in 1991 the Pew Charitable Trusts—seeking an empathetic outsider—invited me to evaluate its Evangelical Scholarship Initiative. Over six months, I got to know many more academics in and around the Evangelical camp, an acquaintance extended and deepened on other occasions in subsequent years. Thus it came about, when *Commonweal* magazine was looking for a writer to describe to its mostly Catholic readers the Evangelical intellectual revival, that Rich Mouw, learned and amiable president of the Evangelical Fuller Theological Seminary, recommended this Catholic boy.

The essay lacks explicit resonance with preceding chapters. Yet attentive readers will discern my interest in how coherent intellectual traditions lay a foundation for fruitful engagement by religious believers with the intellectual life of their time. Curiosity about this phenomenon not only appears and reappears in the historical endeavors composing the first part of this book, but also inspires the two polemics following.

In 1980 the sleeping giant of American politics awoke. Evangelical Protestants make up, along with Catholics (whom they approximate in number), one of the two largest religious blocs in the United States. The entry into electoral politics of a hefty portion of them as a self-conscious Christian Right helped to ensure the triumph of Ronald Reagan and to transform and immensely complicate the affairs of the Republican Party. The story is famous and surely far from the last act in a riveting drama.

Far fewer non-Evangelicals, most of them academics, are aware of a parallel and equally dramatic turning in Evangelical *intellectual* life — though one without the rightward political bent. In 1995 appeared a new bimonthly journal called *Books and Culture*. The magazine is a self-conscious adaptation of the *New York Review of Books*, right down to the newspaper stock on which it is printed; and the editors of *Books and Culture* hoped that their periodical might do for Evangelicals what the *NYRB* has done for secular intellectual life, that is, provide a forum in which academic and freelance intellectuals engage with gusto a general, educated public. Like the *NYRB*, *Books and Culture* has assembled a stable of writers who repeat in its pages, many of them well known to each other. But whereas the *NYRB* came into existence as the more or less chance result of a newspaper strike, *Books and Culture* culminates a kind of Evangelical Long March through American intellectual life.

The names regularly on its pages represent almost a roster of the revolutionaries who have led this struggle. Among them are such widely respected academic intellectuals as the historians Mark Noll of Wheaton College in Illinois and Nathan Hatch and George Marsden of Notre Dame; the philosophers Nicholas Wolterstorff of Yale and Alvin Plantinga of Notre Dame; and Richard Mouw, president of Fuller Theological Seminary. It is more than a curious coincidence that Hatch and Noll were classmates at Wheaton College and that Marsden, Wolterstorff, Plantinga, and Mouw once taught together on the faculty of Calvin College in Michigan (an institution to which we shall have occasion to recur). For Wheaton and especially Calvin have been seedbeds of an intellectual renaissance within American Evangelicalism (broadly defined) that has gone far beyond theology to establish a visible Evangelical presence in literary scholarship, psychology, history, philosophy, and other fields.

Both Plantinga and Wolterstorff have delivered the revered Gifford Lectures (which puts them in company with William James, Etienne Gilson, and Rudolf Bultmann). Hatch's *Democratization of American Christianity* is the standard work on the defining events of the nineteenth-century religious history of the United States. Marsden's *Soul of the American University* ranks among the most talked-about academic books of the past decade. Similar plaudits could be accorded other *Books and Culture* authors. Roger Lundin's *Emily Dickinson* is one of the most sensitive studies of that poet. David Lyle Jeffrey's recent encyclopedic analysis of the Bible in English literature was widely received as a magnificent work of scholarship. These scholars are in no sense confined within some narrow Evangelical discourse; they speak to, and are heeded by, academics of every stripe in their various disciplines. And they strive as well to speak to a wider audience.

Yet, in so speaking, they have had something distinctive to say. They are not standard-issue scholars. As believing Christians, they understand the import of religious faith in everyday lives. They take theological ideas seriously. They refuse to reduce belief to an epiphenomenon of social forces or material circumstances. Thus, while conforming fully to the canons of secular, mainstream scholarship, they have helped to nurture in the academy a heightened sensitivity to Christian faith as a factor important in its own right. They have hardly conquered the high citadels of academe, and they have a long way to go before becoming anything like a major presence in the universities, but they have made their presence felt.

In part the influence flows from organization. Evangelical scholars have developed a cadre of learned societies parallel to the larger disciplinary associations that regulate American academic life. There is a Society of Christian Philosophers to match the American Philosophical Association, Christians in Political Science alongside the American Political Science Association, a Conference on Faith and History affiliated with the American Historical Association, and so on. But these groups, while founded by Evangelicals, no longer exclusively comprise them. A recent president of Christians in Political Science, for instance, is a Roman Catholic. And this indicates another key to the success of the new Evangelical intellectuals: cooperation with other Christians concerned about revivifying Christianity in the life of the mind.

As recently as 1970, probably no credible prophet would have forecast these developments. The dilapidated state in which Evangelical intellectual life found itself during the middle decades of the twentieth century was more than a little ironic. For much of the nineteenth, an informal Evangelical establishment had come close to dominating cultural life in the United States. But in the 1880s and 1890s battles between fundamentalists and modernists (as these two blocs would later come to be called) effectively destroyed this Evangelical near hegemony. In the 1920s—the decade of the infamous Scopes trial—fundamentalism was decisively defeated within the mainline Protestant churches. Thereafter the fundamentalists withdrew into the periphery of American culture, making scarcely any contribution to the nation's intellectual life.

The rise of the so-called New Evangelicalism after World War II loosened the rigidities of fundamentalism and, via the populist revivalism most famously exemplified in Billy Graham, expanded the numbers of Evangelicals; but it did little to bring them back into the intellectual mainstream. As recently as 1994 the distinguished historian Mark Noll could write, in the first sentence of a widely noticed book, *The Scandal of the Evangelical Mind*, that the scandal of the Evangelical mind "is that there is not much of an evangelical mind." Within their own boundaries Evangelicals did, however, nurture distinctive habits of thought. The more unchanging among them retained a nineteenth-century approach to natural science, which led them into creationism, and a "dispensationalist" and literalist biblical hermeneutic, which predisposed them to apocalyptic prediction at the drop of a crisis in the Mideast. It is from this self-enclosed world that the new Evangelical intellectuals have emerged, in the last few decades, into a full engagement with contemporary culture. It is, indeed, *because* of their distress that their fellow believers had so shut themselves off from the larger life of the mind that a small cadre of Evangelical academics decided near the end of the 1980s to struggle explicitly against such anti-intellectual isolationism. *Books and Culture* was one result.

Roman Catholics of a certain age will be inclined to draw an analogy to the experience of American Catholic intellectuals in the wake of the Second Vatican Council and the near simultaneous collapse of the intellectual hegemony of Neo-Thomism. In the 1960s Catholics likewise stepped out of a kind of intellectual ghetto and became full and equal participants in the broader intellectual life of the United States. But, although the structural similarity is remarkable, the parallel is misleading. Whatever the weaknesses of American Catholic culture in the first half of the twentieth century, its intellectual life was rich and vigorous. Neo-Thomism tied it to a deep and sophisticated tradition of philosophic speculation; the international character of the Church connected Americans (even if as distinctly junior partners) with the brilliance of the Catholic Revival—with writers as various and shining as Jacques Maritain, Christopher Dawson, and Georges Bernanos.

There was nothing equivalent in the mainstream of American Evangelicalism. Nineteenth-century Evangelicalism had produced intellectuals of real stature—Charles Hodge, James McCosh, James Dwight Dana—but the churches that nurtured such minds—the Congregationalists, the Presbyterians—went the modernist route in the twentieth century. The denominations from which came the vast majority of fundamentalists and, later, New Evangelicals—such as the Southern Baptists, the Church of Christ, and the various Pentecostal groups—were populist in character, little attuned to the life of the mind, and often suspicious of it. A professorial acquaintance of mine is a loyal member of the Church of Christ who works hard to renew links between Christianity and academic thinking; when asked why he does not pay more attention specifically to the distinctive intellectual traditions of his own denomination, he raised his eyebrows and asked wryly, "Just what would those be?"

Given these facts, the Evangelical intellectual revival seems genuinely puzzling. How did a religious movement that has historically produced preachers rather than professors (and still specializes in the former) manage to generate within a couple of decades a distinguished cohort of scholars? How could so sturdy an intellectual life arise on such feeble intellectual traditions?

The answer to this apparent paradox is that Evangelicals did not build—could not have built—on their own intellectual foundations. Here the curious prominence of Calvin College, alluded to earlier, becomes salient. Calvin is a small institution with a history of having featured on its faculty a surprising number of rather distinguished scholars, especially philosophers and historians. It also, and not coincidentally, has a history of something close to tribalism, though diluted in recent years. Founded in the nineteenth century to serve a recent Dutch migration into the Midwest, Calvin has remained closely bound to the children of those immigrants—reading the names on the faculty roster, one could be forgiven for thinking oneself in Amsterdam—and to their fairly small denomination, the Christian Reformed Church. But, though weak in numbers, the CRC is sturdy in mind. It inherited the same rich Calvinist (or capital-R "Reformed") theological traditions and the same predilection for education that made Presbyterianism probably the most intellectually impressive of the larger American churches.

But it inherited them in a distinctive form, in the Neo-Calvinism of the Dutch politician and theologian Abraham Kuyper (1837–1920), prime minister of the Netherlands from 1901 to 1905 and earlier the founder of the Free University of Amsterdam. Kuyper rejuvenated John Calvin's beliefs in the devastating effect of original sin on the entire human person, including the intellect, and in the power of saving grace to enable the elect to see reality more clearly; he likewise repeated Calvin's insistence on the duty of those whom God had saved to glorify God by working to reform His world. In contrast to Catholic thinkers, who tend to emphasize the common rationality of all human beings, Kuyper thus stipulated a sharp opposition between Christian and non-Christian thought; he also stressed (in George Marsden's words) "the importance of the 'mind' of the age in shaping its culture," and he identified "the Christian task as a broad one of transforming all of culture for God's glory."

Mixed with their hereditary fondness for books and schooling, Kuyperianism made among the Christian Reformed a perfect recipe for cooking up writers and scholars. James Bratt, a historian at Calvin College sometimes associated with the "Evangelical" intellectual revival, has written winsomely about the results in his 1984 book *Dutch Calvinism in Modern America*. From Calvin College itself emerged many of the leaders of the "Evangelical" revival: Mouw, Marsden (who qualifies as an honorary Dutchman from his many years on the Calvin faculty), Plantinga, Wolterstorff, and others. Through Calvin College's influence, Neo-Calvinism stamped its decisive impress on many of the other leaders, including Hatch and Noll.

The quotation marks now appear around "Evangelical" to indicate a certain problem with the term that becomes apparent as soon as one brings in the Calvin College group. As a Calvinist people, the Christian

Reformed have a strong doctrine of the church and a deep attachment to creedal traditions. This sets them apart from the American Evangelical lineage, with its religious individualism and consequently weak ecclesiology and its immediate recourse to the Bible alone as the ground of faith. Shared commitments to doctrinal orthodoxy and a mutually held high view of Scripture have sufficed to ensure hearty cooperation between Christian Reformed and "real" Evangelical intellectuals—between Calvin College and Wheaton College, to phrase the matter in an institutional synecdoche—and in some contexts even to blur altogether the differences between them. But the fact remains that Kuyperian Neo-Calvinism looks very different from most of twentieth-century American Evangelicalism.

Kuyperianism hardly exhausts the resources on which the new Evangelical intellectuals have drawn. Mark Noll notes that recent Evangelical political thinkers have also borrowed "from the Anabaptist heritage, from the mainline Protestantism of Reinhold Niebuhr, or from the neo-conservative Catholicism of Richard John Neuhaus, Michael Novak, and George Weigel." Perhaps the favorite writer among bookish Evangelicals is C. S. Lewis, an Anglican who rarely had kind words for their version of Protestantism. And, while attention to the Kuyperian tradition maps the main highway in recent Evangelical scholarship, for a movement as diverse as American Evangelicalism it is not the only road. Recent stirrings at places like Messiah College (Brethren in Christ), Pepperdine University (Churches of Christ), Baylor University (Southern Baptist), and several Wesleyan, Holiness, and Pentecostal institutions show that renewed concern about intellectual life does not derive only from the Reformed. Such eclecticism helps to explain the suppleness and adaptability of recent Evangelical intellectual life. From my viewpoint, however, the decisive influence on the revival remains Neo-Calvinism.

Whether this judgment is correct or not, the success of these Evangelicals in finding resources outside of their own tradition, in order to enliven the life of the mind within it, is not only one of the more fascinating and impressive episodes in recent intellectual history. It also raises a curious question. To what extent can the Evangelical intellectual revival properly be called Evangelical? The distinctives of Evangelicalism seem to survive more in religious than in intellectual behavior: the new Evangelical intellectuals pray as Evangelicals but think as Calvinists or Anglicans or sometimes even Catholics.

Whether the Evangelical intellectual revival will make serious inroads into the broad culture of American Evangelicalism remains to be seen. Even many Evangelical intellectuals remain skeptical about this. That it has made, and will continue to make, a substantial mark on American academic life seems indisputable, especially in history, philosophy, and, more recently, sociology. But the overall effect will likely be to fortify other, non-Evangelical Christian approaches to scholarship, rather than to generate an original, distinctively Evangelical life of the mind.

CHAPTER EIGHT

The Catholic University in Modern Academe

Challenge and Dilemma

The ghost haunting several of these essays is a historical development first explicitly broached in chapter 3: the fragmentation of academic knowledge following upon the retreat of theistic belief as an axiom of public culture. Seen from a different angle, the "fragmentation" quandary appears as the breakdown of one tradition within which knowledge had been construed, without any other to replace it. That is the form in which this chapter calls the ghost once more from the vasty deep, now as present problem rather than historical event.

The previous essay makes in passing the point that Catholics have long savored their own fertile intellectual traditions. One of these was the Scholastic Thomism of the Middle Ages, revived and given papal sanction in the nineteenth century. This Neo-Thomism structured Catholic higher education, at least in theory, up until about the middle of the last century, playing a part not unlike that of Scottish moral philosophy in Protestant colleges, as discussed in chapters 3 and 5.[1] So distinctive an ideology helped to keep Catholic colleges and universities segregated — intellectually, if not athletically — from the mainstream of learning in the United States. Then, when Neo-Thomism lost its academic hegemony in the later 1950s and 1960s, Catholic higher education quickly moved to clothe itself in standard American garb.

The question at that point became whether Catholic learning still had any distinctive character and, if so, what this might be. Partly as a result of issues raised in the writing and reception of my book on the origins of unbelief, partly out of engagement with the Evangelical intellectuals described in chapter 7, I had myself around 1990 begun to wonder how my early Catholic formation had affected my later work as a professional intellectual. It belatedly dawned on me (a slow learner) that the traditions on which I suckled in my Jesuit high school had permanently shaped some basic patterns of thinking and hence, in part, my adult practice as historian. This was true even though Catholic education had not touched me since high school and even though I had spent all my teaching career happily at state universities.

In the midst of these musings, the University of Notre Dame asked me to speak, during its sesquicentennial year, about the role of Catholic universities in the mostly secular domain of American higher education. All parties understood that I should speak as a denizen of the world of non-Catholic research universities (I was at that time on the faculty of the University of Michigan). I accepted the invitation with trepidation but also with a livelier interest than I should have felt even five years earlier. Predictably, I began on a historical note.

In 1842 Edward Sorin founded his tiny college on the American frontier, christened hopefully the *University* of Notre Dame du Lac. One decade later John Henry Newman did the same thing on a slightly grander scale in Dublin. In that primitive era university development offices had not yet been invented. So Fathers Sorin and Newman both had to figure out for themselves how to work up support for their institutions. Lacking a football team, Father Newman chose a method that would make any development officer cringe. He gave a series of lectures.

Those lectures eventually became a book called *The Idea of a University*.[2] Father Newman's book was the keenest statement of the aims and ideals of university education by any Victorian. It may hold the all-time record in that category. And so it has been a regular embarrassment to all succeeding writers on the aims and ideals of university education, especially those who have the bad luck to be asked to address the challenges and dilemmas of the *Catholic* university. For it was, of course, the animating principles of the new Catholic University of Ireland that Father Newman was particularly concerned to unfold for his listeners.

Much has changed since Newman wrote—fortunately, else I might be reduced to quoting long passages from his book. For instance, we now regard research as a key part of a university's mission: an idea Newman explicitly repudiated. We now think it natural to integrate education for a career (in, say, business or engineering) into a liberal arts education: a notion Newman almost violently rejected. So we are not likely to be startled when Newman says something strange to our ears.

Yet a reader today will still be brought up short by two of Newman's theses. First, it is passing strange that a Roman Catholic priest, the rector of a Roman Catholic university, the great English spokesman of the principle of authority in the church, would stress the separation between church and university, the distinction of their roles, the autonomy of their functions. Yet who, upon reflection, would deny that Newman was right? A Catholic university is a university, not a chapel. And however we may differ about the character of the church, no one with experience of the university will regard it as a divine institution. Its task involves human knowledge, not eternal salvation.

To be sure, a Catholic *college* provides a home for young people in some of their most formative years, and it ought to aid in their formation, as should any other college. Thus, it has a crucial pastoral role—again, like any other college, but with a distinctive Catholic aim. Ideally, a college nurtures moral values, inculcates responsibility for oneself and for others, and—in its specifically Catholic role—helps students develop a maturer and deeper faith. These responsibilities will affect not only extracurricular matters such as dormitory life and athletics, but also the curriculum. Because the Catholic *university* in America normally houses undergraduate *colleges*, its task does in these respects touch on eternal salvation. But it does this work, if I may make the distinction, qua college and not qua university. The university's proper task, to repeat, involves human questions, not divine.

Why, then, does Newman's distinction between Catholic university and Catholic Church sound odd to us? The reason, I think, is convoluted and largely subliminal. In the past century we have grown used to thinking of faith and knowledge as mutually exclusive, almost contradictory, even hostile. So we fear that, in the end, no church would really release its universities from the fetters of doctrine to pursue knowledge. At the back of our minds we suspect that a Catholic university cannot really disentangle itself from the heavy hand of ecclesiastical authority— the long, legendary shadow of the Inquisition—without disengaging itself from Catholicism.

So the challenge of the Catholic university in secular academe is to demonstrate that the phrase "Catholic university" is not an oxymoron; to prove itself *really* a university, and a first-rate one; to make itself a full and distinguished participant in the increasingly international world of scholarship. And that challenge must be felt with special urgency at Notre Dame, for no Catholic university is poised so close to membership in the elite club of major research universities as she.

The dilemma of the Catholic university is the same: to demonstrate that the phrase "Catholic university" is not an oxymoron. Catholic traditions, after all, insist on the integration of faith and learning; modern academic traditions insist on their separation. Many believe that, if a Christian institution plunges headlong into the profoundly secular sea of modern learning, it will unavoidably drown its Christianity. *Ergo*, it seems, a Catholic university must either shun the world of secular scholarship or abandon its Christian beliefs and Roman Catholic intellectual traditions: either cease being Catholic or cease being a university. A dilemma indeed—if it were a real one.

But we may find a clue to lead us out of the apparent impasse if we consider Newman's second puzzling thesis. Newman placed philosophy as the keystone of university education. He thought that philosophy would unify the curriculum, integrate all the subjects of study, provide (as it were) a map of knowledge. Philosophers among my readers will forgive me for pointing out that today this notion sounds downright quaint. Yet Newman would have found few skeptics among his audience.

For the unity of knowledge was still an axiom of European culture when Newman spoke. Knowledge formed a seamless whole because all knowledge referred either to the one Creator or His single Creation. Thus there could exist a discipline like philosophy (in Newman's sense) that showed, in principle at least, how the various specific bodies of knowledge related to each other and to the larger whole. And this explanation of the unity of learning would naturally form the central pillar of university education. Indeed, in American Protestant colleges in Father Newman and Father Sorin's era, the college president conventionally delivered just such a course of lectures to the senior class each year.[3]

But in the last decades of Newman's long life—during the last third of the nineteenth century—doubts about the very existence of a Creator became widespread within the intellectual classes of Europe and America.[4] Disbelief in God washed away the very axiom that gave unity to knowledge, eventually unleashing a flood of doubts that wiped out all those once secure connections that held the pieces of knowledge together.[5] This was not altogether a bad thing. An excess of certainty can make a formidable barrier to the spread of knowledge, especially when the confidence turns into smugness, as it often did in the voices of those old college presidents.

It took almost a century for Victorian epistemological certitude fully to collapse, though Nietzsche was sufficiently crazy to see its end in its beginnings. The Victorian crisis of faith turned out to be equally a crisis of knowledge. We are now living in its splintered, postmodern aftermath. There are actually two distinguishable, but closely related, problems that share the same genealogy (with apologies to Nietzsche). The first is the simple fragmentation of knowledge that makes it difficult, if not impossible, for a molecular biologist to speak intelligibly to a political scientist, or for either to speak intelligibly to an educated layperson. The second is the uncertainty about whether there can be any secure ground for knowledge, which has led to the subjectivism, at times solipsism, that characterizes a lot of recent theory in the humanities and social sciences. The limits and very possibility of knowledge are at stake.[6]

Knowledge lies scattered around us in great, unconnected pieces, like lonely mesas jutting up in a trackless waste. That this fragmentation has impoverished public discourse is a more and more common lament; that it has emaciated education, both undergraduate and graduate, is too painfully obvious a truth to dwell on. So as we try (shifting metaphorical gears) to navigate through waves of uncertainty from one disciplinary island to another, all universities, not just Catholic ones, face the challenges and dilemmas of remapping the world of learning.

Yet Catholic universities may be called to perform a special role in this common task. Traditionally, the great strength of Catholic intellectual life has been just that: tradition. That is, Roman Catholics, even more than other Christian intellectuals, heard their own voices as participants in an unbroken and multisided conversation stretching back continuously over more than two millennia. Catholic writers were as apt to interrogate Aristotle or Anselm or Aquinas as their own contemporaries. During the later–nineteenth century, with the papacy under siege and Catholics fearful of modernity, this respect for intellectual tradition jelled into an artificially rigid, at times even factitious Neo-Thomism. This revived Thomism—which over ensuing decades grew increasingly subtle, increasingly faithful to Aquinas—remained the center of gravity of Catholic intellectual life until the mid–twentieth century. Whatever its defects, Neo-Thomism kept alive among Catholics, even deepened, their powerful sense that intellectual life meant thinking within a tradition.[7]

When the Second Vatican Council opened the church's windows to modernity, the winds of change often drowned out these voices of the past. But Catholic intellectuals are now recovering their sense of the gravity of tradition. (So, too, are many Protestant intellectuals: one of the really interesting and salient facts of the current religious situation.)[8] And older Catholic intellectuals retain powerful memories of what it was like for intellectual life to operate as a self-conscious tradition.

Tradition matters—if we are ever to resolve our common problem of the fragmentation of knowledge. For only within an ongoing framework of shared questions and axioms can we find common ground even for coherent disagreement, much less mutual engagement. This home truth has in recent years been hammered home by some of our most influential philosophers, including notably Alasdair MacIntyre and, in a very different voice, Richard Rorty. One does not imagine MacIntyre and Rorty as teammates, but both agree that real discourse requires a shared framework over time, though Rorty wants to think of the making of such a frame as "continuing a conversation" rather than as engaging a tradition. The distinction serves as a useful reminder that the most intellectually productive traditions are apt to be loose-jointed, encouraging experiment rather than conformity.[9]

That we would need to articulate something so foundational as the salience of tradition speaks volumes about the intellectual condition of the twentieth century. If we are ever to reestablish communication among the scattered realms of scholarship, ever to find a common ground of discourse, ever, in short, to approach anew the lost unity of knowledge, we will do so only by constructing in our new century a new intellectual tradition that we all can share.

This task must remain for now a literally utopian adventure. No one can conceive what such a tradition will look like, though it is hard to imagine that it will be so exclusively European or so overwhelmingly male as the traditions we have grown out of. We are in for (I hope) exciting decades of trial and error, of piecemeal construction, of trying to fit together familiar and unfamiliar pieces into a jigsaw puzzle that will eventually make a picture that would likely startle us out of our socks if we could see it now.

The Catholic university can make a natural home for this experimentation. In common with most other Christian intellectuals, Catholic scholars retain the conviction on which unity of knowledge most comfortably rests: the dual faith in a God who created the universe and in human reason as a reliable God-given instrument for comprehending this creation. Even more than most other Christian intellectuals, Catholic ones retain three other advantages: the living memory of an actual unity; the recent experience of working intellectually on a common ground; and the philosophical and theological resources of the full Catholic intellectual tradition from which to build new connections—resources much more varied and complex than Neo-Thomism liked to admit.

Yet no one would accuse Catholic universities of using these resources to great effect. There are two reasons for this ineptness. First, Catholic universities (like the rest of us) are still stumbling blindly around the problems posed for all universities by the unraveling of the old seamless web of knowledge. But there is a second, specially Catholic fumbling. It arises from the fact that Catholic universities are wrestling with their own identities in the wake of Vatican II's opening to the modern world. They are going through what American Protestant colleges and universities groped through a century earlier: figuring out how to adapt to a thoroughly secular world of learning.

Those Protestant institutions made one of two choices. Most held on to their Victorian confidence that even secular knowledge must ultimately support their religious beliefs: Christianity needed no special nurturing or protection. They therefore welcomed secular modernity without reservation. Harvard had done this by the 1870s, Yale and Princeton a generation later, Duke and Vanderbilt still later. But all eventually shared the experience of the nineteenth-century Yale sociologist William Graham Sumner. Sumner said that one day he put his religious beliefs in a drawer. When he opened the drawer some years later, he found they were no longer there.

Not every Protestant college was Sumner writ large. A few, wary of secular learning, chose differently. They retreated into their Christianity, built up bulwarks against modernity (such as loyalty oaths for their faculties), and thus preserved their religious character. But they paid a heavy price. They cut themselves off from any real hope of influencing the larger world of knowledge—or, indeed, of tempering their own Christian scholarship in the chill waters of modern knowledge.

Catholic universities and colleges today seem poised to repeat the history of their Protestant analogues. Most are rushing to make themselves over in the image of Princeton or Mount Holyoke. A few are throwing up the barricades. At many institutions the debate has become, fortunately, self-conscious and vocal. Some faculty seem embarrassed that a Catholic university should claim any relationship between its religious heritage and its scholarly mission. Others warn that Catholic higher education is sacrificing its Christian birthright for a very messy mess of pottage—that, in fact, it is already sliding down the slippery slope to secularization.[10]

Sometimes the current debate reminds one of Karl Marx's dictum: historical crises that occur first as tragedy repeat themselves as farce. There is something at least quaint, if not comic, in the spectacle of my coreligionists and fellow academics rehearsing the quarrels of the late–nineteenth century about whether a Christian university can preserve its virtue in the potent embrace of secular knowledge—at the dawn of the twenty-first century, when secular knowledge has collapsed in an undignified heap of squirming confusion. One smells a question badly posed. In fact, it is yesterday's question.

Today's question is very different. How can the Catholic university reconstruct itself to bring the resources of Catholic tradition to bear on our *common* task of rebuilding the house of learning? In answering it we need to keep in mind the first of Newman's peculiar peculiarities: his insistence that a Catholic university is not the Catholic Church. Thus, the Catholic university enlists the resources of the Catholic tradition in a human enterprise, which itself is by no means exclusively Catholic or Christian or even religious. Yet *ipso facto* the Catholic university cannot fulfill its part in this enterprise without nurturing its own distinctively Christian and particularly Catholic intellectual traditions.

In short, the Catholic university must become, to borrow a phrase from Sir Thomas Browne, a "great and true *Amphibium*."[11] It must shrink from neither the vast ocean of secular learning nor the old ground of Christian knowledge, but inhabit both domains. Easy enough to say. But how to put this principle into practice? What would a university that was truly Catholic and truly a university look like today—or, better, tomorrow? Let us try to imagine.

What, to begin with, would its faculty look like? At least half of them would be Catholics, though not necessarily devout or even practicing Catholics. For to insist on personal piety is to miss the academic point, which is reflexive familiarity with the intellectual habits and resources of Catholicism, so as to provide a distinctively Catholic matrix for debate and teaching within the university. If one were considering what I earlier called the pastoral function of the *college*, the issues would be posed differently. But, put bluntly, it matters more for the intellectual mission of the *university* that Catholic faculty members be culturally Catholic than sincerely Christian.[12]

At the same time a critical mass of the faculty would be sincerely Christian, though not all Catholic. For only committed Christians are apt to take seriously the work of developing a scholarship deeply informed by Christianity. Much of the Christian tradition is common to all Christians. So Protestant or Orthodox faculty members would in many roles in a Catholic university, perhaps most, prove just as useful as Roman Catholics. Within a somewhat more restricted range, the same would be true of committed Jews or Muslims or other believers. Since neither Catholic Ph.D.s nor Christian scholars are as thick as blackberries (or even as secular academics), the university could not simply trust to the job market. It would need a kind of affirmative action program, such as universities have developed for recruiting minority scholars.

Yet nonbelievers are equally essential. A Catholic university would hire many secular-minded professors. And just as the "Catholic faculty" and "Christian faculty" would overlap, so would the "Catholic faculty" and "secular faculty." After all, a Catholic upbringing is hardly inconsistent with turning out fully secular in adulthood (indeed, some of my more cynical acquaintances would argue that the first condition predisposes to the second). Such overlaps would be important in creating the essential environment. It may well be easier, for instance, for a secularized ex-Catholic to appreciate the peculiar virtues of both Catholic tradition and secular knowledge and thus to act as a bridge between the different viewpoints within the university. The Catholic university would not hire secular scholars reluctantly, on the grudging ground that qualified Christians were too few to fill its faculty. Rather, it would hire them because it needs them. To be blunt, without ongoing synergy between Christians and nonbelievers, the experiment of a Catholic university will fail.

For Catholic and other believing scholars will have to grope their way into a largely untried conversation. They must learn to talk *as religious intellectuals* with colleagues skeptical of religious belief. They must persuade secular scholars that knowledge forged within the Catholic tradition illumines problems of universal import. In historic fact, Christianity has generated—and continues to develop—a broad and complicated set of ways of understanding reality. These overlap and interpenetrate all the major bodies of Western thought: science, philosophy, history, literature, even sociology. Christian scholars ought to be able to show that all this matters.[13]

But, to pull it off, they must not only rediscover and reapply the intellectual resources of Christianity in unimagined ways, but must do so with the constant thought of speaking to the universal university, not just the Catholic university. Sallying forth to conferences four times a year will not suffice. Dailiness is the key. A Catholic university will make itself internally pluralistic not by accident but by design, because only thus can it become effectively Catholic. But the very fact of doing so will make it an attractive home for non-Catholics, for the enterprise will energize and enlighten secular faculty as much as Catholic.

In its teaching, too, the Catholic university would experiment with novel forms of recovering the Christian learned tradition. The curriculum would presumably require theology or biblical studies or ethics, as Catholic colleges often still do. But it would include substantial efforts to relate the full range of university studies to Christian, particularly Catholic, intellectual traditions. This would not be a matter of studying "Christian literature" or "Christian chemistry" (whatever that might be). Rather, students, like faculty, need to explore how to locate modern knowledge within the broad and humane perspective of the Christian intellectual tradition and, still more broadly, within the perspective of theistic transcendence.

We can hardly guess into what curricular forms such explorations might ultimately develop, for the obvious reason that a full-bodied modern instantiation of Catholic learning does not yet exist. But we can imagine how a college might begin. A mathematics requirement might include the philosophical foundations of mathematics. Biology students might hear lectures on natural theology. The history program might include a seminar exploring philosophical and theological understandings of human agency and time. And all students might share a "foundations of knowledge" course, which would achieve what Newman imagined philosophy as doing—and what Victor Cousin actually more or less did in the 1820s at the École Normale, with consequences that still echo in French intellectual life.[14] None of this program would compromise, still less censor, the full range of contemporary mathematical, biological, or historical scholarship. But it would give students practice in thinking about their studies in broader, more interconnected ways that would infuse their knowledge with extra meanings and wider resonance.

That other mission of the modern university, research, is at first tougher to imagine as distinctively Catholic. For it is in research that Catholic scholars engage most directly with colleagues who will raise at least an eyebrow, if not their hackles, at the phrase "Christian scholarship." But the answer to this conundrum is surely not to fabricate a special set of "Christian" standards for research. Down that road lies isolation and intellectual impoverishment: the plight from which Catholic universities really began to extricate themselves only in the 1950s.[15] Catholic academics ought to know better than to think of that problem as a solution. No: researchers in a Catholic university must live fully in the modern academic world, welcoming the hard-wrought standards of specialized professional scholarship, wading into the debates over new methods, new directions, new canons.

What would make research distinctive in a Catholic university is not the methods it applies but the kinds of questions it favors. Some fields of study—theology, biblical criticism, the philosophy of religion—bear directly on Catholic and Christian traditions. A Catholic university would naturally provide a special home for such inquiries. In other fields a Catholic university would probably be indistinguishable from any other. The natural sciences have for the most part taught themselves to operate by shielding inquiry from questions of meaning that lie outside the theoretical structures of the field itself. It is hard to imagine what "Catholic chemistry" might look like, even harder to imagine who would want it.

Still other disciplines have no specifically Christian content yet engage with questions of wider human meaning than the natural sciences: philosophy, literature, history, economics, sociology, anthropology. In these, the humanities and human sciences, the Catholic tradition raises some kinds of questions more urgently than others. A Catholic university would naturally tend to favor these in its research program. One thinks, for instance, of a subfield like medieval intellectual history or an issue like distributive justice in economics. But the focus could not be exclusive. Internal pluralism is essential in research, too, if the Catholic university is to recover the salience of its traditions for the full range of modern knowledge.

Whatever questions are asked, the answers would not be constrained by Christian intellectual traditions but informed by them. The research supported in a Catholic university must remain entirely consonant with secular inquiries in its field, but it would incline to raise issues and suggest interpretations that secular researchers might overlook or play down. A scattering of contemporary examples have begun to demonstrate this. To take one in my own field of history, Christian scholars such as George Marsden and Nathan Hatch of Notre Dame and Mark Noll of Wheaton College have persuaded secular historians that early American Protestantism is better understood as a cultural than a social phenomenon: as a system of belief rather than simply a socially functional one. The fact that these Christian historians themselves take religion seriously as a matter of belief has obviously shaped their attitude toward what matters in the phenomena they study. But their research methods and standards are identical with those of their secular colleagues—a fact that has been essential to their success.

As Christian scholarship matures, it ought to lead, too, toward thicker and thicker connections between fields of study, growing out of the common tradition in which all are embedded. A Catholic university would ultimately reform graduate training in a more integrative mode. But we cannot really conceive what contributions Christian scholarship might make so long as Christian intellectual traditions sit in malnourished isolation from the mainstream of scholarship.

What we can see is that the lingering death of positivism has left us hungry for new modes of knowledge, while postmodern pluralism has offered hospitality to experiments wilder than this one. If the Catholic university grows into its full maturity and power, many more than Catholics stand to gain, just as feminist scholarship has opened eyes far beyond programs in women's studies.

For the stunting of the Catholic tradition in modern intellectual life has excised some of the most important roots of Western thought, including even those of modern natural science. We still read Augustine and Aquinas (or at least some historians do). But we have largely lost their tradition as a living, critical force in intellectual life. We have lost the benefits of the perspectives—radically different from secular ones—that this tradition can give us. We have lost, in short, an illuminating way of viewing reality. Regaining it could help all of us to argue more cogently about where we have come from, where we are, and where we ought to head. Just as the integration of women's ways of knowing into academic knowledge is expanding the university's horizons, so, too, could the resurrection of Catholic ways of knowing help even those of us who have no truck personally with Christianity to bring the isolated islands of human knowledge back into fruitful communication.

Perhaps these benefits become more palpable if we translate them into the classroom. Those of us in higher education worry a great deal about the incoherence of undergraduate education, reflected in persisting arguments about canons and core curricula. We ought to worry a great deal about the incoherence of *graduate education*, from which the incoherence of undergraduate education naturally flows. And therefore we ought to welcome and pay close attention to efforts to tie individual subjects into broader patterns of meaning, to encourage students to think coherently about the interlinkages and mutual resonances of their diverse studies. The University of Michigan could hardly adopt the curriculum of a Catholic university: Michigan, after all, does not believe in God. But, even without submitting to baptism, Michigan might learn a great deal about how to teach students to look for relationships among, say, chaos theory and family psychology and the Russian novel. And that is the first tiny step toward restoring coherence to our intellectual life and public discourse.

Thus far, I have been considering exclusively the Catholic university in its engagement with and service to the larger world of learning. In this I have followed Newman's dictum that the Catholic university is in its nature a university. But Newman firmly believed as well that a Catholic university, in carrying out its functions *as* university, would also serve the church and its people. He was right, for our very different time as well as for his.

As recently as 1960 or so, the phrase "Catholic intellectual," if not considered downright oxymoronic by non-Catholics, connoted a strange person who read Thomas Aquinas and papal encyclicals while harboring deep suspicion of Sigmund Freud and John Locke. This character might be bright, even interesting as a curiosity, but certainly was not someone to engage in debate about contemporary sociology or recent literary criticism. The Second Vatican Council—to oversimplify—exploded the cosy nest within which this odd bird had hatched.

But from the debris vanishingly few recognizably Catholic intellectuals have arisen (leaving aside Catholic theologians, whose trade by its nature *is* Catholic). And this despite the fact that the United States today houses a great many more intellectuals who happen to be Catholic than it used to. Nor has there grown up any vigorous intellectual life among educated Catholics in general—and this despite the rising proportion of college graduates in the Catholic population. College-educated Roman Catholics in this country—doctors, lawyers, business executives—still tend to keep their religious commitments in one box and their intellectual and artistic interests in another.

Neither of these nonevents should surprise us. Catholic universities of the post–Vatican II era have rarely fostered scholarship that plunges Catholicism into the pluralistic intellectual life of our times. So it comes as no great shock that few Catholic intellectuals have appeared. And, likewise, Catholic colleges in recent decades have seldom encouraged their students to think seriously and flexibly about the relationship of their faith to the novels they are reading or the physics they are studying. So it is hardly startling that intellectual life among American Catholics remains torpid.

Yet none of this is inevitable. No Christian people has a richer intellectual tradition. But to activate that tradition in the lives of Catholics, to fulfill its mission to the church, Catholic higher education needs to make a dual move: back to the intellectual resources of Catholicism and out into the larger arena of modern knowledge, so as to bring each to bear upon the other.

But this, as Father Newman might tell us were he writing today, is precisely what the Catholic university must do to fulfill its mission as university.

CHAPTER NINE

Catholic Intellectual Traditions and Contemporary Scholarship

The previous essay argues, *inter alia*, the advantages of carrying Catholic intellectual traditions into the academic public sphere; that is, of bringing them to bear on actual problems, weighty ones, that scholars today grapple with in research. In the chapter at hand I pursue this claim further, both how we might do it and why it might benefit us. The implicit audience is the entire community of scholars, most of it uninterested in Catholicism.

For a professor in Ann Arbor to explain what Catholic universities should do was not only smug but also uncomplicated: he could drive home right afterward. But in 1995 I left the University of Michigan after a stimulating decade to join the faculty of the University of Notre Dame, and this chapter dates from my first years there. The final paragraphs allude to the imminent founding of a center for research, the Erasmus Institute, aiming to put a little practical flesh on the theoretical skeleton rattling through this and the previous chapter. What I did not in the least expect at the time of writing was how many leading scholars, many not Catholic, would join in the Erasmus Institute's projects in varied fields. When I pitched the value of Catholic traditions for the whole world of scholarship, I felt my words to be a little utopian. They turned out to be the starkest realism.

Among the most striking of recent developments on the American academic scene is a sharply rising interest in the relationship of religion and higher education. The reasons for this growing attention are far from clear. Possibly it is simply a response to a general increase in the volubility of religion in American public life, heard in sectors ranging from the so-called Religious Right to the Catholic bishops' interventions on issues of peace and social justice. Perhaps it springs from dissatisfactions with the academy, with failures in the moral education of students and in the coherence of curriculum.[1] Perhaps it has something to do with multiculturalism and postmodernism, which have encouraged more explicit attention to the perspectival character of knowledge and to the influence of values on academic discourse. Whatever its sources, the fact of growing interest in the nexus of religion and learning is patent. Nothing quite like this has been seen on campuses since the 1950s, the heyday of the Danforth Fellows.

Rising interest does not necessarily imply rising enthusiasm. Optimism among many believers about an enhanced role for religion in classrooms and in research mingles with fear among others (believers as well as non-believers) of ecclesial oppression or intellectual narrowness. The points of tension are numerous. Should church-related colleges and universities have a distinctive role? If so, what? Should university teachers pay attention to the gap between the religious worldviews that American students often bring to higher education and the typically secular character of academic knowledge? If so, how? Does a largely secularized academy still have a valid role in the broad "formation" of students, and should we as teachers help in forming students as whole human beings rather than as disembodied intellects? If so, how? Does religion make legitimate cognitive claims? If so, what is the relation of these claims to academic knowledge? More specifically, should a scholar's religious beliefs influence her or his academic research? How should and how could the integrative tendency of religious belief comport with the highly professionalized, specialized, disciplinary nature of academic knowledge?

As this list suggests, within the general concern about the place of religion in colleges and universities, the point of greatest tension is probably the conflict between the knowledge claims made by religion and the decidedly nontheistic, secular understanding of knowledge characteristic of modern colleges and universities. This epistemological tension has attracted more and more explicit attention recently. And, within the general problem of religion and knowledge, the most sensitive question—but also the key question—is the possible bearing of religious commitments and religious traditions on academic research.

The prevailing view within academe is that religion properly has nothing to do with research—except, of course, in fields where religion provides the subject matter under study, as in theology, philosophy of religion, religious studies, and so forth. Otherwise, religion is understood to be a private matter, standing apart from the necessarily public discourse of an academic discipline: religion being no more relevant to sociology or political science than is an enthusiasm for fly-fishing or membership in the Girl Scouts. This is not to say that sociology or political science or economics or biology are somehow innately hostile to religion; indeed, most practitioners of these and other academic disciplines presumably recognize the need for deeper philosophic grounding or larger philosophic perspectives than their discipline can provide from its own resources—and recognize, too, that science cannot produce all the values that we need to live by and even to guide our academic research. Some would seek grounding, perspectives, values in religious traditions. The "warfare of science and religion" is a late-Victorian conceit best buried with the Victorians.

Yet religion ought not to be mingled with academic research as such. This opinion is not just that of scholars without religious beliefs; it is probably the view of most academics who are themselves churchgoers. Some professors would go further and argue that religion ought to be quarantined from intellectual life because it is dangerous, even toxic, to rational thought. Richard Dawkins of *Selfish Gene* fame calls religion "a virus" threatening rational discourse (a claim unfortunately not without some historical basis).[2] Dawkins's is perhaps an extreme statement, but it reflects a commonplace and understandable unease within academe.

The importance of guarding intellectual life against all kinds of irrational fanaticism goes, I hope, without saying. Further—let me lay my epistemological cards on the table—I want to insist on the great value of liberating academic research insofar as humanly possible from personal biases and extramural pressures. Put differently, I do not join in the so-called postmodern flight from objectivity. This is not because I have been napping for the past century. I know that knowledge is never pure, never isolated from the social conditions under which it is produced, never seen from a God's-eye view undistorted by individual or group perspectives, never free from political agenda and power plays, and always necessarily the product of an interpretative community. But I also believe that human beings, however deeply flawed, remain capable of decent behavior sometimes and of partial communication across cultural frontiers, that the ideals of a pure knowledge and of universal canons of knowledge are worth striving for, and that the closer we can come to those ideals (which may never be very close) the more valuable will knowledge be to the human race. Therefore, whenever religion becomes a threat to the academic enterprise, whenever religious presuppositions or ecclesiastical authorities try to put blinders on scholarship, as notoriously has sometimes happened, then that threat must be warded off—just as must the heavy hands of political or economic coercion.

Having said all this, I also want to insist that consigning religion to epistemological irrelevance is not merely needless; it is positively detrimental both to contemporary scholarship and to religious believers. Now, this is a very broad claim. It presents an enormous—and enormously complicated—series of questions. In this essay I intend only to outline a couple of problems and to map broadly, in a suggestive and tentative spirit, some approaches to dealing with them. A reader fond of Kant might call this essay "A Prolegomenon to [a rough draft of a sketch of] Some Possible Future Research Agenda." A little more precisely, I would like us to reflect on the relationship between Catholic intellectual traditions and contemporary academic research.

This focus specifically on Catholic intellectual traditions is in no way meant to denigrate or marginalize the intellectual heritage of other faiths; it simply recognizes my background and my (rather recently acquired) role as a teacher in a Catholic university. I am ignorant enough of my own traditions, but at least they are mine; I do not want to blunder in an offensive way into other people's. Still, it should be acknowledged that a great deal of the wisest recent thinking in this area comes from Protestant thinkers and that most of what I shall say about Catholic scholarship might be said about other Christian traditions, much of it about Jewish and Islamic scholarship as well. Moreover, a lot of the most original and profound work even on Catholic intellectual traditions has been accomplished by scholars whose backgrounds and beliefs are far distant from Catholicism, such as the late Amos Funkenstein.

With this prologue, then, let us ask two symmetrical questions. First, would contemporary scholarship, despite its fundamentally secular character, benefit from closer attention to Catholic intellectual tradi-

Catholic Intellectual Traditions | 147

tions? Second, would Catholics benefit—qua Catholics, with their own worldview—from closer attention to the relations between their intellectual traditions and contemporary scholarship?

Any attempt to answer these questions must begin by acknowledging the very distant relationship at present of Catholic thinking and the academy. On the one hand, there exists a growing, complex, rich body of Catholic thinking and scholarship stretching back almost two millennia. This is no simple corpus; it is rife with disputation, disagreement, development, divergence. Heterogeneity and many-sidedness are among the great strengths of Catholic intellectual traditions, one of the reasons why they have provided such rich resources for human reflection, so flexible and open-ended a source of possibilities for understanding. Recently however—at least recently as historians measure these things—Catholic intellectual traditions have pretty much become the proprietary preserve of theological scholars, a category broadly understood to include scripture scholars, ethicists, and so forth. Self-consciously Catholic thinking seems to have limited itself to two tasks: (1) deepening scriptural, theological, and philosophical understanding of the Christian faith, and (2) providing guidance in matters of personal and social morality.

These are crucial tasks, but, to put the case baldly, the intellectual work expected of Catholics no longer includes participating *as Catholics* in the human race's common task of expanding the range of understanding of the world and adding to the stock of knowledge. A great many academic intellectuals happen to be Catholic; they are growing in number and in distinction. But their Catholic beliefs, however important to them personally, usually make no difference to them as intellectual resources in their research as sociologists, historians, literary scholars, economists, anthropologists.

On the other hand, there exist vibrant, growing, complex, rich bodies of contemporary research in a wide variety of academic disciplines. A certain amount of research crosses disciplinary boundaries. Yet the prevailing axiom is that one intellectual boundary cannot be crossed: the frontier between academic knowledge, with its secular assumptions, and religious *thought* (a lot of academics would not call it "knowledge"), with its theistic assumptions. And so one sees at present almost no connection between these two impressive bodies of thought, Catholic intellectual traditions and contemporary scholarship—except, as mentioned earlier, where religion itself forms the subject matter of research.

Habit inures us to anything, but, if we could look with fresh eyes, this situation would appear more than slightly weird. Two lively and sophisticated groups of thinkers and researchers, each with well developed institutions for advancing and propagating ideas, often working on similar problems—and they pay virtually no attention to each other. Strange indeed.

The reasons for this peculiarity are, however, familiar to historians of higher education and academic knowledge. Until about a century and a half ago, scientists and scholars commonly assumed that knowledge formed a coherent whole; more precisely, they assumed that all parts of knowledge ultimately could be connected because every area of knowledge focused on some aspect of one single divine creation. Under these circumstances, it was relatively easy for specialists to pursue their specialized researches through the lens of Christian intellectual traditions (including specifically Catholic ones), whether they studied economics, biology, history, or whatever subject. The best scientific and humanistic knowledge was Christian in its assumptions, and Christian intellectual traditions helped learned people to understand the reality they studied.

Yet in the course of the nineteenth century knowledge came to be reconfigured along very different lines. Academic knowledge was divided into "disciplines." These different specialized areas of knowledge became separate from each other, entirely distinct fields rather than special aspects of a single whole. And once academic disciplines lost their connections with any larger reality, the idea of placing them within some transcendent Christian perspective became absurd. In the course of the twentieth century, broadly similar assumptions migrated out from academe into general understandings of knowledge.

The problem created was not specialization as such (which is very old); it was the cutting-off of knowledge within each discipline from larger, integrating structures of knowledge. While it is, strictly speaking, possible to work within a disciplinary structure and in addition connect one's intellectual work to larger religious meanings, this has proved very difficult. In American Protestant intellectual life, Christianity and learning were already well on the way to divorce in the early 1900s. For a while, among Catholic intellectuals, official Neo-Thomism retarded the separation of learning from Catholic intellectual traditions, although at the cost of isolating Catholic thought from the mainstream. But after

Vatican II the secularization of knowledge vastly accelerated for Catholic intellectuals as well.

The effect of this transformation was to create boundaries dividing "real knowledge," of a modern sort, from the theistically grounded "speculation" of earlier eras and of contemporary theology. Speaking broadly and too crudely, one can say that the line was drawn chronologically at roughly the end of the Enlightenment (with the large exception of philosophy, which presents a more complex case). Thinkers of earlier eras— Aquinas or Averroës or Anselm—might make interesting objects of historical study, but they were not to be taken seriously as live sources of theoretical understanding; nor were living theologians. An economist or literary critic or sociologist might plausibly draw on Marx or Nietzsche or Weber for the concepts that framed her research, but rarely could she derive conceptual underpinnings explicitly from Augustine and expect to be taken seriously in the secular academy. And whatever solvent effect postmodernism may have had on professorial conceptions of knowledge—less, I suspect, than is sometimes touted—this dividing line between knowledge and religion remains pretty nearly standard in academic thinking and deeply embedded in academic institutions. As a result, in almost all fields of knowledge it is now very difficult, if not impossible, to approach the understanding of reality from a Catholic point of view. Someone may be both a Catholic and a political scientist, but she can be a Catholic political scientist only by swimming vigorously against the stream—a bravura act that vanishingly few are able or wish to perform.

It is important to stress that this configuration of knowledge is relatively recent: we should not regard the present state of things as natural or inevitable. Indeed, the arguments today over postmodernism, perspectival knowledge, and antifoundationalist epistemologies remind us just how historically contingent and subject to change our present-day conceptions of knowledge are. Nonetheless, our present conceptions are our present conceptions—at present.

I hasten to add, too, that these exclusionary attitudes do not arise from blind prejudice or secularist animus. The academy's problem with Christianity is genuine and fundamental. Scholars need to share at least minimal assumptions about what qualifies as "knowledge" if they are going to engage in a common search for it. The fact is that academic knowledge does not recognize the existence of God, and this does make

Augustine problematic for any scholar fully enmeshed in an academic discipline today.

Problematic is not, however, the same as useless. We may well ask whether, in secularizing knowledge, the modern academy has gone too far in almost totally excluding religiously grounded thinkers as serious interlocutors: whether, even from a secular point of view, it has thrown out the baby with the bath water. But as soon as we raise the possibility of some link between Catholic intellectual traditions and contemporary scholarship, we face an obvious question. Anselm or Duns Scotus might provide intriguing objects of study for intellectual historians or maybe theologians or conceivably a few philosophers. But, really, are they not part of a past long dead? And does not even a live Catholic thinker, thinking as Catholic, operate from axioms foreign to the academy? What resources could Catholic intellectual traditions possibly have to offer to contemporary scholars? That is the first question to approach.

Let us put aside for a moment the assumption that thinkers who think qua Catholics must be excluded from academic discourse on secular principle. Let us simply ask, rather, whether contemporary scholarship might have something to learn from Catholic intellectual traditions, even without buying into theistic axioms. If we frame the question in these terms, then the answer in my view is "Of course!" We are talking, after all, about nearly two thousand years of human intellectual effort, of grappling with problems of human psychology, social organization, political power, and aesthetic imagination, of thinking and writing by some enormously gifted people, including at least two individuals, Augustine and Aquinas, who rank among the most profound, prolific, and creative minds of all eras. Granted, much of what these earlier scholars wrote has grown outmoded, perhaps even more would need to be recast and reinterpreted in terms accessible to contemporary scholars. But it would be the rankest prejudice to pretend that this vast and complex intellectual heritage contains nothing of value to us, and it would be the wildest hubris to claim that we have already assimilated all of its riches. To believe that Christianity has run out of steam intellectually strikes me as unwarranted bias arising from the hangover effect of the Victorian ideology of scientific progress; put differently, it is to take Auguste Comte's positivist schema of world-historical evolution far more seriously than any competent historian would.

One does not have to be Catholic to want to look afresh at the contemporary academic relevance of Catholic intellectual traditions. (Nor, conversely, does being a Catholic intellectual imply any interest or duty in this direction.) Clearly, personal belief does give one a special view of religious intellectual traditions: an Orthodox Jew will look upon rabbinic traditions differently than a Christian, and both will look upon them differently than an atheist. Nonetheless, religious intellectual traditions are productions of human cultures and are accessible to everyone in the same way and to the same extent as other productions of human cultures. We can all comprehend Aquinas or Lonergan in roughly the same way as we do Marx or Engels: you do not have to be Catholic or Marxist to understand their writings (though you might understand them somewhat differently if you were the one or the other).

Still, why should some political scientist or economist bother to comprehend Aquinas or Lonergan? What difference could attention to Catholic intellectual traditions make in contemporary knowledge? What would a Catholic approach to knowledge have to offer? There is more than one type of answer.

The first is *critique*. Catholic intellectual traditions offer a standpoint outside of the conventional wisdom of academic disciplines, a well thought-out and carefully articulated alternative perspective from which the contemporary researcher can criticize effectively the limits imposed on thinking by axioms underlying work in a field. One thinks, for instance, of commonplace, yet almost self-evidently feeble, models of human nature that direct research in psychology and sociology, such as rational-choice theory. Augustine's understanding of the mind is not likely to displace present models of cognition in experimental psychology, but it might well help a researcher to see more clearly aspects of mental activity that present models fail to account for adequately. And one recalls the enormous influence that Reinhold Niebuhr had, in the middle of the last century, on American historians and social scientists, many of them "atheists for Niebuhr"; he redirected them away from simplistic notions of the plasticity of human beings, simply because the doctrine of original sin profoundly informed his otherwise not terribly profound writings.[3]

Second, scholars can recover from Christian intellectual traditions *analytic devices* or conceptual apparatus useful in developing their own theories or approaches. Charles Peirce is today regarded as perhaps the greatest of American philosophers, and his semiotic theory of knowledge as his greatest achievement. Peirce was in his lifetime notoriously eccentric, eventually sadly isolated. It may have been sheer idiosyncrasy that led him to the decidedly unfashionable (outside of Catholic circles at least) Scholastic philosopher Duns Scotus: an encounter crucial in Peirce's working-out of his semiotic.[4] Today a sociologist trying to figure out why Americans react differentially to police officers, clergy, politicians, and teachers might develop a new model of response to authority by contemplating late-antique and medieval discourse on modes of authority and belief. A literary theorist might turn to Augustine's numerous writings on language for models of interpretation. A historian trying to understand competing conceptions of knowledge in the nineteenth century, the tensions and fusions between natural science and philology, might gain insight from studying biblical hermeneutics.

Third, certain *developed bodies of thought* in the Catholic heritage still offer scholars rich resources. Perhaps the prime recent instance is the revival of just-war theory in the past two decades. Whatever one thinks of its virtues—and many Catholics of pacifist inclination have criticized it harshly—just-war theory has undeniably emerged as an academic discourse as significant for secular political theorists as for Christian ones. And just as undeniably it has drawn very heavily on Catholic thinkers, notably Augustine.[5]

Finally, Catholic traditions, precisely because they are often foreign to the current wisdoms of the various disciplines, offer contemporary scholars something less easily definable but perhaps more important: a reflective *interlocutor who thinks in very different terms* than most of us do now, offering fresh approaches to problems we grapple with. Wittgenstein's long tangle with Augustine may not have left him fond of the Bishop of Hippo, but it did provide an anvil on which he hammered out a lot of his own thinking about language.[6]

Such examples, I hope, suggest useful ways in which scholars today might approach Catholic intellectual traditions. They certainly suggest something worth recovering there. This work of recovery has already begun, as the revival of just-war theory indicates, and one of the chief voices in that discourse, Jean Bethke Elshtain, in her lectures published in 1995 as *Augustine and the Limits of Politics*, suggests still broader relevance of Augustine for political theory.[7]

Yet might not one make similar claims for Buddhist or Hindu traditions? Certainly, but not with equal force. In the first place, Judaeo-Christian thinking was foundationally implicated in European thought from its late-antique origins until the Enlightenment (as in the medieval period was Islamic); because of this history, Jewish and Christian (perhaps especially Catholic) traditions still have, for European and American intellectuals, broader resonance and more specific applicability than do any analogues in other religions. In the second place, Catholic intellectual traditions have certain traits that suggest distinctive, though not necessarily unique, resources for academic work (which is by no means to deny that other traditions have their own special strengths). I would not pretend to anything like a comprehensive listing. But one might notice the highly rational and argumentative character typical of Catholic intellectual life through the centuries; its pluralistic nature and indeed multicultural bases; the hierarchic character of its approach to knowledge, anti-reductionist almost in principle; its tendency, especially in more recent centuries, to stress development over time; and its powerfully institutional orientation, which has produced a rich body of thinking about the nature of institutions, their relations to individuals and vice versa, and the issues of duty and right. These qualities (none individually unique to Catholicism) do not necessarily make Catholic thinking better or worse than other thinking; but they do collectively provide it its own intellectual tool kit—one, I would argue, of value for many areas of scholarly work.

Of course, for many problems of knowledge, especially in areas developed after the divorce between religion and academic learning, Catholic traditions would prove irrelevant. What does a molecular biologist trying to understand retroviruses have to learn from a theologian like David Tracy? Or an engineer trying to develop quantum machines from Albertus Magnus? Not much. How would Catholic traditions help a historian studying American electoral behavior under the second party system of the 1830s, 1840s, and 1850s? I see no way. But at present we can only imagine the range of connections that *could* be made between Catholic thought and current knowledge. It would be a serious error to think them few or trivial.

As must be obvious from the examples cited, such a project would be catholic with a lowercase *c* as well as with a capital C. We owe our intellectual as well as religious foundations to the ancient Hebrews; we share with Jews and Muslims as well as with other Christians crucial axioms of monotheism; much of our Christian tradition belongs to Protestant and Orthodox believers as well; and unbelievers might also benefit from and participate actively in the recovery of Catholic intellectual traditions for contemporary knowledge.

But now I want to turn the question around: what might Catholics—as believing Christians—have to gain from an ongoing conversation between contemporary knowledge and their own intellectual traditions? Here discussion can be much briefer because, unfortunately, the answer is certainly more obvious, probably less controversial.

Catholics, like other religious believers in the contemporary intellectual world, live with divided minds. We have one set of beliefs about reality as constituted by divine creation and expressing God's providential will. But this comprises, so to speak, only our "Sunday knowledge." For we have another set of beliefs about reality, taught in schools and colleges, in which God does not exist, and this provides our knowledge for most everyday purposes, including our work as scholars. Our most fundamental understanding of the world thus does not cohere with most of what we actually know in detail about it. Such a plight is hardly healthy for a faith seeking knowledge.

From this predicament we can hope for no easy exit. A divided mind simply *is* the condition of religious believers in the twenty-first century. I do not, however, find in this quandary occasion for despair. Our state is, after all, not unlike the situation of the earliest Christians, who lived with an even wider ravine between their creed and their culture. And, if Catholics can start to see points of connection between the God-centered world of Augustine or Lonergan and the world they learn about in school, then they can at least begin the long and arduous task of trying to understand the world in terms compatible with their beliefs about its most fundamental character. It is even possible that they will find their own understanding of the faith enriched by close encounter with secular knowledge, as Augustine famously did as a result of his confrontation with classical culture.

If, then, we might all of us—Catholics, scholars, Catholic scholars—have something to gain from reengaging Catholic intellectual traditions with contemporary scholarship, what is to be done?

The crucial first step is the creation of institutions to foster investigations bringing Catholic intellectual traditions to bear on issues in contemporary scholarship. The climate, in most graduate schools and research centers, for work along these lines is still only a few degrees above frigid. So for the time being the project of recovering the Catholic heritage for mainstream academic work will require its own structures to encourage established scholars and nurture new ones. But it must be understood that such a strategy does not signal retreat into a Catholic fortress; it begins, rather, an attempt to discover how those of us interested in Catholic traditions, by no means all of us Catholics, working as collaborators not only with each other but with the great, bustling, pluralistic world of scholarship, can best contribute as fellow citizens to the prosperity of the republic of learning.

One such effort has recently begun at Notre Dame, the Erasmus Institute. The Institute sponsors residential fellowships, graduate seminars, conferences and colloquia, working groups, and publications. It does not toil in splendid isolation, nor restrict its programs to the Notre Dame campus, for the job is not one that any university can take on by itself, but only in cooperation with institutions and individual scholars elsewhere. Probably most people inclined to take part are Catholic, but neither can such an institute be sectarian if it hopes to succeed. It welcomes not only other Christians, Jews, and Muslims who are pursuing parallel work in the intellectual traditions of their own faiths; it invites the collaboration of scholars of all faiths and none. If the intent is to reconnect Catholic intellectual life with mainstream academic thought, we can hardly hope to succeed without the partnership of leaders in it.

At the same time, operations like the Erasmus Institute do offer one type of answer to the "identity" dilemma that puzzles Catholic campuses. Like more established centers at Notre Dame—the Cushwa Center for the Study of American Catholicism, the Medieval Institute, the Center for the Philosophy of Religion—this new institution proceeds from the axioms that Christian and Catholic traditions have great value and that a Catholic university bears special responsibility to bring them to the contemporary world. But such centers for research and study are not a source of unwelcome pressure on faculty, only of opportunity. They do not retreat into a Catholic ghetto, but try to identify the common ground that can be shared with mutual benefit by Catholic and secular intellectuals. They are not exclusionary in attitude, but welcome anyone interested in their work, for whatever reason, from whatever angle. Indeed, few other university activities make clearer how central to the mission of a Catholic university are those among our colleagues who are fully secular and even skeptical about claims of the intellectual value of Catholic traditions. For Catholic scholars need that skepticism—to save us from sentimentalism, to keep us honest, to force us to sharpen our research and hone our thinking as we work to reclaim the riches of our traditions. We will not get far if we talk only to ourselves.

Notes

Introduction

1. John Maynard Keynes, *The General Theory of Employment, Interest and Money* (London, 1936), p. 383.
2. This last conclusion rests on a very informal survey of Ph.D.s and doctoral students in my acquaintance. I invite the skeptical reader to repeat the experiment.
3. For anthropology, see Thomas R. Trautmann, *Lewis Henry Morgan and the Invention of Kinship* (Berkeley, Calif., 1987); for art history, James Turner, *The Liberal Education of Charles Eliot Norton* (Baltimore, Md., 1999).
4. See chapter 3 and Jon H. Roberts and James Turner, *The Sacred and the Secular University* part 2 (Princeton, N.J., 2000).
5. The very existence of this lost language was undreamed of before Sir William Jones noticed affinities between Greek and Sanskrit in the late—eighteenth century, yet nineteenth-century philologists inferred much of the grammar and vocabulary of Indo-European by comparing its daughter languages.
6. Three important scholars who do treat philology as part of the intellectual history of the United States are Stephen G. Alter, Michael O'Brien, and Caroline Winterer. There exist "internalist" historical studies of such fields as linguistics, classical scholarship, and English literature in the United States. But, to the best of my knowledge, the first major study to take serious account of philology as a force central in the larger intellectual life of the American nineteenth century was Trautmann's *Morgan* (1987). It is probably no coincidence that its author was not originally an American historian but rather an anthropologist and historian of ancient India, who made himself into a superb nineteenth-century intellectual historian.

Chapter 1. Language, Religion, and Knowledge in
Nineteenth-Century America

Originally delivered as a lecture at the University of Michigan in 1985, then put in a drawer, the essay was pulled out several years later at the urging of Maurice Olender, a philologist at the Ecole des Hautes Etudes en Sciences Sociales. Slightly revised, it was published in *Revue de l'histoire des religions* 210, no. 4 (1993) : 431–62. It appears here for the first time in English.

I thank my sometime colleagues Stephen G. Alter, James McIntosh, and Thomas R. Trautmann for erudite advice.

1. Charles Darwin, *On the Origin of Species by Means of Natural Selection, or The Preservation of Favoured Races in the Struggle for Life* (London, 1859), pp. 116–17, 422; Thomas R. Trautmann, *Lewis Henry Morgan and the Invention of Kinship* (Berkeley, Calif., 1987).

2. See, e.g., two works of very different character: Maurice Olender, *Les langues du Paradis: Aryens et Sémites, un couple providentiel* (Paris, 1989); and Martin Bernal, *Black Athena: The Afroasiatic Roots of Classical Civilization*, vol. 1, *The Fabrication of Ancient Greece, 1785–1985* (New Brunswick, N.J., 1987).

3. The pioneer in the intellectual-historical approach has been Hans Aarsleff; see *The Study of Language in England, 1780–1860* (Princeton, N.J., 1967) and *From Locke to Saussure: Essays on the Study of Language and Intellectual History* (Minneapolis, Minn., 1982). A representative example of the approach through the history of academic knowledge is Michel Espagne and Michael Werner, eds., *Philologiques I: Contribution à l'histoire des disciplines littéraires en France et en Allemagne au XIXe siècle* (Paris, 1990). In focusing on the period after about 1750, I do not mean to slight the much more developed body of scholarship on early–modern philology, currently enjoying a burst of energy. Here, to single out one among several fine scholars, the work of Anthony Grafton is as exemplary as it is prolific.

4. The closest approach to a general survey is Julie Tetel Andresen, *Linguistics in America, 1769–1924: A Critical History* (London and New York, 1990); there are also a relatively small number of special studies, some cited below.

5. On the transformation of the teaching of Latin and Greek in American colleges into the discipline of classics, see Caroline Winterer, *The Culture of Classicism: Ancient Greece and Rome in American Intellectual Life, 1780–1910* (Baltimore, Md.: Johns Hopkins University Press, 2001), the most important study of the influence of philology in higher education. On Gildersleeve himself, see the several books edited by Ward W. Briggs Jr., which go a long way toward remedying the lack of a full biography. Absent comparable editions, the want of a biography of Child is a more serious flaw; pending its rectification, see Jo McMurtry, *English Language, English Literature: The Creation of an Aca-*

demic Discipline (Hamden, Conn., 1985), which treats him at length. On Whitney, see the forthcoming intellectual biography by Stephen G. Alter, which will upon publication take its place as the weightiest study of philological scholarship and its intellectual resonances in nineteenth-century America (though the book's significance transcends the United States). Another American by birth, Fitzedward Hall, was an important Sanskritist, but Hall's entire career was spent in India and England, so he hardly qualifies as "American" for present purposes. It was not just the Indo-European project that Americans neglected; there were vanishingly few comparative philologists of any stripe in the United States—the Anglo-Saxonist Francis A. March (1825–1911) of Lafayette College being a notable exception—though leanings in that direction could be found around the Modern Languages Association and American Oriental Society.

6. The other two were Moses Stuart of Andover Seminary and Charles Hodge of Princeton Seminary. See Jerry Wayne Brown, *The Rise of Biblical Criticism in America, 1800–1870: The New England Scholars* (Middletown, Conn., 1969). On Stuart, see John H. Giltner, *Moses Stuart: The Father of Biblical Science in America* (Atlanta, Ga., 1988); on Hodge, John W. Stewart, "The Tethered Theology: Biblical Criticism, Common Sense Philosophy, and the Princeton Theologians, 1812–1860" (Ph.D. diss., University of Michigan, 1990), and *idem, Mediating the Center: Charles Hodge on American Science, Language, Literature, and Politics,* Studies in Reformed Theology and History, vol. 3, no. 1 (Princeton, N.J., 1995).

7. See especially Lilian Handlin, "*Babylon est delenda*—The Young Andrews Norton," in Conrad Edick Wright, ed., *American Unitarianism, 1805–1865* (Boston, 1989), pp. 53–85, a very perceptive assessment of Norton.

8. A biography of Norton is a desideratum. Handlin's "*Babylon est delenda*" is very good but covers only the earlier phase of Norton's life. His whole existence is treated in my biography of his son, *The Liberal Education of Charles Eliot Norton* (Baltimore, Md., 1999), but incidentally to the younger Norton. The fullest account can be found in a longer, unpublished version of this latter book; copies of it are deposited in the C. E. Norton papers in Houghton Library, Harvard University, and in the Department of Special Collections, Hesburgh Library, University of Notre Dame. Easier of access are my sketch of Andrews Norton in the *American National Biography* and another in the older *Dictionary of American Biography*. Among unpublished sources, far and away the most important is the collection of Andrews Norton papers in Houghton Library. Uncatalogued as of this writing, the collection, in seventeen boxes, can be located under the call number bMS Am 1089. Unless otherwise indicated, all manuscripts cited are from this collection. "Andrews Norton" will be abbreviated "AN."

For the piety of Norton and his family, see his correspondence with his father, Samuel, and sister, Jane; for his Italianist ambitions, see AN to Samuel

Norton, 24 June 1803. Strictly speaking, the term "Unitarian" is an anachronism, since the word was not usually applied to the liberal theological faction within the New England Congregationalist establishment until after about 1815.

9. For these years, see AN's journal, 1804; AN-Samuel Norton correspondence; Samuel Thacher to AN, 12 January 1811; Henry Ware to AN, 5 September 1809 and 23 April 1810; and the AN-Levi Frisbie correspondence, 1809–10, in Harvard University Archives.

10. AN to Samuel Norton, 4 May 1814, 20 July 1814, and 29 February 1815 [sic]; AN-George Bancroft correspondence; AN to Josiah Quincy, 1 March 1842; AN to John Gorham Palfrey, September 1818; AN to Joseph Story, 2 August 1823; Samuel A. Eliot to AN, 27 January 1820; Levi Frisbie to AN, 27 January 1820; resolution of directors of Harvard Divinity School, 12 April 1830; AN to John Gorham Palfrey, [1828] and [27 January 1831]; Palfrey to AN, 28 January 1831; Ephraim Peabody to Catharine Eliot Norton [Mrs. AN], 10 January 1854; AN to James Savage et al., 25 August 1840, Letterbook B. The tax bills preserved in the AN papers show AN to have been perhaps the wealthiest private resident of Cambridge. For AN and Bancroft, see Lilian Handlin, *George Bancroft: The Intellectual as Democrat* (New York, 1984). An account of the Harvard reform effort of the 1820s appears in David B. Tyack, *George Ticknor and the Boston Brahmins* (Cambridge, Mass., 1967).

11. [George Ripley], "Martineau's Rationale of Religious Enquiry," *Christian Examiner* 21 (1836): 225–54.

12. Andrew Preston Peabody, *Harvard Reminiscences* (Boston, 1888), pp. 75–76; AN to editor of *Christian Examiner,* 1 November [1836], and to [Harm J. Huidekoper?], [March 1837]; *Boston Daily Advertiser,* 5 and 9 November 1836.

13. Emerson published it in the fall of 1838 as *An Address, Delivered before the Senior Class, in Divinity College, Cambridge, Sunday evening, 15th July 1838.*

14. *Boston Daily Advertiser,* 27 August, 28 September, 5, 15, and 18 October 1838; *Christian Register,* 29 September 1838; Samuel A. Eliot to AN, 10 and 21 October 1838. Articles by other hands appeared in other Boston papers.

15. Published in 1839 in pamphlet form as *A Discourse on the Latest Form of Infidelity* and reprinted in AN, *Tracts Concerning Christianity* (Cambridge, Mass., 1852), pp. 229–68.

16. AN to John Gorham Palfrey, [c. 1819] and [21 September 1822?], Palfrey Family Papers, Houghton Library. The motto plays on the words supposedly repeated by Marcus Porcius Cato (Cato the Elder), unyielding foe of Carthage, in every speech he made in the Roman senate—a tag known to every nineteenth-century schoolboy: "Delenda est Carthago" (Carthage must be destroyed).

17. Perry Miller, *The Transcendentalists: An Anthology* (Cambridge, Mass., 1950), p. 158.

18. On Unitarian epistemology, see Daniel Walker Howe, *The Unitarian Conscience: Harvard Moral Philosophy, 1805–1861* (Cambridge, Mass., 1970), esp. chap. 1.

19. On Norton and the literary style of the New England Renaissance, see notably Lawrence Buell, *Literary Transcendentalism: Style and Vision in the American Renaissance* (Ithaca, N.Y., 1973).

20. AN to editor of *Christian Examiner*, 1 November [1836]; *Boston Daily Advertiser*, 27 August 1838, 15 October 1838.

21. Ironically, De Wette's son-in-law, Karl Beck, joined the Harvard faculty in 1832 as Professor of Latin, taught Norton's son Charles there in the 1840s, and seems to have gotten on well with Norton.

22. AN, "Remarks on the Modern German School of Infidelity" (1839); reprinted in AN, *Tracts*, pp. 269–368. Quotations are from pp. 274, 277.

23. Ibid., pp. 277, 279–80, 281, 285, 286.

24. AN to John Gorham Palfrey, 22 April 1840, Palfrey Papers; AN to William Ware, 18 March 1840 and [spring 1840]; *Boston Daily Advertiser*, 9 November 1836; Joseph Henry Allen, *Our Liberal Movement in Theology: Chiefly As Shown in the History of Unitarianism in New England*, 2d ed. (Boston, 1883), p. 68.

25. AN to Blanco White, 7 November 1837, Letterbook B; AN, *Discourse*, p. 263; [George Ripley], *"The Latest Form of Infidelity" Examined: A Letter to Mr. Andrews Norton* (Boston, 1839), p. 55.

26. AN, *Discourse*, pp. 239, 240, and "Remarks," p. 276.

27. AN, "A Defence of Liberal Christianity," reprinted in AN, *Tracts*, pp. 17–18. Donald A. Crosby and Philip F. Gura have, from different perspectives, partially explicated Norton's ideas about language, though neither of them in the context discussed here; neither raises the issues central to my discussion. See Crosby, *Horace Bushnell's Theory of Language in the Context of Other Nineteenth-Century Philosophies of Language* (The Hague, 1975), pp. 180–89; Gura, *The Wisdom of Words: Language, Theology, and Literature in the New England Renaissance* (Middletown, Conn., 1981), pp. 24–30.

28. Peabody, *Reminiscences*, p. 78; William Ware to AN, 26 July 1833. Letterbook C in the AN Papers contains a number of his poems, conventionally romantic in theme and execution.

29. Never published, these lectures are preserved in the AN Papers. See especially lectures 5 and 10.

30. Reprinted in AN, *Tracts*; see especially pp. 69–70.

31. Dexter lecture 10.

32. Dexter lectures 5 and 10; AN, Notebook [c. 1811–13?]; AN, *Inaugural Discourse*, esp. pp. 86–88.

33. AN to John Ware, 23 June 1834.

34. In 1967 a scholarly conference marked the centenary of Johnson's death: not all contributors agreed with Drake as to Johnson's genius, but even at that date his solitude seemed well established. See Charles L. Todd and Russell T. Blackwood, eds., *Language and Value: Proceedings of the Centennial Conference on the Life and Works of Alexander Bryan Johnson* (New York, 1969). See also Charles L. Todd and Robert Sonkin, *Alexander Bryan Johnson: Philosophical Banker* (Syracuse, N.Y., 1977); and Alexander Bryan Johnson, *A Treatise on Language*, ed. David Rynin (Berkeley, Calif., and Los Angeles, 1947), especially Rynin's "Critical Essay on Johnson's Philosophy of Language."

35. Theologians had never lost sight of this aspect of Bushnell's work, though naturally treating it in a theological, not a philological, context. Charles Feidelson's *Symbolism and American Literature* (Chicago, 1953) awakened interest in Bushnell among literary scholars and intellectual historians. Since then Bushnell studies have become a cottage industry among the linguistically inclined, of which the most substantial product is Crosby, *Bushnell's Theory of Language*. See also James O. Duke, *Horace Bushnell on the Vitality of Biblical Language* (Chico, Calif., 1984).

36. Hazard made a cameo appearance in Gura, *Wisdom of Words*, and got more sustained attention in Crosby, *Bushnell's Theory of Language*. Crosby had been anticipated in linking Bushnell and Hazard by Harold Durfee, "Language and Religion: Horace Bushnell and Rowland Gibson Hazard," *American Quarterly* 5 (1953): 57–70. Gura says a good deal about Kraitsir. Cardell appears fleetingly in both Crosby and Gura.

37. Elizabeth Flower and Murray G. Murphey, *A History of American Philosophy*, 2 vols. (New York, 1977).

38. Crosby and Gura come closest, but the former's theological focus and the latter's dogged pursuit of Thoreau and Melville's metaphors seem to have inoculated them against other dimensions of their subject. This may explain Gura's otherwise incomprehensible neglect of Norton's anti-Transcendentalist screeds when he comes to discuss that gentleman.

39. See Brown, *Rise of Biblical Criticism*.

40. This story can be traced in Aarsleff, *Study of Language in England* and *Locke to Saussure*. The situation in England, though turning out ultimately rather like the Continental one, was more complex, involving protracted entanglements with radical politics centered on John Horne Tooke and his disciples. On this, see, besides Aarsleff, Olivia Smith, *The Politics of Language, 1791–1819* (Oxford, 1984). The English struggles seem to have had little resonance in America.

41. Trautmann, *Morgan*, p. 74.

42. James Turner, *Without God, Without Creed: The Origins of Unbelief in America* (Baltimore, Md., 1985), pp. 160–62.

43. J. B. Stallo, *The Concepts and Theories of Modern Physics*, ed. Percy W. Bridgman (1884; reprint of 2d ed., Cambridge, Mass., 1960), pp. xix, 3, 9–10.

44. Reprinted in Chauncey Wright, *Philosophical Discussions*, ed. Charles Eliot Norton (New York, 1877).

Chapter 2. Charles Hodge in the Intellectual Weather of the Nineteenth Century

Originally delivered at an interdisciplinary conference assessing the legacy of Charles Hodge, convened at Princeton Theological Seminary to commemorate his two-hundredth birthday in 1997; this essay will be published in a forthcoming collection of essays from that conference by William B. Eerdmans Publishing Company.

BRPR signifies the *Biblical Repertory and Princeton Review*, which Hodge edited from 1825 to 1868 (under variant titles). Most *BRPR* articles, conventionally for such journals in the period, masqueraded as book reviews, rarely carrying formal titles; I have identified them by abbreviated running title. I am grateful to Raymond Cannata for supplying photocopies of many of Hodge's articles in the *BRPR*.

1. "Stuart on the Romans," *BRPR* 5 (July 1833): 382–85. This was for Hodge fairly mild stuff; cf. the savage ridicule heaped on the High Church Episcopal bishop George W. Doane in "Bishop Doane and the Oxford Tracts," *BRPR* 13 (July 1841): 451–52. The rules of engagement were well known; e.g., regarding an article signed "A Friend to the A[merican] E[ducation] Society," known to those *au courant* with the controversy in question to have come from the pen of Moses Stuart, Hodge mentioned in replying to it that "we were not authorized to know the writer" until Stuart himself had publicly acknowledged his authorship. "Professor Stuart's Postscript," *BRPR* 2 (January 1830): 125.

2. Edward Everett and George Bancroft laid similar foundations but turned to other careers soon after returning from Germany. A high proportion of Americans who attended German universities in the first two-thirds of the nineteenth century merely brushed German erudition, owing to deficiency of language or brevity of exposure.

3. "England and America," *BRPR* 34 (January 1862): 147; "What is Christianity?" *BRPR* 32 (January 1860): 135; "Professor Park's Sermon," *BRPR* 22 (October 1850): 657. My emphasis.

4. John W. Stewart, *Mediating the Center: Charles Hodge on American Science, Language, Literature, and Politics*, Studies in Reformed Theology and History, vol. 3, no. 1 (Princeton, N.J., 1995), pp. 7–9. I am in general much indebted to Stewart for my understanding of Hodge, though I do not want to implicate him in my misunderstandings.

5. In the case of most thinkers whose careers spanned as many decades as Hodge's, the historian would take care to respect the evolution of the subject's thought and distinguish accordingly between earlier writings and later. So far as I can tell, however, the lineaments of Hodge's worldview changed remarkably little over his lifetime, becoming only clearer and, as usual in middle and old age, more rigid. In this overview I have therefore drawn on his work without regard to dates of composition.

6. "Bishop Doane," 456 and passim; "Theories of the Church," *BRPR* 18 (January 1846): 145, 157; "Is the Church of Rome a Part of the Visible Church?" *BRPR* 18 (April 1846): 341, 343, 344; "Schaf's [sic] Protestantism," *BRPR* 17 (October 1845): 630; "Oxford Tracts," *BRPR* 10 (January 1838); "Dr. Schaff's Apostolic Church," *BRPR* 26 (January 1854).

7. "The Church and the Country," *BRPR* 33 (April 1861): 323, 375; "Voluntary Societies and Ecclesiastical Organizations," *BRPR* 9 (January 1837): 106; "Preaching the Gospel to the Poor," *BRPR* 42 (January 1871): 87, 90; "Claims of the Free Church of Scotland," *BRPR* 16 (April 1844): 258.

8. "Bushnell on Christian Nurture," *BRPR* 19 (October 1847): 535, 502, 504.

9. "Christian Nurture," 510, 521–22. "They are called *American* revivals," Hodge noted. "There is nothing American however in true religion. It is the same in its nature, and in its means of progress in all parts of the world." Ibid., 520.

10. Some, though by no means all, Whigs belonged in this tradition; one gets some sense of its parameters in the essay on Rufus Choate in Daniel Walker Howe, *The Political Culture of the American Whigs* (Chicago, 1979). A classic statement by a younger figure is [Charles Eliot Norton], *Considerations on Some Recent Social Theories* (Boston, 1853), which is helpful in that it explicitly treats at a theoretical level contemporaneous European political ideas.

11. "The Princeton Review on the State of the Country and of the Church," *BRPR* 37 (October 1865): 628; "Slavery," *BRPR* 8 (April 1836): 270, 289; "Emancipation," *BRPR* 21 (October 1849): 597. In his early writings on the subject, Hodge tended to minimize ill-treatment by slave owners and to accept the "wage-slavery" argument that English factory workers were worse off than American slaves ("Abolitionism," *BRPR* 16 [October 1844]: 576–77). His opinion changed during the crisis years following the Mexican War; the 1849 article "Emancipation" was a turning point.

12. E.g., "Emancipation," 605, and "Slavery," 300.

13. "Emancipation," 599; "Abolitionism," 562; "The State of the Country," *BRPR* 33 (January 1861): 13.

14. "Emancipation," 593. I say "help to explain": Hodge had other clear objections to utilitarianism. His communitarianism was very obviously rein-

forced by his belief in "the participation of the life of Adam by the whole race, and of the life of Christ, by all believers" ("Christian Nurture," 502–3).

15. "Civil Government," 138, 133, 132, 134, 139, 143, 151, 152. More precisely, Hodge claimed that the right of revolution was "a necessary inference" from the fact that God willed "that government should exist" but "left the form to be determined" by "those to whom the general command is given," as well as from "the end which God designs government to answer," viz., "the welfare of the people." Ibid., 152–53.

16. "Professor Stuart's Postscript," 132.

17. "Introductory Lecture," *BRPR* 1 (January 1829): 76–77, 87; "Slavery," 299; "The Church and the Country," *BRPR* 33 (April 1861): 340. Curiously, Hodge did believe that, "as one of the necessary adjuncts of the right of private judgment," Christians should "have a voice" (though not necessarily more than a veto) in choosing their pastor ("Church of Scotland," 241). Given his strong version of the religious role of the state, his failure to extend this right to the choice of political rulers was probably a lapse in logic.

18. "Schaf's Protestantism," 627; "Civil Government," 145.

19. "Abolitionism," 551, 553.

20. "Schaf's Protestantism," 627; "Oxford Tracts," 113; "Church of Rome," 332–33; "Theories of the Church," 147; "Schaff's Apostolic Church," 152.

21. "Schaff's Apostolic Church," 159, 157, 179, 165. My emphasis. Hodge was inconsistent in capitalizing "Scripture," and I have let his inconsistencies stand.

22. "Stuart on the Romans," 382; "Oxford Tracts," 102–3; "The Latest Form of Infidelity," *BRPR* 12 (January 1840): 35.

23. "Civil Government," 137; "Abolitionism," 554.

24. "Bushnell on Vicarious Sacrifice," *BRPR* 38 (April 1866): 172; "Stuart on the Romans," 382.

25. "Thornwell on the Apocrypha," *BRPR* 17 (April 1845): 270–72; "Slavery," 276; "Inspiration," *BRPR* 29 (October 1857): 664, 663, 679.

26. "Latest Form of Infidelity," 54, 68. How little Hodge was affected by historical criticism is shown by his enthusiasm for one argument for the reliability of the biblical account of the creation and fall. Accepting literally the ages of Adam and the patriarchs recorded in the Old Testament, Hodge was much taken by the idea that Adam could have related the story directly to Methuselah, Methuselah to Noah's son Shem, and Shem to Jacob, in whose epoch "minute and particular history commences." "Neill's Lectures on Biblical History," *BRPR* 18 (July 1846): 456–61.

27. "Princeton Review on State of the Country," 652.

28. "Theology in Germany," *BRPR* 25 (July 1853): 449; "Cousin's Philosophy," *BRPR* 28 (April 1856): 339, 347; "Latest Form of Infidelity," 69–70. For

Hodge's views of the Germanized Americans, see especially "Park's Sermon," "Bushnell on Sacrifice," and, for Nevin, "What is Christianity?"

29. "Inspiration," 688.

30. "Inspiration," 689; "Park's Sermon," 642, 658, 673; "Latest Form of Infidelity," 38, 59.

31. "Park's Sermon," 646; "Inspiration," 693. Hodge was not referring specifically to Bushnell in the second passage quoted, but in general to theologians who took a position like his.

32. "Can God be Known?" *BRPR* 36 (January 1864): 134, 143, 148; "Bushnell on Sacrifice," 161; "Latest Form of Infidelity," 33–34.

33. "Park's Sermon," 645; "Oxford Tracts," 118, 102. I use quotation marks to distinguish the nineteenth-century American (and to some extent British) understanding of Francis Bacon's views from how Bacon or others might have understood them. See especially Theodore Dwight Bozeman, *Protestants in an Age of Science: The Baconian Ideal and Antebellum American Religious Thought* (Chapel Hill, N.C., 1977). "The Unity of Mankind," *BRPR* 31 (January 1859), exemplifies Hodge's "Baconianism."

34. "Bushnell on Sacrifice," 184–85.

35. "Unity of Mankind," 104–6. I omit consideration of Hodge's famous encounter with Darwinism, because the key issue there seems to me to have been Darwin's naturalism rather than historicism, although Darwin's evolutionary hypothesis certainly had profoundly historicist implications for knowledge. Hodge's *What Is Darwinism?* has recently been reissued (together with related writings) with an illuminating introduction by Mark A. Noll and David N. Livingstone (Grand Rapids, Mich., 1994).

Chapter 3. Secularization and Sacralization

First published, with other papers from a 1990 conference at Duke University, in George Marsden and Bradley Longfield, eds., *The Secularization of the Academy* (Oxford University Press, 1992). I continued these explorations in somewhat different directions in Jon H. Roberts and James Turner, *The Sacred and the Secular University* (Princeton University Press, 2000).

1. I have been censured—though never by anyone versed in the history of American higher education—for ignoring Catholic colleges. In extenuation of admitted guilt I plead two facts. First, little is known about the history of Catholic higher education before 1900 (though this little suggests a fascinating intellectual alternative to Protestant colleges and richly merits further research). It was impractical for me to undertake the amount of archival digging needed even to construct a plausible context within which to comprehend data excavated—

historiographic contexts already well developed for the Yales, Oberlins, Wisconsins, and Vanderbilts of the nineteenth century. Second, the great majority of students, and even greater weight of subsequent academic influence, rested with institutions historically Protestant in ethos (a category that includes state universities). Throughout the twentieth century, Catholic colleges and universities gravitated toward this "mainstream" model. After the grip of official Neo-Thomism relaxed during the 1950s and 1960s, the drift became a riptide. Cf. Philip Gleason, *Contending with Modernity: Catholic Higher Education in the Twentieth Century* (New York, 1995).

2. The standard history, despite ever more apparent deficiencies, is still Frederick Rudolph's *The American College and University: A History* (New York, 1962), which, on the specific subject at hand, Rudolph amplified in *Curriculum: A History of the American Undergraduate Course of Study since 1636* (San Francisco, 1977). Post-Rudolph historians of higher education have tended to follow Laurence R. Veysey (*The Emergence of the American University* [Chicago, 1965]) in concentrating on graduate training, research, and the exfoliation of "university" structures around the undergraduate college—understandably, since the most significant changes *seemed* to lie in such developments—or they have explored the social functions of the college. It is high time for a new general history of American higher education.

3. Rudolph, *Curriculum*, chap. 2, briefly discusses the curriculum of the early American colleges; but the best study of the curriculum transported to the colonies remains Samuel Eliot Morison, *The Founding of Harvard College* (Cambridge, Mass., 1935), chaps. 1–10.

4. Henry F. May, *The Enlightenment in America* (New York, 1976), remains the most effective broad study of Scottish intellectual influence in America; Douglas Sloan, *The Scottish Enlightenment and the American College Ideal* (New York, 1971), is a good initial approach to its educational role. When first introduced, moral philosophy was not necessarily taught to seniors; but it quickly assumed this place. On the origins of the moral philosophy course, see Lawrence A. Cremin, *American Education: The Colonial Experience, 1607–1783* (New York, 1970), pp. 400–466. Of all the comprehensive histories of individual institutions, the most sensitive to the role of Scottish philosophy in the curriculum—and one that in general sets a high standard for the genre—is Mark A. Noll, *Princeton and the Republic, 1768–1822* (Princeton, N.J., 1989).

5. D. H. Meyer, *The Instructed Conscience: The Shaping of the American National Ethic* (Philadelphia, Pa., 1972) is an acute and comprehensive analysis of moral philosophy textbooks. The most illuminating study of instruction in moral philosophy in any antebellum American college, though ranging far beyond the course itself and even the college, is Daniel Walker Howe, *The Unitarian Conscience: Harvard Moral Philosophy, 1805–1861* (Cambridge, Mass.,

1970). The best-selling American textbook of moral philosophy, by the president of Brown University, is available in a modern edition: Francis Wayland, *The Elements of Moral Science* (1837), ed. Joseph L. Blau (Cambridge, Mass., 1963).

6. The example comes from Wayland, *Elements*, p. 272.

7. I thank Thomas Trautmann for suggesting this remarkably exact metaphor.

8. I have addressed this development and its relationship to the fragmentation of knowledge in *Without God, Without Creed: The Origins of Unbelief in America* (Baltimore, Md., 1985). Most professors—including natural scientists, the group reputedly most riddled with doubters—seem to have remained believers, even Christians, well into the twentieth century. Possibly most still are believers, in some plausible sense. The point is that, absent a consensus on the existence of God, it became increasingly difficult to construct the framework of knowledge around theistic assumptions.

9. Some of these programs and the novel degrees awarded at their completions are noted in Rudolph, *Curriculum*, p. 138. Many others can be discovered in the histories of particular institutions, including a number in subjects that later returned to the ordinary liberal arts curriculum (like the School of Political Science at Michigan, discussed in chapter 4).

10. Gleason, *Contending with Modernity*.

11. To cite specific examples of a generic inclination would be invidious, but I do want to stress that the landscape is not utterly waste and barren and to acknowledge the great help I have found in the exceptions to this generalization, such as the work of Hugh Hawkins.

12. There is, for instance, nothing comparable to the work cited above on moral philosophy courses and the role of Scottish common-sense philosophy in the antebellum curriculum. Yet, at least in the college and university archives that I have visited, evidence of classroom instruction, in the form of lectures and syllabi by professors and lecture notes by students, is more voluminous for the period after 1860 than for the decades before.

The pioneering study by Thomas Le Duc, *Piety and Intellect at Amherst College, 1865–1912* (New York, 1946), did try seriously to examine teaching, notably in the chapter on Charles E. Garman; but Le Duc made surprisingly little use of material revealing what actually occurred in the classroom. More generally, courses in English literature (added to traditional instruction in rhetoric from circa 1860) are also now a partial exception to this rule with the publication of Gerald Graff, *Professing Literature: An Institutional History* (Chicago, 1987), which contains some acute comments on the early teaching of English literature in American colleges and universities, as well as fascinating illustrations of it. Graff's book is, unfortunately for present purposes, constructed around aims tangential to those of this chapter. Moreover, in some instances where I know the material (all from before 1900) independently, Graff's evidence seems to me shaky, his categories anachronistic. But, especially because I question Graff's interpretation of early college teaching, I do wish to acknowledge that his willingness to pioneer deserves applause and, in particular, that his work led me to several of the cases I cite.

In contrast to Graff's work, other recent studies of the academic discipline of English have little to say about teaching: see Kermit Vanderbilt, *American Literature and the Academy: The Roots, Growth, and Maturity of a Profession* (Philadelphia, Pa., 1986), and Jo McMurtry, *English Language, English Literature: The Creation of an Academic Discipline* (Hamden, Conn., 1985). An older book, Arthur N. Applebee, *Tradition and Reform in the Teaching of English: A History* (Urbana, Ill., 1974), devotes two chapters to the teaching of English before 1900 but stays away from what actually happened in the classroom.

It is typical of the state of the historiography of American higher education that we know more about the teaching of rhetoric and composition before the Civil War than we do about the teaching of literature after it. See, e.g., Wallace Douglas's chapter on Harvard, "Rhetoric for the Meritocracy," in Richard Ohmann, *English in America: A Radical View of the Profession* (New York, 1976), pp. 97–132. It is, by the way, also typical of the historiography of American higher education that we know more about the teaching of rhetoric (and almost everything else) at Harvard than anywhere else—Yale coming a close second. I cannot claim to be much help in this respect in this chapter. *Mea culpa*.

13. The key works on undergraduate education at Harvard in this period are Hugh Hawkins, *Between Harvard and America: The Educational Leadership of Charles W. Eliot* (New York, 1972) and Samuel Eliot Morison, ed., *The Development of Harvard University since the Inauguration of President Eliot, 1869–1929* (Cambridge, Mass., 1930). Given the volume of writing about Harvard's history and the quality and accessibility of the sources available for it, it is more than a little surprising that there is neither a full scholarly history of Harvard nor a modern biography of Eliot himself, though Hawkins's book goes a long way toward remedying the latter defect. Michigan has been as stingily served by historians as Harvard has generously. Scholarly inquirers must resort primarily to Wilfred B. Shaw, ed., *The University of Michigan: An Encyclopedic Survey*, 4 vols. (Ann Arbor, Mich., 1942)—which has been supplemented by later volumes covering later years—and Burke A. Hinsdale, *History of the University of Michigan*, ed. Isaac N. Demmon (Ann Arbor, Mich., 1906), both encyclopedic in nature and erratic in coverage. There is also a more popular history by Howard H. Peckham, *The Making of the University of Michigan, 1817–1967* (Ann Arbor, Mich., 1967), of which a new edition, updated to 1992, was published by the university's Bentley Historical Library in 1994.

14. Michigan and Harvard happen to be the two institutions on which I had done substantial primary research at the time this chapter was written—research eventuating in the former case in chapter 4 of this book, in the latter case in my biography *The Liberal Education of Charles Eliot Norton* (Baltimore, Md., 1999). The evidence from the two schools is thus skewed in predictable directions: I tend to treat Michigan rather generally and personify Harvard quite particularly.

15. Personal communication, 26 February 1990.

16. The Sheffield School did not actually acquire that name until 1860. I rely for these generalizations on the leading secondary works cited earlier, confirmed through browsing in histories of individual institutions. I will restrict attention to courses of study regarded by contemporaries as providing what we would term a liberal arts education; i.e., a nonprofessional, nonvocational, unspecialized, undergraduate general education. This standard would include Nott's "scientific course," but exclude the Sheffield School. Harvard's experience with the elective system was hardly unusual—indeed, the other leading character in this chapter, Michigan, moved in exactly the same direction somewhat earlier—but it is particularly well documented. See esp. Hawkins, *Between Harvard and America*, chaps. 3 and 9.

17. Hugh Hawkins suggests this; personal communication, 26 February 1990. The classic statement of these educational aims was a celebrated and much-quoted sentence from the influential Yale Report of 1828; most of the report is printed in Richard Hofstadter and Wilson Smith, eds., *American Higher Education: A Documentary History*, 2 vols. (Chicago, 1961), 1:275–91; the sentence in question is on p. 278.

18. Admirably analysed in Louise L. Stevenson, *Scholarly Means to Evangelical Ends: The New Haven Scholars and the Transformation of Higher Learning in America, 1830–1890* (Baltimore, Md., 1986), esp. chap. 4. Stevenson also calls my attention to similar Christian versions of the liberal arts at other institutions (personal communication, 4 June 1990).

19. On philosophy at Harvard in this period, see Bruce Kuklick, *The Rise of American Philosophy: Cambridge, Massachusetts, 1860–1930* (New Haven, Conn., 1977), parts 1–3, as well as Ralph Barton Perry, *The Thought and Character of William James*, 2 vols. (Boston, 1935). There is nothing on Michigan (or any other university) remotely comparable to Kuklick; but, besides the sources mentioned above for Michigan's history, the work on John Dewey's early career, spent partly at Michigan, gives a useful picture.

20. *Calendar of the University of Michigan for 1886–87* (Ann Arbor, Mich., 1887), pp. 51–52. I have omitted Dewey's psychology courses, also taught within the philosophy department. I take "speculative philosophy" to be metaphysics.

21. Absent a prosopography of philosophy professors, I rely on impressions from biographical accounts. But these suspicions gain confidence from the closest thing to such a source for this issue: the collation by Bruce Kuklick of the reasons given for undertaking graduate study in philosophy by Harvard Ph.D. candidates in response to the department's post-1906 request for such information. In the first five years (1907–1911), nineteen students mentioned religious problems or doubts, as compared to seven who gave other reasons for studying philosophy and four whose motives could not be determined. The comparable figures for the next five years (1912–16) are twelve, nine, and two. (Kuklick, *Rise of American Philosophy*, pp. 464–65). I see no reason why such concerns should have been less prominent in the late nineteenth century; if anything, the reverse.

22. I exclude Charles Peirce because his truncated teaching career hardly qualifies him to be identified as primarily a college professor.

23. I owe this suggestion to David Hollinger, who cites George T. Ladd of Yale, Charles E. Garman of Amherst, George H. Howison of Berkeley, Jacob G. Schurman and James E. Creighton of Cornell, George S. Morris and Robert M. Wenley of Michigan, and George H. Palmer and Josiah Royce of Harvard (personal communication, 19 April 1990).

24. On Palmer, see Kuklick, *Rise of American Philosophy*, chap. 12; on Garman, Le Duc, *Piety and Intellect*, chap. 8, and George E. Peterson, *The New England College in the Age of the University* (Amherst, Mass., 1964), pp. 134–36, 172–74. The quotation about Garman is from Palmer, quoted in Peterson, *New England College*, p. 173.

25. *Catalogue of the Officers and Students of the University of Michigan: 1854–55* (Ann Arbor, Mich., 1855), p. 33. (These catalogues, published annually under a variety of slightly differing titles, will henceforth be identified simply as UM, *Catalogue*, with the academic or calendar year as printed.) My unsystematic survey of rhetoric and composition courses reveals *Paradise Lost* as the champion entry for parsing purposes. Is it possible that the poem owed its later prominence in the literary canon partly to its ubiquity in "preliterary" college teaching? Longfellow was teaching modern European literature at Harvard in the 1830s but seems not to have dealt with English topics, except for some lectures on the Anglo-Saxon language. Simply because more information is available about the teaching of English than of foreign literatures (English being much more widely taught, as it still is), this chapter focuses on English literature. The very scattered information that I have indicates that the teaching of foreign literature did not significantly deviate from the patterns in English.

26. Rudolph, *Curriculum*, pp. 134, 140; George Wilson Pierson, *Yale College: An Educational History* (New Haven, Conn., 1952), p. 299.

27. But not until 1868–69 did "English" appear as a distinct field of study in the Harvard catalogue. Charles H. Grandgent, "The Modern Languages,

1869–1929," in Morison, *Harvard University*, pp. 66–67. White added the "History of English Literature" and the "Masterpieces of our Literature" to his sophomore rhetoric classes at Michigan—apparently not merely as examples of style. UM, *Catalogue*, 1858, p. 39. In 1861 White severed literature entirely from rhetoric, making it a distinct course for second-semester sophomores, and included a "weekly exercise" in the plays of Shakespeare. The plays studied were the histories along with four tragedies—*King Lear, Hamlet, Macbeth,* and *Othello*—to be "critically examined" in connection with "Reed's English History." In the following year White added "the criticisms of Coleridge and Hazlitt" to Reed's work. Whereas only students in the "scientific course" had studied rhetoric, all Michigan undergraduates now studied literature. After 1863, however, when White switched to history (his real love), English literature virtually disappeared for a few years. "English Literature" did remain in the catalogue in 1864–65 as a senior elective taught by Erastus O. Haven, who doubled as president of the university and professor of rhetoric and English. But the catalogue described it as "a brief course of lectures on Logic and General Literature" (UM, *Catalogue*, 1861, pp. 43–44; 1862, pp. 39–40; 1864–65, p. 47).

28. McMurtry, *English Language*, pp. 65–110; Howard Mumford Jones, *The Life of Moses Coit Tyler* (Ann Arbor, Mich., 1933).

29. Child seems from the beginning of his tenure as Boylston Professor of Rhetoric in 1851 to have met informally with students to discuss early English texts. Hawkins, *Between Harvard and America*, p. 11 n. 20. But his official teaching was confined to the traditional routine of rhetoric and composition until after Lowell had opened the door for literature. In 1867, about the time that Child was gearing up English literature at Harvard, Moses Coit Tyler appeared at Michigan to fill the chair of rhetoric and English literature left vacant by President Haven two years earlier. From the first he apparently chafed more vocally than the long-suffering Child under the burden of freshman comp. But in his first years in Ann Arbor he seems to have assuaged these miseries only by resurrecting the second-term sophomore course in English literature, invented by White. (UM, *Catalogue*, 1867–68, pp. 48–49.) This pattern continued through 1874–75.

30. Grandgent, "Modern Languages," pp. 66–67, 74–75, 80–81; UM, *Calendar*, 1874–75, p. 34; 1875–76, pp. 37–38; 1878–79, pp. 32–33. (The title of the university's catalogue changed to *Calendar* in the 1870s and will henceforth be referred to as such.) It was the development of the elective system that opened the Michigan courses to all students.

31. A great need in both European and American intellectual history is for an imaginative, comprehensive history of philology and its influence during the nineteenth century. The existing works on the subject, often worthy scholarship, are almost all narrowly conceived disciplinary histories. Hans Aarsleff's writing on theories of language begins to break out of this mold (notably *The Study of*

Language in England, 1780–1860 [Minneapolis, Minn., 1983]) but is tangential to the main thrust of philology. The line to follow is more nearly that laid down in Thomas R. Trautmann, *Lewis Henry Morgan and the Invention of Kinship* (Berkeley, Cal., 1987), and in Stephen G. Alter, *Darwinism and the Linguistic Image: Language, Race, and Natural Theology in the Nineteenth Century* (Baltimore, Md., 1999).

32. Francis A. March, "Recollections of Language Teaching," *PMLA* 8 (1893), app., p. xx; Robert Morss Lovett, *All Our Years* (New York, 1948), p. 37; Tyler to George H. Putnam, 9 August 1875, quoted in Jones, *Tyler*, p. 176. Lovett's unflattering and largely uncomprehending description of Child's teaching, recorded decades later, gives some measure of how thoroughly philology was detested, stamped on, and finally suppressed by its methodological successors—for Lovett, in his day, was a prominent professor of English literature and Child, in his, an admired and sought-after teacher.

33. March, *Method of Philological Study*, p. 8, cited in Graff, *Professing Literature*, pp. 38–39; UM, *Calendar*, 1875–76, pp. 37–38, 1878–79, pp. 32–33, 1890–91, pp. 52–54. The Hopkins instructor was Albert S. Cook, associate in English from 1879 to 1881. The *Calendar* gives no indication of the content of Tyler's American literature course, for which I rely on his books.

The overwhelming dominance of medieval and early modern literature in these first literature courses draws a sharp distinction between the use of literature for teaching of rhetoric, on the one hand, and philological teaching of literature on the other, contra Graff's efforts (*Professing Literature*, passim) to assimilate the two modes. Relatively recent works—Burke's, for instance—were quite commonly used to teach rhetoric, while it made little sense to offer Chaucer as a model of style to Victorian undergraduates. Philologists, unlike rhetoricians, did teach literature for its own sake.

34. It does seem that the line-by-line "linguistic analysis" inflicted on students at Lafayette College by Francis March made Francis Child look methodologically broader than Northrop Frye. March, "Recollections," p. xx; also March, *Method of Philological Study of the English Language* (New York, 1879), p. 8, cited in Graff, *Professing Literature*, pp. 38–39. (Graff makes this claim less equivocally. I say "seem" because March's "Recollections" are not very specific, and I have been unable to lay hands on March's *Method*.) Branders Matthews reported an even less inspiring routine at Columbia circa 1870 under Charles Murray Nairne. Matthews, *These Many Years: Recollections of a New Yorker* (New York, 1917), pp. 108–9. But it is hard to know what to make of such recollections, given the contempt of the next generation of professors for discarded philology. The contempt seems to have been passed on to their intellectual progeny. Cf. Graff, *Professing Literature*, which is riddled with it: an attitude that Graff sustains by grouping the more broad-gauged philologists, such as Lowell,

with "generalists." Part of Graff's problem seems to be that, equipped with the dismissive prejudices of modern interpretative literary study, he does not make the necessary discriminations but conflates all philology: comparative philology in linguistics courses is the same to him as the philological study of literature.

35. The dichotomy between generalist and specialist, between professors of the genteel tradition devoted to culture and professors of the new Ph.D. ideal devoted to research, is a very common one among historians who write about this period in American higher education. See, e.g., Laurence Veysey's perceptive essay "The Plural Organized Worlds of the Humanities," in Alexandra Oleson and John Voss, eds., *The Organization of Knowledge in Modern America, 1860–1920* (Baltimore, Md., 1979), pp. 53–54. Without denying all validity to the distinction, I should nevertheless insist that it is much overdrawn or, to be more precise, that there commonly coexisted in the same professor a high valuation of serious specialized research and an insistence on broad culture as the proper context for that research. Child is a perfect example. His friend Lowell, though never guilty of dogged research himself (despite his considerable erudition), was by no means hostile to the enterprise.

I believe that historians have sometimes confused complaints about pedantry or excessive narrowness in research (laments still heard today, after we have all presumably become convinced of the virtues of specialization) with a general hostility to research. Charles Eliot Norton, often cited as a genteel critic of the research ideal, did carp incessantly at academics whom he regarded as dry-as-dust pedants. Yet, in other contexts, Norton warmly praised tomes reporting highly detailed research that could not possibly have interested anyone beyond a small circle of scholars. He himself published both technical scholarship and general works intended for a cultured laity; even some of the latter reflected massive archival research. Veysey conveniently, if inadvertently, exemplifies this point about the coexistence of the culture ideal and the research ideal. He first cites Norton as a prominent "generalist" (p. 54) and then mentions (p. 89) the American School of Classical Studies at Athens—founded by Norton, though Veysey may have been unaware of this—as the first research institute in the humanities.

36. Horace Elisha Scudder, *James Russell Lowell: A Biography*, 2 vols. (Boston, 1901), 1:393–94. For a fuller account, see Barrett Wendell's memoir "Mr. Lowell as a Teacher" in his *Stelligeri and Other Essays concerning America* (New York, 1893), pp. 205–17.

37. Cf. Lowell's 1889 presidential address to the Modern Language Association, "Address," *PMLA*, 5 (1890): 5–22. Graff's reading of this address is more than slightly strained (*Professing Literature*, p. 88). He regards it as an attack on philologically oriented teaching. In fact, the address is a vindication of the study of modern languages and literatures as against the traditional primacy of classical

studies. Toward the end Lowell does briefly address the relation in college teaching of modern languages and modern literature. Graff oddly interprets Lowell's plea at this point (p. 21) for the study of literature *as well as* language—and of language as a doorway to literature—as antiphilological. This makes sense only if one assumes that philology was only the narrowly construed study of language, opposed to the study of literature, rather than that philology was one approach to the study of literature as well as of language. The former assumption certainly was not Lowell's. In fact, in the passage Graff cites, Lowell was referring specifically to courses in "comparative philology," not to a philological approach to literature. Moreover, so far as I know there is no hint of skepticism on Lowell's part about Child's teaching, and Lowell was not a notably reticent man in his letters.

38. "Imaginative writers" is my term. "Poets" was Lowell's; he meant it largely.

39. Lowell, "Address." Cf. his "Dante" and "Spenser," in *Literary Essays*, Riverside Edition of the Writings of James Russell Lowell, vol. 4 (Boston, 1897).

40. [Dwight C. Miner, ed.], *A History of Columbia College on Morningside* (New York, 1954), p. 25; Pierson, *Yale College*, p. 298; Arthur Richmond Marsh to Charles Eliot Norton, 27 November 1888, in Charles Eliot Norton Papers, Houghton Library, Harvard University; Hiram Corson, *The Aims of Literary Study* (New York, 1901), p. 13.

41. I cannot omit that, after having committed this last trope, I learned that Logan Pearsall Smith, a Harvard student in this era, not only read devoutly "the works of Matthew Arnold" but "used to pore for hours" over "a little book of Rosicrucian doctrine." I cite this passage as a warning of the risks of loose-cannon prose: your wildest metaphors may turn literal on you. Smith, *Unforgotten Years* (Boston, 1939), p. 128.

42. See, e.g., Carl L. Johnson, *Professor Longfellow of Harvard* (Eugene, Oreg., 1944), p. 89.

43. R. Freeman Butts, *The College Charts Its Course: Historical Conceptions and Current Proposals* (New York, 1939), p. 141; Shaw, *Encyclopedic Survey*, pp. 575–76; Rudolph, *Curriculum*, pp. 140–43; Pierson, *Yale College*, passim.

44. Ephraim W. Gurney to Norton, 11 February 1874, Charles William Eliot to Norton, 5 May 1875; and Howells to Norton, 19 April 1895, in Norton Papers. On Norton, see Turner, *Liberal Education of Charles Eliot Norton*. Norton's art-historical scholarship was more considerable than now credited, but it is clear that his national reputation did not rest on it. As to his stature at Harvard, one sometimes reads that Norton's courses owed their enormous popularity to the fact that they were (in the local dialect) roaring guts—which they certainly were, apparently because Norton chose to lure football-obsessed philistines into the halls of "culture" by liberal dispensation of the gentleman's C. But even cursory reading of student comments, both contemporaneous and retrospective,

makes clear that the influence and reputation of Norton's courses went far beyond this.

45. Lovett, *All Our Years*, p. 38; Samuel Warren Davis to Norton, 27 July 1898, and Mary Elizabeth Blake [mother of two Harvard graduates] to Norton, 1 June 1898, in Norton Papers. The fire-escape tale has been questioned.

46. Garrison to Norton, 30 December 1895, in Norton Papers; Ellery Sedgwick, *The Happy Profession* (Boston, 1946), p. 71.

47. Woodberry to Norton, 17 July 1886, and Hart to Norton, 4 March 1898, in Norton Papers; Copeland, "Norton in His Letters," *Harvard Bulletin*, 29 October 1913. Copeland was the "Copey" of hundreds of repetitive Harvard tales.

48. Norton to Nathan Haskell Dole, 21 April 1894, in Norton Papers; [Norton], *Report of the Committee on the Fine Arts*, October 1900, in *Reports of Visiting Committees of the Board of Overseers of Harvard College, I to CIX*, Harvard University Archives; Norton to Leslie Stephen, 20–23 December 1897, in Stephen Papers, Berg Collection, New York Public Library.

49. Norton to Ruskin, 10 February 1874, and Norton to Charles H. Moore, 7 January 1870, in Norton Papers; Norton, "Lectures on Roman and Mediaeval Art 1894. Oct. 1894," in Norton Papers, box 1; Norton paraphrased in Constance Grosvenor Alexander, "An Evening in the Library of Charles Eliot Norton, 11 May 1905," TS, 1942, in Norton Papers (MS Am 1088.7).

50. Norton, "The Culture of the Imagination," lecture, TS, 1899, in Norton Papers, box 1; Norton to C.H. Moore, 7 January 1870, in Norton Papers.

51. Norton, "Lectures on Roman and Mediaeval Art" and "Culture of the Imagination."

52. The relation of the vagueness of this "religion" to its role in the curriculum gains plausibility from the fact that other late Victorians created much more specific doctrines of secularized religion. David Hollinger observes that, in contrast to teachers of the humanities, scientists and "science–advocates" in this period "managed to select from the Protestant heritage some fairly specific and consistent themes for perpetuation as 'the scientific spirit'" (personal communication, 19 April 1990). This judgment is entirely consistent with my own; and it is particularly interesting to note that even Norton, *outside of the classroom*, advanced quite specific secular-religious teachings. See Turner, *Without God, Without Creed*, esp. chaps. 8–9 and, for Norton in particular, pp. 199, 212, 215, 235–38, 244, 252–54.

53. Samuel A. Eliot, "Some Cambridge Pundits and Pedagogues," *Proceedings of the Cambridge Historical Society* 26 (1941): 34; *The Christian*, November 1908 (clipping in Norton Papers, box 6).

54. Although Curtius, citing H. Oppel (*Kanon*, 1937), says that the concept of a canon was introduced into philology in the eighteenth century by David Ruhnken, the definitions of "canon" and examples of its usage in the

Oxford English Dictionary do not suggest that the word was used in English with respect to nonscriptural texts before the transformation in humanities teaching described herein. Ernst Robert Curtius, *European Literature and the Latin Middle Ages,* trans. Willard R. Trask (1948; Princeton, N.J., 1953), p. 256 n; *Oxford English Dictionary,* s.v. "canon."

55. Such a sense of shared purpose—however vague—may go some way toward explaining a mystery alluded to by Laurence Veysey: how the humanities came to seem an entity when in fact the term covers a congeries of unrelated subjects and approaches to knowledge having far less in common methodologically than the natural or social sciences. Veysey, "Worlds of the Humanities," pp. 56–57.

Chapter 4. The "German Model" and the Graduate School

This essay was originally written for the fiftieth-anniversary symposium of the University of Michigan's Rackham School of Graduate Studies in 1987; published in a longer version in *Rackham Reports* (1988–89): 6–52; then in its present slightly abridged form in *History of Higher Education Annual* 13 (1993): 69–98; and reprinted in Roger L. Geiger, ed., *The American College in the Nineteenth Century* (Vanderbilt University Press, 2000). Anyone hungry for even more details of the history of the University of Michigan should refer to the first publication.

My coauthor, Paul Bernard, was at that time a doctoral student in the Program in American Culture at the University of Michigan; he went on to write a fine dissertation on the history of the discipline of economics in the United States before choosing a career in the law. This chapter benefited also from the comments of several colleagues—Bernard Bailyn, Hugh Hawkins, David Hollinger, Joel Howell, George Marsden, Jonathan Marwil, Nicholas Steneck, and Stephen Tonsor—and from the financial support of the Rackham School of Graduate Studies of the University of Michigan and the moral support of its then dean, the late John D'Arms.

1. The most cogent summing-up of the story remains Laurence R. Veysey's justly influential *The Emergence of the American University* (Chicago, 1965), esp. pp. 10, 12–13, 125–33, 153–58.

2. See, e.g., James McLachlan, "The American College in the Nineteenth Century: Toward a Reappraisal," *Teachers College Record* 80 (1978): 287–306. There are three especially consequential figures whose personal visions and intellectual progeny, while recognized in the historical literature, have not yet been sufficiently taken into account: Eliphalet Nott of Union College, Francis Wayland of Brown, and Henry P. Tappan of Michigan. Because university history, even more than military history, is written from the standpoint of the victors, the importance of an institution like Harvard is exaggerated all out of

contemporary proportion, while that of a place like Union is diminished into anachronistic insignificance. Brown and Michigan were probably the most talked-about and influential exemplars in the formative decade preceding the emergence of modern universities (c. 1855–65), and the presidents who gave them prominence, Wayland and Tappan, were both nurtured by Nott at Union and freely acknowledged their debt to him. Wayland and Tappan, in turn, were each mentors of the founding president of Cornell, Andrew Dickson White, influencing his educational ideas far more than did the teachers at White's alma mater, Yale. White, along with Daniel Coit Gilman of Johns Hopkins University, was the key figure in the creation of the modern American university.

3. Some uncertainty prevails about who went first to Germany and when. This confusion about priority matters little, for it is clear that significant scholarly pilgrimages to Germany began immediately after the War of 1812 when men like George Ticknor and Edward Everett studied in Germany and then returned to apply their foreign learning (at least temporarily, often without much effect) in American colleges. Ultimately some nine or ten thousand Americans matriculated in German universities between the end of the Napoleonic Wars and the outbreak of the First World War—seemingly, however, often only for a term. The statistical data are not full enough to permit more than broad generalizations about patterns of American attendance at German universities. The University of Göttingen appears to have been at first the most popular destination, owing both to its receptivity to English speakers—its Hanoverian rulers happened also to be kings of England until 1837—and to its calculated efforts to make itself attractive to *Ausländer*. (On this policy, essentially mercantilist in intent, see, e.g., Ilse Costas, "Die Sozialstruktur der Studenten der Göttinger Universität im 18. Jahrhundert," in *Anfänge Göttinger Sozialwissenschaft* [Göttingen, 1987], pp. 128–29.) Long before midcentury, however, Berlin, Halle, and Leipzig had achieved parity with Göttingen in numbers of American students. Heidelberg also became popular after about 1850. By the 1860s Berlin had become preeminent in attracting Americans.

There is no thorough study of the whole phenomenon, despite its importance to the German model of American university history. But see Carl Diehl, *Americans and German Scholarship, 1770–1870* (New Haven, Conn., 1978), esp. chap. 3; and Jurgen Herbst, *The German Historical School in American Scholarship: A Study in the Transfer of Culture* (Ithaca, N.Y., 1965), esp. chap. 1; the footnotes in Diehl and Herbst provide a reliable guide to older sources. Histories of the relevant German universities themselves do not have much to say about American students—not even the flood of books celebrating the 250th anniversary of Göttingen in 1987 (though some of this latter batch are helpful in understanding the subjects Americans went to study there, notably Bernd Moeller, ed., *Theologie in Göttingen: Eine Vorlesungsreihe* [Göttingen, 1987], especially the essay by Rudolf Smend that discusses the great magnet J. G. Eichhorn). The records of the "American Colony" in Göttingen (a sort of nondueling *Burschenschaft* for U.S. students) have been printed: P. G. Buchloh and W. T. Rix, *American Colony of Göttingen* (Arbeiten aus der Niedersächsischen Staats- und Universitätsbibliothek Göttingen, vol. 15 [Göttingen, 1976]). They provide some sense of what life was like for Americans at the university—and of how superficial their connection with German academic life commonly was.

One of the greatest obstacles to serious work on German influence in American universities is the dilapidated state of German university history itself, fallen upon hard times since the pioneering work of Friedrich Paulsen around the turn of the last century. It is often difficult simply to find out what professors and students actually did in the German universities where Americans studied. See James Turner, "German University History in Comparative Perspective: The Case of Göttingen," *Archiv für Sozialgeschichte* 29 (1989): 482–87.

4. Among these educational investigators were Charles W. Eliot, the creator of modern Harvard, Daniel Coit Gilman, founder of Johns Hopkins, and Michigan's founding president, Henry P. Tappan. Travelers with other purposes who nevertheless devoted considerable time to studying German universities while on their journeys included Andrew Dickson White, founding president of Cornell, and Charles Kendall Adams, White's successor at Cornell (1885–92) and then president of Wisconsin (1892–1902).

5. The most helpful monographs on the episodes mentioned are David Tyack, *George Ticknor and the Boston Brahmins* (Cambridge, Mass., 1967), chap. 3; Hugh Hawkins, *Pioneer: A History of Johns Hopkins University, 1874–1889* (Ithaca, N.Y., 1960); idem, *Between Harvard and America: The Educational Leadership of Charles W. Eliot* (New York, 1971); and Robert A. McCaughey, "The Transformation of American Academic Life: Harvard University, 1821–1892," *Perspectives in American History* 8 (1974): 239–332.

6. Influential examples include Burton J. Bledstein, *The Culture of Professionalism: The Middle Class and the Development of Higher Education in America* (New York, 1976); Thomas L. Haskell, ed., *The Authority of Experts: Studies in History and Theory* (Bloomington, Ind., 1984), part 2; and Magali Sarfatti Larson, *The Rise of Professionalism* (Berkeley, Calif., 1977). Professionalization and historiographically related concepts like the search for cultural authority are useful, for professionalization was certainly *one* of the things involved in the emergence of the modern professoriate and research university, with all of the specialization involved in both. Whether professionalization is really the key to understanding these developments is, to say the least, debatable. In any case, professionalization makes a poor organizing theme for university history: it is too blunt an instrument, misses too much of what was going on within colleges and universities. In part, this latter defect arises because the sociological concept of

professionalization developed (obviously) with reference to the structure of certain adult careers (initially, the traditional professions). Professionalization thus refers only secondarily and *selectively* to education, however important education may be in the processes of professionalization. Conceptually "external" to education, referring primarily to broad social-structural trends, professionalization fails to take account of much that is distinctive within universities.

7. A study sensitive to both the pull of German example and American deviation from it is Nathan Reingold, "Graduate School and Doctoral Degree: European Models and American Realities," in *Scientific Colonialism: A Cross-Cultural Comparison*, ed. Nathan Reingold and Marc Rothenberg (Washington, D.C., 1986), pp. 129–49.

8. "Qualified" means that the student had studied at a Gymnasium and earned an *Abitur*, also institutions of which real American equivalents never developed, though the University of Michigan moved in the direction of promoting them in the 1870s and 1880s. It has been argued that the elective system was the American equivalent of *Lernfreiheit*, but this seems a pretty faint shadow of the real thing.

9. Charles William Eliot, *A Turning Point in Higher Education: The Inaugural Address of Charles William Eliot as President of Harvard College, October 19, 1869* (1869; reprint, Cambridge, Mass., 1969), p. 7. This distance from the German model did not much lessen during the remainder of Eliot's career: see Hawkins, *Between Harvard and America*, passim.

10. See, e.g., Veysey, *American University*, pp. 158–59. The best study of the first decades at Hopkins is Hawkins, *Pioneer*.

11. Robert Morris Ogden, ed., *The Diaries of Andrew D. White* (Ithaca, N.Y., 1959), pp. 98–108. Cf. Buchloh and Rix, *American Colony*, passim.

12. Richard Hofstadter and Wilson Smith, eds., *American Higher Education: A Documentary History*, 2 vols. (Chicago, 1961), 1:256, 262–63; Motley to his mother, 1 July 1832, in G. W. Curtis, ed., *The Correspondence of John Lothrop Motley* (New York, 1900), 1:19–23.

13. The Yale Report was published (slightly abridged) as "Original Papers in Relation to a Course of Liberal Education," *American Journal of Science and Arts* 15 (1829): 297–351. Most of it is reprinted in Hofstadter and Smith, *American Higher Education*, 1:275–91, from which the quoted phrase is taken (p. 278).

14. Veysey, *American University*, comes close to this model, identifying three paradigms ("Liberal Culture," "Utility," and "Research") as competing with the old "Mental Discipline" for the soul of the university. Veysey neglects the longer historical context and meaning of the old classical curriculum (which he identifies solely with its antebellum defense as "mental discipline"). His category of "research" probably had less to do with *educational* programs than with other faculty activities, at least until very near the end of the century. This was, at

any rate, true at Michigan, as appears below. To say that "the liberal arts ideal" had taken shape by the 1880s is to ignore a host of difficulties as to what it was: see Bruce A. Kimball, *Orators and Philosophers: A History of the Idea of Liberal Education* (New York, 1986).

15. Charles Eliot Norton, "Harvard University," in *Four American Universities: Harvard, Yale, Princeton, Columbia* (New York, 1895), pp. 32–35 [sic: pp. 33–34 are occupied by a photograph]. The relation of this educational ideal to the broader Victorian ideal of "culture" goes without saying.

16. Quotation from Reingold, "Graduate School," p. 135. For White's reliance on Tappan's vision, see Glenn C. Altschuler, *Andrew D. White: Educator, Historian, Diplomat* (Ithaca, N.Y., 1979), p. 42. White's student and successor as professor of history at Michigan, Charles Kendall Adams, followed him as president of Cornell and then went on to become one of the two presidents who transformed Wisconsin into a research university. The other was Thomas Chamberlin, who received graduate training at Michigan in the afterglow of the Tappan years. See Merle Curti and Vernon Carstensen, *The University of Wisconsin: A History, 1848–1925*, 2 vols. (Madison, Wis., 1949), esp. 1:545–46, 561–79.

17. For the early history of the university, see Wilfred B. Shaw, *The University of Michigan: An Encyclopedic Survey* (Ann Arbor, Mich., 1942), 1:10–38, and Burke A. Hinsdale, *History of the University of Michigan*, ed. Isaac N. Demmon (Ann Arbor, Mich., 1906), chaps. 2–6. In general, Shaw is stronger on politics, Hinsdale on curriculum; both have the encyclopedic quality, if not always quantity, promised in Shaw's title. See also John D. Pierce, "Origin and Progress of the Michigan School System," *Pioneer Collections: Report of the Pioneer Society of the State of Michigan* 1 (1877): 37–45, and Charles Kendall Adams, *Historical Sketch of the University of Michigan* (Ann Arbor, Mich., 1876), p. 12.

One point here is that Henry P. Tappan's zeal for Cousin's version of Prussia was not innovative. Another point, however, is that the initial Michigan version of the "Prussian system" involved the relations between the university and other educational institutions in the state, rather than the character of the university itself. Adams, in *Historical Sketch*, p. 16, disclaims any Prussian influence on the university's internal organization or curriculum before Tappan's arrival, a conclusion supported by the other available evidence.

18. Hinsdale, *History*, p. 76; *University of Michigan Catalogue of the Officers and Students in the Department of Arts and Sciences, 1843–44* (Ann Arbor, Mich., [1843?]).

19. George Bancroft, Henry Barnard, and a New York minister, the Rev. William Adams, possibly others, turned down the job before the regents finally named Tappan. It was Bancroft who raised Tappan's name, having heard of him initially, it seems, from none other than Cousin. Shaw, *Encyclopedic Survey*,

1:39–40; Charles M. Perry, *Henry Philip Tappan: Philosopher and University President* (Ann Arbor, Mich., 1933), pp. 169–71.

20. Hinsdale, *History*, pp. 42–43; Perry, *Tappan*, pp. 169–70; Adams, *Historical Sketch*, pp. 15–16. The quotation is from the first catalog issued under Tappan's direction (1852–53), which proudly declared that Michigan had copied its educational system from the Prussian. *Catalogue of the Corporation, Officers and Students in the Departments of Medicine, Arts and Sciences in the University of Michigan, 1852–53* (Detroit, Mich., 1853), p. 19.

21. Henry P. Tappan, *A Discourse . . . on the occasion of his Inauguration as Chancellor of the University of Michigan, December 21st, 1852* (Detroit, Mich., 1852), pp. 37, 40. For the course of events during Tappan's administration, see Hinsdale, *History*, chap. 7, and Shaw, *Encyclopedic Survey*, pp. 39–53.

22. Hinsdale, *History*, pp. 43–44; *Catalogue, 1852–53*, p. 20; Tappan, *Discourse*, pp. 42–45; Adams, *Historical Sketch*, p. 17. In his long-term ideal of American Gymnasia feeding real American universities, and in his shorter-term goal of making the university at least a respectable Gymnasium, Tappan closely resembled George Ticknor at Harvard in the 1820s. See Tyack, *Ticknor*, chap. 3.

23. Tappan, *Discourse*, pp. 21–22, 35. These were the traditional four faculties of the German university. Medicine, law, and philosophy (i.e., the arts and sciences faculty, called at Michigan Literature, Science, and the Arts), Tappan pointed out, were already organized. Recognizing that in an American state university theology must "be left to the different denominations," Tappan urged them to set up theological schools in Ann Arbor. (They did not take up his invitation.) Tappan, *Discourse*, pp. 47–48; *Catalogue, 1860–61*, p. 32.

24. *Catalogue, 1852–53*, p. 21.

25. *Catalogue, 1852–53*, p. 21; Yale Report, in Hofstadter, *Higher Education*, 1:278.

26. *Catalogue, 1852–53*, pp. 21, 26.

27. *Catalogue, 1852–53*, pp. 21, 26. A decade later, in 1863, Harvard's president, Thomas Hill, inaugurated a superficially similar innovation called "University Lectures." Although regarded by Charles W. Eliot as ancestral to the graduate school, this program differed from the University Course both in its more occasional nature and in its intended audience: a mélange of curious citizens and interested postgraduates, as distinguished from graduate and equivalently prepared students pursuing a regular course. Charles H. Haskins, "The Graduate School of Arts and Sciences, 1872–1929," in Samuel Eliot Morison, ed., *The Development of Harvard University Since the Inauguration of President Eliot, 1869–1929* (Cambridge, Mass., 1930), p. 453.

28. *Catalogue, 1852–53*, p. 26. Tappan probably could not read German at this period of his life (indeed was not at ease even in French). Most of his crucial

notions about German education seem to have come from Cousin's report on the Prussian system, itself more a reflection of Humboldt's ambitions than Prussian realities.

29. *Catalogue, 1852–53*, p. 28; Tappan, "Annual Report of the Chancellor [October 1854]," in *University of Michigan Regents' Proceedings . . . 1837–1864* (Ann Arbor, Mich., 1915), p. 599; Hinsdale, *History*, p. 88; Alan Creutz, "From College Teacher to University Scholar: The Evolution and Professionalization of Academics at the University of Michigan, 1841–1900" (Ph.D. diss., University of Michigan, 1981), 2:232, 243–48; Tappan, "Annual Report [1854]," p. 599. It is unclear whether Tappan originally expected students in the University Course to be examined or to take a degree, though the master's became explicitly linked to it in 1858–59 when the University Course took on rather scrawny flesh as the "Programme of Studies for the Degrees of A.M. and M.S."

30. The use of the phrase "the University proper" to refer to the University System occurs in *Catalogue of the Officers and Students of the University of Michigan: 1854–55* (Ann Arbor, Mich., 1855), p. 33.

31. Henry P. Tappan, *University Education* (New York, 1850), p. 11; idem, "Report of the President [October 1856]," in *Regents' Proceedings, 1837–1864*, pp. 664–66; Tappan, *The University; Its Constitution: A Discourse Delivered June 22, 1858* [to the Christian Library Association of the University of Michigan] (Ann Arbor, Mich., 1858), pp. 17–18. In this president's report, Tappan made a distinction between *teaching* undergraduates and *lecturing to* graduates.

32. The catalogues list specific courses beginning in 1858–59, when the rubric of "Programme of Studies for the Degrees of A.M. and M.S." replaced the old "University Course" section with its hopeful listing of twenty broad subjects under which instruction was eventually anticipated. Cf. *Catalogue, 1858–59*, p. 47. Names of students, including "resident graduates," were printed in the catalogues.

33. Cf. E. O. Haven, *Universities in America: An Inaugural Address Delivered in Ann Arbor, Michigan, October 1st, 1863* (Ann Arbor, Mich., 1863), esp. pp. 3–5. Haven (mostly) tells his own story in the posthumous *Autobiography of Erastus O. Haven, D.D., LL.D.*, ed. C. C. Stratton (New York, 1883); see esp. chaps. 5, 7, 8.

34. *Catalogue, 1863–64*, p. 18; 1867–68, p. 12; 1868–69, p. 11; and 1870–71, p. 11. The catalogues from 1864–65 through 1866–67 do not list graduate students; this does not prove there were none.

35. Frieze's most lasting contribution to the university, not directly relevant here, was the admission of women on a basis of near equality with male students. There is no biography; see the accounts in the general university histories and James B. Angell, *A Memorial Discourse on the Life and Services of Henry Simmons Frieze, LL.D.* (Ann Arbor, Mich., 1890); quotation from p. 16.

36. Hinsdale, *History*, p. 60; Creutz, "College Teacher," 1:96–99, 156–57; and correspondence from school principals in the James B. Angell Papers, Michigan Historical Collections, Bentley Library, University of Michigan.

37. The only substantial biography is Shirley W. Smith, *James Burrill Angell: An American Influence* (Ann Arbor, Mich., 1954); see also James B. Angell, *Reminiscences* (New York, 1912).

38. Angell did see some good things in the German university, and, at least in his earlier years, he showed sympathy for research. His increasingly cautious attitude in later career toward research is evident in, e.g., his book *The New Era in Higher Education* (Ann Arbor, Mich., 1902).

39. Angell, *Frieze*, pp. 14, 21–22.

40. Adams to Herbert Baxter Adams, 9 February 1886, in W. Stull Holt, ed., *Historical Scholarship in the United States, 1876–1901: As Revealed in the Correspondence of Herbert B. Adams* (Baltimore, Md., 1938), p. 79; *Catalogue, 1858–59*, p. 40; cf. *Catalogue, 1859–60*, p. 49. On White at Michigan, see Ruth Bordin, *Andrew Dickson White: Teacher of History*, Michigan Historical Collections Bulletin no. 8 (Ann Arbor, Mich., 1958). It is important to stress how great the change in college education was when its basis shifted from recitations to lectures—and how closely identified this method was with the German universities.

41. Adams taught both history and Latin from 1863–1867. The only biography is Charles Forster Smith, *Charles Kendall Adams: A Life Sketch* (Madison, Wis., 1924), about as full an account as the subtitle suggests. Adams's twenty-four years at Michigan get thirteen pages, the bulk of which, fortunately for present purposes, concerns the method and character of his teaching, including the famous seminar. Adams's career is likely to remain obscure, for Smith (who based his own account largely on recollections of Adams's colleagues) noted that all personal papers were destroyed in a fire at Wisconsin. Information on Adams as president of Cornell (where he pretty clearly tried to transplant a version of the University System that he and Frieze had developed at Michigan) is in Morris Bishop, *A History of Cornell* (Ithaca, N.Y., 1962), esp. chaps. 15–17, and on Adams as president of Wisconsin in Curti and Carstensen, *Wisconsin*, esp. 1:561–79.

42. *President's Report to the Board of Regents, for the Year Ending June 30, 1872* (Ann Arbor, Mich., 1872), pp. 32–33. Adams later described the purpose of the course as "to direct the student in the work of original historical investigation" rather than to "impart actual instruction"; but he apparently meant that students were set to work in standard collections of printed sources to find data for their class essays, not that they were expected to come up with new ideas or information. *President's Report*, 1874, pp. 27–28.

Henry Adams (who himself had approached, though never quite embraced, study at Berlin) was apparently teaching his students at Harvard by similar methods from 1870–71, though the class seems not to have been called a seminar and never to have adopted training in original research as an explicit goal. Adams did introduce a postgraduate seminar, as such, in 1875. See Ernest Samuels, *The Young Henry Adams* (Cambridge, Mass., 1948), esp. pp. 211–12, 215; Adams's own inimitable account is in *The Education of Henry Adams* (Boston, 1918), pp. 299–304. William C. Russel apparently did something similar in constitutional history courses at Cornell from 1868, though it is unclear whether his students were sent to primary sources. Bishop, *Cornell*, p. 163.

Charles K. Adams later gave the date of his introduction of the seminar as 1868 (Adams, *The Part of the University of Michigan in Higher Education* [n.p., (c. 1885)], p. 10) and as 1869 (Adams to H. B. Adams, 9 February 1886, in Holt, *Historical Scholarship*, p. 79). Likely, Adams's memory was tricked by recalling his intentions upon his return from Germany (which did occur in 1868). It is possible that some sort of informal seminar was in operation before 1871. But contemporary evidence, including Adams's own account in the *President's Report* supports the date of 1871 for the first seminar officially offered.

On the introduction of the seminar more generally, see Veysey, *American University*, pp. 153–58.

43. *President's Report*, 1874, pp. 27–28.

44. E.g., the reference to *Quellen* in Moses Coit Tyler to George H. Putnam, 9 August 1875, quoted in Howard Mumford Jones, *The Life of Moses Coit Tyler* (Ann Arbor, Mich., 1933), p. 176. Tyler was Adams's first imitator.

45. White to Angell, 30 September 1874, in Angell Papers; Angell, *President's Report*, 1883, pp. 9–10; Jones, *Tyler*, pp. 161, 164. Given the character of Adams's seminar, it was not at all surprising that a graduate of it, Mary D. Sheldon (later, Barnes), thought it feasible "to apply the 'Seminary' method" in high schools. (She graduated with a bachelor's degree in 1874 and seems not to have taken a higher degree, at least not at Michigan.) Mary D. Barnes to Angell, 2 January 1886, in Angell Papers.

46. See, e.g., R. Steven Turner, "The Growth of Professorial Research in Prussia, 1818 to 1848—Causes and Context," *Historical Studies in the Physical Sciences* 3 (1971): 146.

47. This was, of course, not "teacher training" as in later education faculties. Cf. Wilhelm Erben, "Die Entstehung der Universitäts-Seminare," *Internationale Monatsschrift für Wissenschaft, Kunst, und Technik*, 7 (1913): 1248–60. Erben's two-part article is the only substantial history of the German seminar, though hardly a satisfactory one. Less full but more easily available is the account in Friedrich Paulsen, *Geschichte des gelehrten Unterrichts*, 3d ed., ed. Rudolf Lehmann (Berlin and Leipzig, 1921), which sketches the history of the seminar in 2:258–59, 270–75, and passim.

48. "Probably" because existing scholarship reveals little about standard practice inside German seminars. For hints about internal workings of German seminars before the late–nineteenth century, see Erben, "Entstehung der Semi-

nare," 1251, 1253; H. B. Adams to Daniel Coit Gilman, 21 May 1876, in Holt, *Historical Scholarship*, p. 31; Hartmut Boockmann, "Geschichtsunterricht und Geschichtsstudium," in *Geschichtswissenschaft in Göttingen: Eine Vorlesungsreihe* (Göttingen, 1987), pp. 172–76; Walter C. Perry, *German University Education; or, the Professors and Students of Germany* (London, 1845), pp. 97–98. *Übungen*, not *Forschung*, is the word that recurs in descriptions of seminar work. Fred M. Fling, "The German Historical Seminar," *The Academy* (1889): 129–39, 212–19, gives a detailed account of the routine in Maurenbrecher's Leipzig seminar in the late 1880s and can be used cautiously to interpret the more scattered bits of information about earlier seminars if one remembers that by the 1880s German seminars had shifted decisively to their mature research orientation.

Part of the difficulty in exploring the seminar is that historians tend to take programmatic statements, especially seminar statutes, as representing practice — rather as if students of American politics drew their evidence from party platforms. This is true even of the best scholars of German university history (see, e.g., Turner, "Professorial Research," 145; idem, "The Prussian Universities and the Concept of Research," *Internationales Archiv für Sozialgeschichte der deutschen Literatur* 5 [1980]: 88). Anthony Grafton is a notable exception ("Polyhistor into *Philolog*: Notes on the Transformation of German Classical Scholarship, 1780–1850," *History of Universities* 3 [1983]: 163–69) but unfortunately not helpful on the point in question here.

To say that seminars before the last quarter of the century were typically not focused on serious original research is of course not to deny the exceptional seminar, the exceptional student in the ordinary seminar, and certainly not the importance of original research in the careers of German professors and of their students intending to proceed to habilitation.

49. The final abolition of the "in course" master's and the awarding of the first Ph.D. both occurred in 1874. *Catalogue, 1874–75*, p. 18. The twenty-one candidates are mentioned in Frieze to Angell, 9 October 1880, in Angell Papers.

50. *Catalogue, 1874–75*, p. 18; *Catalogue, 1879–80*, p. 65. But note the absence of any such express requirement before 1879. The most explicit statement of faculty expectations in the first years is a report of a faculty committee "to consider what steps should be taken in regard to examination of candidates for the degree of Doctor of Philosophy," 29 May 1876, in Records of the Registrar, University of Michigan, Michigan Historical Collections. This report contains no mention of original research and no indication that the thesis was required to show such. Frieze and Adams were two of the three members of the committee.

51. See, e.g., George B. Groff to Angell, 8 and 24 September and 15 November, 1876, and C. K. Adams to [?], 15 June 1878, in Angell Papers. The reports on examinations of candidates for advanced degrees, in Records of the Registrar, provide helpful instances of what sort of work was done.

52. Angell, *Frieze*, pp. 26–27; Smith, *Adams*, p. 19; Henry S. Frieze, *The President's Report to the Board of Regents, for the Year Ending June 30, 1880* (Ann Arbor, Mich., 1880), p. 10.
53. Angell, *Frieze*, p. 29; Frieze, *President's Report*, 1880, pp. 10–11.
54. Frieze to Angell, 9 July 1881, in Angell Papers.
55. *Calendar of the University of Michigan for 1881–82* (Ann Arbor, Mich., 1882), pp. 74–82; Frieze, *President's Report*, 1881, pp. 2–4; C. K. Adams to Angell, 6 July 1881, in Angell Papers.
56. Alexis Angell to J. B. Angell, 10 October 1881; Martin L. D'Ooge to Angell, 29 November 1881; W. H. Pettee to Angell, 28 November 1881; Frieze to Angell, 25 October and 26 November 1881, in Angell Papers; packet marked "Relations of the School of Political Science to the Literary Department," in Reports and Resolutions, 2d semester, 1881–82, Records of the Registrar. Curiously, the opposition was initially led by the classicist Martin L. D'Ooge, the only Michigan professor at the time who held a German Ph.D. (Leipzig, 1872). D'Ooge came around to the support of Frieze's proposed University System later in the fall and served on the committee that devised it.
57. Adams to Angell, 6 March 1881, in Angell Papers; Frieze, *President's Report*, 1881, pp. 4–18. These pages comprise the fullest statement of Frieze's idea of a university and are essential to understanding what happened in 1880–82.
58. Frieze to Angell, 26 November 1881; "Relations of the School," in Reports and Resolutions, 2d semester, 1881–82, Records of the Registrar; Frieze, *President's Report*, 1881, pp. 4–18.
59. *Calendar*, 1882–83, pp. 63–65; subsequent *Calendars*; and Angell to Helen Magill, 3 May 1882, in Angell Papers.
60. Curiously, Johns Hopkins, supposed by historians of higher education to have set the most widely emulated example for American graduate programs, never appears in the records of the debate. It should, however, immediately be said that the records are pretty skimpy.
61. Angell to Magill, 3 May 1882; *Calendar*, 1882–83, pp. 63–65.
62. The Hopkins requirements for the Ph.D. in history and political science, for example, retained the German idea of a major field and two minors but insisted that a student's minors both be "akin to his major course." Holt, *Historical Scholarship*, pp. 14–15.
63. Frieze, *President's Report*, 1881, pp. 2–3; Adams to J. T. Moore, 2 February 1882, and Moore to Adams, 7 February 1882, in Charles Kendall Adams Papers, Michigan Historical Collections. Bert James Loewenberg notes how this stress on public service distinguished Adams from the "scientific historians" like Herbert Baxter Adams: *American History in American Thought: Christopher Columbus to Henry Adams* (New York, 1972), p. 468.

64. *The University Record* 2 (1892): 58–59.

65. No more than thirteen undergraduates ever took degrees on the University System in any one year; by the end of the eighties, the number had dwindled to three or four annually. Most of these few students came, in fact, from Adams's School of Political Science. When Adams departed for Cornell in 1885, that trickle soon dried up. These data are compiled from the *President's Reports* and the (incomplete) records of examinations under the University System in Records of the Registrar.

66. Angell, *President's Reports*; *University Record* 2 (1892): 78.

67. Angell, *President's Report, 1892*, pp. 13–15.

68. *University Record* 1 (1891) and 2 (1892): passim; *Announcement of the Graduate School, 1892–93* (Ann Arbor, Mich., 1892), pp. 14–38, and subsequent years; *Calendar, 1893–94*, pp. 119–20.

69. Likewise, "the most important work of the university professor, ideally considered, is the advancement of science. His calling is to work on the frontier and his best work will necessarily be done with a few students who are themselves preparing to be investigators." *University Record* 2 (1892): 79.

70. See, e.g., *University Record* 2 (1892): 2–3; *Announcement of the Graduate School, 1892–93*, p. 13.

71. This is not to deny the obvious fact that the theory, as well as practice, of applied skills formed part of the curriculum of these professional schools. The formulation here refers advisedly to "divinity schools" (with their pastoral emphasis) rather than theology faculties, since theology has commonly been construed as "pure" rather than "applied" knowledge. Theology faculties, of hoary antiquity, in their practice also come closer, perhaps, than any other academic entities to Tappan's ideal of advanced, but broadly integrated, education. Possibly their marginal relation to modern knowledge—put differently, their old-fashioned form of knowledge—helps to explain this.

72. To say that German example was persistently influential in this half century is, of course, neither to deny that it had its ups and downs in every institution nor to claim that there was no institution with a secular trend of rise or decline. See Hawkins, *Pioneer*; idem, *Between Harvard and America*; Bishop, *Cornell*; Louise L. Stevenson, *Scholarly Means to Evangelical Ends: The New Haven Scholars and the Transformation of Higher Learning in America, 1830–1890* (Baltimore, Md., 1986); and Veysey, *American University*.

Chapter 5. The Forgotten History of the Research Ideal

This essay was originally delivered as a Horning Lecture at Oregon State University in 1994, having first been tested on colleagues in the Michigan Society of Fellows, and subsequently evolved in other venues. It has not been previously published.

1. See chapter 4.
2. For a fuller account, see chapter 3.
3. The only complete narrative remains Laurence R. Veysey, *The Emergence of the American University* (Chicago, 1965), though many historians would now dissent from a number of his characterizations. One can get some sense of how Veysey's story might be rewritten today by browsing through Bruce Kimball, "Writing the History of Universities: A New Approach?" *Minerva* (1986): 375–89; Roger Geiger, "The Ten Generations of American Higher Education," in *American Higher Education in the Twenty-First Century*, ed. Philip G. Altbach et al. (Baltimore, Md., 1999); the second half of Geiger, ed., *The American College in the Nineteenth Century* (Nashville, Tenn., 2000); Louise L. Stevenson, *Scholarly Means to Evangelical Ends: The New Haven Scholars and the Transformation of Higher Learning in America, 1830–1890* (Baltimore, Md., 1986); Caroline Winterer, *The Culture of Classicism: Ancient Greece and Rome in American Intellectual Life, 1780–1910* (Baltimore, Md., Johns Hopkins University Press, 2001); and Julie A. Reuben, *The Making of the Modern University: Intellectual Transformation and the Marginalization of Morality* (Chicago, 1996).
4. See chapter 4.
5. Graff, *Professing Literature: An Institutional History* (Chicago, 1987), pp. 40–41, 66, 88–90.
6. "Culture" here is an anachronistic term, but convenient. An American in the second half of the nineteenth century would have said "civilization" to designate what readers today would recognize as "culture" in the broad anthropological sense of the word.
7. Graff, *Professing Literature*, p. 88; Lowell's 1889 presidential address was printed as "Address," *Publications of the Modern Language Association of America* 5 (1890): 5–22; the discussion of modern languages and literatures occurs on p. 21.
8. Graff, *Professing Literature*, p. 40.
9. Lowell, "Address," 14.
10. *Jahrbücher für Kunstwissenschaft*, ed. A. von Zahn, 5 (1872): 66–90; Norton, *Historical Studies of Church-Building in the Middle Ages: Venice, Siena, Florence* (New York, 1880; reprinted 1902).
11. Norton, "The Text of Donne's Poems," *Studies and Notes in Philology and Literature* 5 (1896): 1–19; Norton to Charles W. Eliot, January 15, 1874, Norton Papers, Houghton Library, Harvard University. Norton's publications on Dante (which included a pioneering English translation of the *Vita Nuova* and what was for long a standard prose translation of the *Divina Commedia*) are too numerous to list here; see the list of his writings appended to James Turner, *The Liberal Education of Charles Eliot Norton* (Baltimore, Md., 1999). On the significance of his Donne scholarship, see Dayton Haskin, "New Historical

Contexts for Appraising the Donne Revival from A. B. Grosart to Charles Eliot Norton," *ELH* 56 (1989): 869–95.

12. Laurence Veysey, "The Plural Worlds of the Humanities," in *The Organization of Knowledge in Modern America, 1860–1920*, ed. Alexandra Oleson and John Voss (Baltimore, Md., 1979), pp. 53–54, 88–89.

13. The first version has been reprinted in a modern edition: Victor Cousin, *Cours de philosophie: Introduction à l'histoire de la philosophie* (1828; reprint, Paris, 1991).

14. Jean-Louis Fabiani, *Les philosophes de la république* (Paris, 1988), pp. 45–55.

Chapter 6. Catholicism and Modern Scholarship

This essay was originally delivered as the opening address at the conference "Catholic Intellectual Traditions in the Humanities and Social Sciences," convened in celebration of the 575th anniversary of the Katholieke Universiteit Leuven (Catholic University of Louvain) in 2000. It was first published in the European journal *Ethical Perspectives* 7, no. 4 (2000): 279–87.

1. For one such example of sensitivity to this link, see Thomas Albert Howard, *Religion and the Rise of Historicism: W. M. L. De Wette, Jacob Burckhardt, and the Theological Origins of Nineteenth-Century Historical Consciousness* (New York, 2000).

2. Robert E. Sullivan has reminded me that Acton uttered the dictum with reference to the papacy, in his correspondence with Mandell Creighton regarding the latter's history of the Renaissance popes: Acton to Creighton, 5 April 1887, in J. Rufus Fears, ed., *Selected Writings of Lord Acton* (Indianapolis, Ind., 1985), 2:383.

3. Walter Rüegg, "Themes," in *Universities in the Middle Ages*, ed. Hilde de Ridder-Symoens vol. 1 of *A History of the University in Europe* (Cambridge, Mass., 1992), p. 32.

4. Rainer Christoph Schwinges, "Admission," in ibid., pp. 172–73, 200–201; Walter Rüegg, "Epilogue: The Rise of Humanism," in ibid., p. 443 (quotation).

5. Willem Frijhoff, "Patterns," in *Universities in Early Modern Europe (1500–1800)*, ed. Hilde de Ridder-Symoens vol. 2 of *A History of the University in Europe* (Cambridge, Mass., 1996), pp. 75–77; *Anfänge Göttinger Sozialwissenschaft* (Göttingen, 1987).

6. Peter A. Vandermeersch, "Teachers," in *Universities in Early Modern Europe*, ed. Hilde de Ridder-Symoens, p. 223.

7. Ibid., pp. 223–24, 226–27.

8. Richard Mathes, *Löwen und Rom: Zur Gründung der Katholischen Universität Löwen unter besonderer Berücksichtigung der Kirchen- und Bildungspolitik Papst Gregors XVI* (Essen, 1975). To stress the ecclesiastical motive is not to deny the force of Belgian nationalism in the refounding of Leuven, a force patent in, e.g., [Pierre François Xavier] de Ram, *Considérations sur l'histoire de l'Université de Louvain (1425–1797)* (Brussels, 1854).

9. "London University" (now University College, London) having been refused a royal charter when founded in 1828, the University of London began, strictly speaking, in 1836 when both the original dissenting college and the new Anglican King's College were placed under its newly chartered and pretty ethereal wing. Spain's universities remained under clerical control through the century, as did those of some of the Italian principalities.

10. These two generalizations are well exemplified in the new collective work, *A History of the University in Europe*, ed. Walter Rüegg (Cambridge, Mass., 1992–), which seems destined to become the standard general history of the subject, as well as in an earlier collaborative landmark, *The University in Society*, ed. Lawrence Stone, 2 vols. (Princeton, N.J., 1974). For elaboration of the point, see James Turner, "German University History in Comparative Perspective: The Case of Göttingen," *Archiv für Sozialgeschichte* 29 (1989): 482–87.

11. For fuller development of this point and its effects on academic knowledge in the United States, see Jon H. Roberts and James Turner, *The Sacred and the Secular University*, (Princeton, N.J., 2000), part 2.

12. E. Harris Harbison, *The Christian Scholar in the Age of the Reformation* (New York, 1956), p. 92.

13. Amos Funkenstein, *Theology and the Scientific Imagination from the Middle Ages to the Seventeenth Century* (Princeton, N.J., 1986), p. 11; Maurice Mandelbaum, "Historicism," in *The Encyclopedia of Philosophy*, ed. Paul Edwards (New York, 1967) 4:22. (Mandelbaum is restating Ernst Troeltsch's definition). For a brief and helpful recent introduction to philological historicism (my term, not his) in the eighteenth and nineteenth centuries, see Paul Hamilton, *Historicism* (London, 1996), chaps. 2–3. The classic work is Friedrich Meinecke, *Die Entstehung des Historismus*, 2 vols. (Munich and Berlin, 1936). English trans. J. E. Anderson, (London, 1972).

14. [Andrews Norton], "Character of Rev. Joseph Stevens Buckminster," *General Repository and Review* 1 (1812): 307–8. For Andrews Norton, see chapter 1.

15. Charles Eliot Norton to Goldwin Smith, 14 June 1897, Norton Papers, Houghton Library, Harvard University; student notes by S. G. Morley on Professor George Foot Moore's History of Religions, 1906, HUC 8906.338.56, Harvard University Archives. On Moore see his entry in the *American National Biography*. On Norton see James Turner, *The Liberal Education of Charles Eliot Norton* (Baltimore, Md., 1999).

16. On the separation of morality from knowledge and the rise of an ideal of value-free knowledge in the United States, see Julie A. Reuben, *The Making of the Modern University: Intellectual Transformation and the Marginalization of Morality* (Chicago, 1996).

17. *Oxford English Dictionary*, s.v. "discipline."

18. John Henry Newman, *The Idea of a University*, ed. Martin J. Svaglic (Notre Dame, Ind., 1960), pp. 52–53.

19. I have essayed this in the American context in *Without God, Without Creed: The Origins of Unbelief in America* (Baltimore, Md., 1985).

20. Goldwin Smith, *A Plea for the Abolition of Tests in the University of Oxford* (Oxford, 1864), esp. pp. 9, 12.

21. The often closely related traditions of Islam played little role in European universities after the High Middle Ages.

22. Geoffrey Hartman, *A Life of Learning* (Charles Homer Haskins Lecture for 2000, American Council of Learned Societies Occasional Paper, no. 46 [New York, 2000]), pp. 9–10.

Chapter 7. The Evangelical Intellectual Revival

This essay was originally published in *Commonweal* 76 (January 15, 1999): 11–13, under the title "Something to be Reckoned with: The Evangelical Mind Awakens."

1. Readers curious about these historians, all in some way involved with the Institute for the Study of American Evangelicals at Wheaton College in Illinois, can find a sampling of their work in D. G. Hart, ed., *Reckoning with the Past: Historical Essays on American Evangelicalism from the Institute for the Study of American Evangelicals* (Grand Rapids, Mich., 1995), to which I contributed a foreword—in my by then accustomed role of sympathizing outsider.

Chapter 8. The Catholic University in Modern Academe

Originally delivered at a 1992 symposium celebrating the 150th anniversary of the University of Notre Dame, this lecture circulated among Catholic academics as a sort of *samizdat* (to my astonishment when I became aware) and was finally published in *Catholic Education*, March 1998.

1. That such unity was realized more often as ideal than practice—another similarity to Protestant moral philosophy—is pointed out in Philip Gleason's magisterial *Contending with Modernity: Catholic Higher Education in the Twentieth Century* (New York, 1995).

2. John Henry Newman, *The Idea of a University Defined and Illustrated* (London, 1873). The 1873 edition is usually considered the definitive one, al-

though the first book publication of the lectures (published as separate pamphlets during the course of their delivery in 1852) came in 1853.

3. The bestselling example exists in a modern edition: Francis Wayland, *The Elements of Moral Science*, ed. Joseph L. Blau (1837; reprint, Cambridge, Mass., 1963). On the genre see Donald H. Meyer, *The Instructed Conscience: The Shaping of the American National Ethic* (Philadelphia, Pa., 1972).

4. Surprisingly, given its consequences for European culture and its importance in intellectual history, most of this story remains to be written. But see James Turner, *Without God, Without Creed: The Origins of Unbelief in America* (Baltimore, Md., 1985).

5. Perhaps the most compelling overall analysis of this development, though carried through from a point of view different from mine, is by the Canadian Catholic philosopher Charles Taylor, *Sources of the Self: The Making of the Modern Identity* (Cambridge, Mass., 1989).

6. Both this epistemological crisis and the fragmentation of knowledge would seem to have consequences for the structure and function of universities. Yet the people who administer them and write about their present problems have mostly maintained a (politic? puzzled? distracted?) silence. If my diagnosis is right (and it is at least unoriginal), then university leaders are missing the boat.

7. Alasdair MacIntyre's rendition of nineteenth-century Neo-Thomism in his Gifford Lectures, *Three Rival Versions of Moral Enquiry: Encyclopedia, Genealogy, and Tradition* (Notre Dame, Ind., 1990), strikes me as overly charitable, though I hasten to add that his judgment is certainly better informed than my own. For an instance, as amusing as it is revealing, of the contortions and distortions entailed in the Vatican's pretense that Thomism was a timeless panacea, see Robert E. Sullivan, "Modernizing Traditions: Some Catholic Neo-Scholastics and the Genealogy of Natural Rights," in *Religion and the Authority of the Past*, ed. Tobin Siebers (Ann Arbor, Mich., 1993). Philip Gleason has written a sensitive, more general account of the American career of Catholic medievalism: "American Catholics and the Mythic Middle Ages," in his *Keeping the Faith: American Catholicism Past and Present* (Notre Dame, Ind., 1987), pp. 11–34.

8. For a good example, see Thomas C. Oden, *Systematic Theology*, vol. 1, *The Living God*; vol. 2, *The Word of Life* (San Francisco, 1987–89).

9. The quoted phrase is from Richard Rorty, *Philosophy and the Mirror of Nature* (Princeton, N.J., 1979), p. 373.

10. Perhaps the most sharp-edged, and literally the weightiest, indictment of Catholic universities for deserting their posts (extending the critique to Protestant institutions) is James Tunstead Burtchaell, *The Dying of the Light: The Disengagement of Colleges and Universities from Their Christian Churches* (Grand Rapids, Mich., 1998).

11. Thomas Browne, *Religio Medici and Other Works*, ed. L. C. Martin (Oxford, 1964), p. 33 (*Religio Medici* [1642], sec. 34).

12. I am evading here an important, indeed potentially crippling, subsidiary problem. With the decline in number of Catholic schools and colleges, and with the decreasing attention in their curricula since Vatican II to specifically Catholic intellectual traditions, recruiting younger faculty members who were raised as Catholics and may still be devout ones does not guarantee getting professors who are "culturally Catholic." Catholic colleges today are beginning to show renewed interest in Catholic intellectual traditions, notably in programs of "Catholic Studies," which may help to ease the problem in coming decades. Were Catholic universities and colleges to accept the curricular prescriptions that I offer later in this paper, that, too, would help. But, then, one's own advice is usually a fine nostrum.

13. See, for a major example, Amos Funkenstein, *Theology and the Scientific Imagination from the Middle Ages to the Seventeenth Century* (Princeton, N.J., 1986), and Stanley L. Jaki, *The Road of Science and the Ways to God* (Chicago, 1978).

14. On Cousin's legacy, see especially Jean-Louis Fabiani, *Les philosophes de la république* (Paris, 1988).

15. This is not to deny the intellectual rigor and the special strengths — especially in its philosophic bent — of Catholic education in the earlier period, but only to point to its inability to benefit from full engagement with contemporary knowledge.

Chapter 9. Catholic Intellectual Traditions
and Contemporary Scholarship.

This essay was originally delivered as a lecture under the auspices of the Cushwa Center for the Study of American Catholicism at the University of Notre Dame in April 1997 and published as an occasional paper by the Center. It was reprinted in *Catholic Education*, September 1998.

1. Dennis O'Brien, president emeritus of the University of Rochester, reported that, as a Phi Beta Kappa lecturer during the 1996–97 academic year, the lecture topic most often chosen by the institutions he visited was one on the "moral curriculum." *Key Reporter* 62, no. 4 (June 1997): 1.

2. *Chronicle of Higher Education*, 29 November 1996, sec. A, pp. 14–15.

3. Those of us *d'un certain âge* need no help in recalling Niebuhr's resonance; younger readers may wish to consult Richard Wightman Fox, *Reinhold Niebuhr: A Biography* (New York, 1985).

4. See especially Peirce's 1871 "review" of A. C. Fraser's edition of the works of Berkeley, *North American Review* 113 (1871): 449–72 (reprinted in James Hoopes, ed., *Peirce on Signs* [Chapel Hill, N.C., 1991], pp. 116–40) and, for a

recent assessment, Susan Haack, "'Extreme Scholastic Realism': Its Relevance to Philosophy of Science Today," *Transactions of the Charles S. Peirce Society* 28 (1992): 19–50.

5. Readers can sample the debate in Jean Bethke Elshtain, ed., *Just War Theory* (New York, 1992).

6. The experience of scholars associated with the Erasmus Institute since it began full operation in fall 1998 suggests at least three broad areas in which Catholic intellectual traditions have proven especially important in major problems in "secular" research: (1) providing analytic categories for rethinking the nature, role, and limits of the state at a time when the old master trope of "sovereignty" is increasingly at odds with political reality; (2) exploring the historical origins (and hence present meanings) of "Enlightenment reason" and modern conceptions of rationality; (3) emending axioms (often implicit) about "human nature" underlying research in psychology, economics, and political science, particularly conceptualizations of motivated behavior. This list by no means exhausts the research carried out up to now under the Institute's auspices by literary historians and critics, historians, anthropologists, psychologists, political scientists, philosophers, and art historians.

7. Notre Dame, Ind., 1995.

Index

academic professionalization. *See* professionalization in academia
Adams, Charles Kendall
   biography, 83, 181n16, 187n63
   influence on others, 185n44
   influences on, 82–83, 179n4
   School of Political Science (UM) role, 86–87, 188n65
   seminar as instructional method, 83–84, 184n42, 185n45
   University System (UM) developed by, 85–91
AIA (Archaeological Institute of America), 103–4
American Evangelicalism, 121–28
American intellectual history, 59
American intellectual tradition, 26–27, 51–52
American language theory, 26–30
American Philological Association, 13, 97
American university history. *See* university history, American
Angell, James B., 82, 85, 87, 89
Archaeological Institute of America (AIA), 103–4
art history, history in liberal arts education, 63–67

Augustine and the Limits of Politics (Elshtain), 152

Bancroft, George, 15, 163n2
biblical criticism. *See also* philology, textual
   historicist, 38, 42–45, 47–49
   influence on research ideal, 99–100
   philological origins of, 13
   role in university development, 97
Biblical Repertory and Princeton Review (BRPR), 33
Books and Culture, 122–23, 124
Bridgman, Percy, 29
Bushnell, Horace, 26, 36, 44–47

Calvin College, 122, 125–27
the Catholic intellectual contemplated, 141–42
Catholic intellectual scholarship. *See also* university, Catholic
   applicability to contemporary research, 146–56
   Catholics, benefit from reengaging in, 154–55
   challenging fragmentation of knowledge, 133–35, 148–49

Erasmus Institute, 155–56, 195n6
  history of, 124–25, 129
  institutional sponsorship in
    fostering, 155–56
  secularization of education and,
    148–50
Catholic intellectual tradition. *See
    also* university, Catholic
  belief shaping research, 138–40,
    147–48
  contribution to scholarship,
    151–54, 195n6
  future of, 134–35
  history of, 147
  importance of, 134
Chamberlain, Thomas, 181n16
Child, Francis J. (Stubby)
  Lowell, compared to, 97–98, 101,
    174n35
  as philological educator, 59–61,
    172n29, 173n32
  in philological history, 13
Christian Examiner, Norton-Ripley
    controversy, 16–17
Christian Nurture (Bushnell), 36
classical studies vs. utilitarian,
    paradigm of, 73–77, 79–80, 92,
    180n14. *See also* curriculum
    evolution
college history, American. *See also*
    curriculum evolution;
    education
  antebellum colleges, 52, 63, 70, 73
  Catholic schools, 53, 166n1
  Colonial (unified) curriculum, 51
  liberal arts colleges, 80
  the Scottish Enlightenment in,
    100
  utilitarian vs. liberal arts paradigm
    in reform, 73–77, 79–80, 92,
    180n14

*Concepts and Theories of Modern
    Physics* (Stallo), 29–30
Cooley, Thomas M., 86
Copeland, Charles T., 65
Cornell University, 70, 185n42
Corson, Hiram, 63, 64
Cousin, Victor, 75–76, 105–6, 181n17,
    181n19
curriculum evolution, classical
  the antebellum curriculum,
    52, 63
  the Colonial (unified) curriculum,
    51
  fragmentation/diversification in,
    52–58, 66–67, 74
  unifying factor, 52–53, 66–67, 98,
    105
  utilitarian paradigm vs., 73–77,
    79–80, 92, 180n14
curriculum evolution, liberal arts
  art history role, 63–67
  the elective system in, 56, 170n16,
    172n30
  fine arts study in, 56–57
  moral philosophy course, role
    in, 52–54, 56, 57–58, 96, 98,
    105
  secular, 6–7, 52–57, 59–67
curriculum evolution, unifying
    element
  liberal culture as, 56–57, 63
  the moral philosophy course,
    52–53, 66–67, 98, 105
  philosophy study as, 132

Dawkins, Richard, 145
"A Defense of Liberal Christianity"
    (Norton), 23
*Democratization of American
    Christianity* (Hatch), 123
Dexter Lectures (Norton), 23–24

discipline specialization. *See also* knowledge, fragmentation of
  fragmentation resulting from, 98, 148–49
  generalist-specialist dichotomy, 96–98, 101–4, 174n35
  in graduate education, 92–94, 188n71
  in institutional secularization, 117–18
  Lowell-Child comparison (example), 97–98, 101–2
  Norton, Charles Eliot (example), 102–5
  in university history, 96–97, 117–18
A Discourse on the Latest Form of Infidelity (Norton), 17, 18, 160n15
Dissertation on the Origin of Languages (Smith), 29
Dutch Calvinism in Modern America (Bratt), 126

education, graduate. *See also* Michigan, graduate education; university history, American
  discipline specialization in, 92–94, 188n71
  the graduate school, origins of, 92–94
  lectures, use as instructional method, 78–79
  the masters degree, 80, 87–90, 183n29, 183n32, 186n49
  origins, 69–71
  undergraduate education vs., 80, 183n31
  utilitarian paradigm in, 92
education, higher. *See also* college history; university history
  religion, role/conflicts in, 131–32, 143–47
  Scottish common-sense philosophy influence on, 51–52, 74, 105–6
education, high school, 76–77, 81, 185n45
education, secularization of
  beginnings, 52–55
  in Catholic intellectual scholarship, 148–50
  definition, 109–10
  gains/losses from, 6–7
  generalist-specialist dichotomy, 99–105
  institutional, 111–12, 135–36, 191n9
  intellectual, 112, 114–20
  liberal culture as unifying principle, 56–57, 63, 66–67
  of literary scholarship, 119
  Scottish common-sense philosophy influence on, 51–52
education, undergraduate. *See also* college history, American
  elective system in, 84
  graduate education vs., 80, 183n31
  the *Gymnasium* concept for, 70, 76–77, 182n22
  instructional method, lecture/seminar, 83–84, 184n40, 184n42, 185n45
  purpose of, 77
Eliot, Charles W., 72, 78, 179n4, 180n9
Eliot, Samuel, 15, 16
Eliot, Samuel A., 17
Elshtain, Jean Bethke, 152
Emerson, Ralph Waldo, Rev., 14, 17, 19, 25–26
Emily Dickinson (Lundin), 123
Enlightenment, 11, 27–28, 149. *See also* Scottish Enlightenment
Erasmus Institute, 155–56, 195n6
Evangelical intellectual revival, 122–28

Everett, Edward, 15, 163n2, 178n3
"The Evolution of Self-Consciousness" (Wright), 30

fine arts study in curriculum evolution, 56–57
Frieze, Henry Simmons, 81, 82, 85–91, 183n35

Garman, Charles E., 58
Garrison, William Lloyd Jr., 64
generalist-specialist dichotomy. *See* discipline specialization
General Repository and Review (Norton, ed.), 15
The Genuineness of the Gospels (Norton), 16
German educational model
   faculty research, expectations for, 88–89
   four elements of, 70–71
   Gymnasia for preparatory studies, 70, 76–77, 81, 182n22
   of higher learning
      in American university history, 70–73, 178n3, 188n71
      discipline specialization in, 117–18
      four faculties of, 182n23
      transmogrification of, 93–94
      University Course resemblance to, 78–79
   instructional method, lecture/seminar, 78–79, 83–84, 184n40, 186n48
   at Michigan, 75–77, 79–81, 86, 93–94, 181n17, 182n20
   in origin myth of American university, 96, 97
   Ph.D. program/requirements, 85, 88–89
   Prussian system, 75–77, 79–81, 93–94, 181n17, 182n20
   purpose in career development, 71, 84, 185n47
German idealist theology, 19–20, 22, 25, 43–45, 74
Gildersleeve, Basil L., 13, 105
Gilman, Daniel Coit, 178n2, 179n4
God
   and government, 38, 165n15
   and knowledge, 46–47, 116–17
   and language of communication, 21–22, 25
Graff, Gerald, 97–98, 100–102

Hart, Albert Bushnell, 65
Hartman, Geoffrey, 119
Harvard University
   elective system at, 170n16
   English literature at, 59–60, 61, 171n25, 171n27
   Ph.D. program, 88
   role of German universities in history of, 70
   seminar as instructional method, 184n42
   University Lectures program at, 78
Hatch, Nathan, 122–23, 126, 140
Haven, Erastus O., 81, 172n27
Hawkins, Hugh, 55
Hazard, Rowland Gibson, 26, 162n36
Historical Studies of Church-Building in the Middle Ages (Norton), 102
historicism
   biblical authenticity vs., 38, 42–45, 47–49
   defined, 3
   Hodge's repudiation of, 40–48
   individualism and, 40–41
   philological origins of, 99–100, 115–16
   radical theological, 45–46

historicism (*cont.*)
  unity of knowledge vs., 46–47, 115–18
The History of American Literature, 1607–1765 (Tyler), 59
Hodge, Charles
  about, 1–2, 31–34, 37, 48–49, 164n5
  biblical authenticity, belief in, 38, 42–44, 47–49
  Bushnell and, 36, 46, 47
  character traits, 32, 33–34, 37
  on contextual nature of knowledge, 46–47
  on German idealist theology, 44–45
  historicism, repudiation of, 40–48
  individualism/hyperindividualism and, 36–41, 44–46, 164n9
  Norton relationship, 31
  politics of, 36–40, 165n17
  and religion, 35–37, 38–39, 41–42, 46–48, 164n 14
  on slavery, 37–38, 39, 164n11
  on Stuart, 32, 163n1
  on utilitarianism, 38, 164n 14
Howells, William Dean, 64
hyperindividualism as heresy, 36–38, 44–46, 164n9

idealist theology, German, 19–20, 22, 25, 43–45, 74
imagination
  as central to moral life, 65
  knowledge vs., 47
Inaugural Discourse on the Extent and Relations of Theology (Norton), 25
individualism/hyperindividualism, 36–41, 44–46, 164n9
intellectual history, America, 59
intellectual scholarship. *See* Catholic intellectual scholarship

intellectual tradition. *See also* Catholic intellectual scholarship; Catholic intellectual tradition
  American, 26–27, 51–52
  Evangelical intellectual revival, 122–28
intuitionism, 16, 18, 25

Jeffrey, David Lyle, 123
Johns Hopkins University
  English literature at, 61
  Ph.D. program, 88, 187n60, 187n62
  role of German universities in history of, 70, 72
Johnson, Alexander Bryan, 26, 162n34

knowledge
  academic vs. religious thought, 147, 149–50
  Catholic approach to, 151–54
  contextual nature of, 25, 46–47
  as cumulative, 46
  German university in advancement of, 70–71
  historicist, 100, 116–17
  imagination vs., 47
  and language, relationship to, 21–22, 25–26
knowledge, fragmentation of. *See also* discipline specialization
  Catholic university challenge for resolving, 133–35
  in curriculum evolution, 52–58, 66–67, 74
  from discipline specialization, 57–58, 92–94, 98, 148–49, 188n71

from liberal culture as unifying
    principle, 56–57, 63
  in philosophy coursework, 57–58
knowledge, religious
  academic knowledge vs., 147,
    149–50
  religious language and, 21–22
knowledge, secularization of
  gains/losses from, 6–7
  institutional, 112–14, 191n9
  intellectual, 112, 114–20
  origins, 111–12
knowledge, unity of
  Catholic university role in
    recreating, 133–35
  historicism vs., 46–47, 115–18
  moral philosophy course and
    belief in, 52–53, 66–67, 98
Kuperianism, 126–27

Lafayette College, 59, 61
language. *See also* linguistics
  and knowledge, 21–22, 25–26
  processing theory of, 24–25
  religious, 21–23, 25, 29
  of Transcendentalism, 14, 19–23,
    25–26
language theory, American, 26–30
learning, higher. *See* education,
  higher
Das Leben Jesu (Strauss), 44
liberal arts education vs. utilitarian,
    paradigm of, 73–77, 79–80, 92,
    180n14. *See also* curriculum
    evolution; individual
    disciplines, e.g. art history
liberal arts movement, 74
linguistics, origination of, 99. *See also*
  language
linguistic writers, antebellum
  America, 26–27

*The Literary History of the American
  Revolution* (Tyler), 59
literature, American, 59, 61
literature, English (study/teaching of)
  curriculum evolution, role in, 57
  history, in American education,
    58–59
  inspiration, not information in,
    63, 67
  morality learned in study of,
    62–63
  philological approach to, 59–63,
    67
Lounsbury, Thomas R., 59
Lowell, James Russell
  antiphilological interpretation of,
    101–2, 174n37
  Child, compared to, 97–98, 101,
    174n35
  as philological educator, 59,
    62–63
Lundin, Roger, 123

March, Francis A., 59, 60, 61, 173n34
Marsden, George, 122–23, 126, 140
May, Henry, 11
Michigan, University of
  admission-by-diploma, 81
  beginnings, 75–76, 80
  credit-system program, 87
  elective system at, 84, 170n16,
    172n30
  research university evolution,
    influenced by, 75, 77, 88,
    178n2, 186n50
  women, admission of, 183n35
Michigan, coursework (specific)
  art history, 64
  English literature, 59–60, 61,
    171n25, 171n27
  philosophy coursework, 58

Michigan, German educational model at
  graduate education influenced by, 79–81, 88–89, 91
  the *Gymnasium* concept used, 76–77, 81
  Ph.D. program and, 86
  of the Prussian system, 75–77, 79–81, 93–94, 181n17, 182n20
Michigan, graduate education
  basis of, 84
  as career preparation, 88–90
  German university model influence, 79–81, 88–89, 91
  growth of, 91
  the masters degree, 78, 80, 87–90, 183n29, 183n32, 186n49
  Ph.D. program, 85–92, 186nn49–50, 187n56, 187n60
  purpose of, 90
  School of Political Science, 86–87, 188n65
  the University Course, 77–81, 82, 88–89, 92, 183n29
  University System, 85–92, 186nn49-50, 187n56, 187n60, 187n63, 188n65
  utilitarian paradigm in, 92
Michigan, undergraduate education
  admission-by-diploma, 81
  bachelor's degree requirements, 87
  credit-system program, 87
  elective system at, 84, 170n16
  the *Gymnasium* concept, 76–77, 81
  instructional method, lecture/seminar, 78–79, 83–84, 184n40, 184n42, 185n45
the miracles controversy, 16–19, 25–26

moral philosophy (study of). *See also* philosophy (study of)
  art history as substitute for, 63–67
  curriculum evolution, role in, 52–54, 56
  demise, 57–58, 98
  inspiration, not information in, 63
  Scottish common-sense philosophy and, 52, 105–6
  secularized parallel (France), 105–6
  as unifying factor in college curriculum, 52–53, 66–67, 96, 105
Morgan, Lewis Henry, 12, 29
Mouw, Richard, 122, 126

Nature (Emerson), 26
Newman, John Henry, 42, 118, 130–32, 141
Noll, Mark, 122, 124, 126
Norton, Andrews
  background, 1–2, 13–16
  character, 16, 17, 21
  Emerson conflict, 14, 17, 19, 25–26
  Hodge relationship, 31
  and language
    American language theory, role in, 28–29
    his background, 23–24, 28–29
    of German idealist theology, 20–22
    knowledge, relationship to, 21–22, 25–26
    of Transcendentalism, 14, 19–23, 25–26
  and miracles, 13–14, 16–19, 21, 25–26
  motto, 18, 160n16
  as poet/poetry and, 23
  Ripley conflict, 14, 16–19, 21–22

Transcendentalism, 13–14, 16–23, 25–26
Unitarianism and, 14, 21
Norton, Andrews (works)
"A Defense of Liberal Christianity," 23
Dexter Lectures, 23–24
"A Discourse on the Latest Form of Infidelity," 17, 160n15
General Repository and Review (founder), 15
The Genuineness of the Gospels, 16
Inaugural Discourse on the Extent and Relations of Theology, 23, 25
"Remarks on the Modern German School of Infidelity," 19
Norton, Charles Eliot
about, 40, 174n35
art history, scholar/teacher, 64–66, 102, 175n44, 176n45
generalist-specialist dichotomy, 102–5
influence on others, 64–65, 103
on the liberal arts paradigm, 74
religious affiliation, 65–67
Notre Dame University, 132
Nott, Eliphalet, 56, 178n2

Paradise Lost (Milton), 60, 171n25
Peirce, Charles Sanders, 30, 152, 171n22
philological scholarship. *See also* biblical criticism; language
contempt for, 173n34
founders of, 27
philology
classical, 13, 99–100
comparative historical, 3, 28–29, 99, 157n5
disciplines originating from, 99

historicism's origination from, 99–100, 115–16
history of, 2–3, 12–13, 26–30, 157n6, 173n32
humanistic, 115
Renaissance, 115
the research ideal in, 100–101
in teaching (of English literature), 59–63, 67
textual, 3, 25, 99, 100, 115. *see also* biblical criticism
philosophy (study of). *See also* moral philosophy (study of)
curriculum evolution, role in, 56–57, 132
in liberal arts education, 58
professors, reasons for teaching, 58
by students, reasons given for enrolling, 170n21
as a unifying curricular element, 132
Plantinga, Alvin, 122–23
professionalization in academia
discipline specialization in, 92–94, 96–98, 101–4, 117–18, 174n35
in research university evolution, 71, 88, 178n2, 179n6
Transcendentalist controversy in, 18

Rationale of Religious Enquiry (Martineau), 16
religious intellectual traditions, intellectual traditions
"Remarks on the Modern German School of Infidelity" (Norton), 19
the research ideal
generalist-specialist dichotomy, 99–105
of philology, 100–101

research university. *See also* university history, American
  Catholic scholarship relevance in the, 146–56
  Catholic university as, 131–32, 139–40, 143–47
  the comprehensive model, 77
  German university model, 78–79, 94
  origins, 75, 77, 82, 88, 94, 186n50
  professionalization in, 71, 88, 178n2, 179n6
Ripley, George, Rev., 14, 16–19, 21–22
Rüegg, Walter, 111

The Scandal of the Evangelical Mind (Noll), 124
Schaff, Philip, 33, 42
scholarship. *See also* Catholic intellectual scholarship
  Evangelical, 121–28
  philological, 27, 173n34
Scottish common-sense philosophy
  of contextual nature of knowledge, 46–47, 49
  influence on American intellectual life, 51–52
  liberal arts paradigm, influenced by, 74
  moral philosophy course and, 105–6
  in resolving moral questions, 39–40
  Unitarianism and, 18
Scottish Enlightenment. *See also* Enlightenment
  culture as context and, 100
  influence in America, 11, 12, 28
  realism of, 46
secularization in education
  beginnings, 52–55
  in Catholic intellectual scholarship, 148–50
  definition, 109–10
  gains/losses from, 6–7
  generalist-specialist dichotomy, 99–105
  institutional, 111–12, 135–36, 191n9
  intellectual, 112, 114–20
  liberal culture as unifying principle, 56–57, 63, 66–67
  of literary scholarship, 119
  Scottish common-sense philosophy influence on, 51–52
Selfish Gene (Dawkins), 145
Sheffield School, 56, 59, 170n16
Smith, Goldwin, 119
Soul of the American University (Marsden), 123
Stallo, J. B., 29–30
Stewart, John W., 33–34
Strauss, David Friedrich, 44
Stuart, Moses, 27, 32, 163n1
Sumner, William Graham, 104, 135

Tappan, Henry P.
  career, 76, 181n19, 182n28
  Gymnasium model for the college, 76–77, 182n22
  influence on others, 82, 86, 177n2
  influences on, 77, 177n2, 179n4
  the Prussian system used by, 76–77, 79–81, 181n17
  University Course of graduate education, 77–81, 82, 88–89, 92, 183n29
theological seminaries, role in university development, 97, 188n71
Ticknor, George, 73, 178n3, 182n22

Transcendentalism
  controversy/rebellion, 14, 16–19, 25–26
  language of, 14, 19–23, 25–26
Treatise on Language (Johnson), 26
Trinitarian Congregationalists, Norton on, 23
Turner, James, 121, 129–30
Tyler, Moses Coit, 59–60, 61, 172n29, 185n44

UM (University of Michigan). See Michigan
Unitarianism, miracles controversy, 14, 16–19, 25–26
United States. *See also* university history, American
  American Evangelicalism, 121–28
  American intellectual tradition, 26–27, 51–52
  American language theory, 26–30
  hyperindividualism in, 36–38, 164n9
  individualistic utilitarian liberalism in, 38
  linguistic writers in history of, 26–27
  religion in, 110
university, Catholic. *See also* Catholic intellectual scholarship; Catholic intellectual tradition
  Catholic intellectual scholarship place in, 134–35
  challenge/dilemma of the, 131–32, 133, 155–56
  in fostering Catholic scholarship, 155–56
  history of, 118–20, 129, 166n1
  purpose, 131
  reconstructed future of, 137–41, 194n12
  research component in, 139–40
  separation of church from, 131–32, 143–47
University Education (Tappan), 76
university history
  Catholic, 118–20, 129, 166n1
  the church in, 111–12
  European, 114–20, 191n9
university history, American. *See also* college history, American; curriculum evolution; education; research university
  admission practices, 81
  beginnings, 96–97
  domestic influences on, 97
  the German model influence on, 70–73, 93–94, 178n3, 188n71
  the modern university model, 75, 97, 179n2
  origin myths
    the German model adopted, 69–70, 96, 97
    the research ideal as central motif, 95–106
  overview, 69–70
  people significant in, 177n2
  secularization in, 135–36
  state universities in, 77, 182n23
  university president's role, history of, 82
  the university professor, 92, 188n69
University of Michigan (UM). *See* Michigan, University of
utilitarianism, 38, 164n14
utilitarian studies vs. classical paradigm, 73–77, 79–80, 92, 180n14

Veysey, Laurence, 104

Wayland, Francis, 77, 177n2
Wheaton College, 122, 127
White, Andrew Dickson
    about/career, 59, 82–83, 172n27
    German university study, experience of, 72
    influence on others, 82–83, 86
    influences on, 75, 178n2, 179n4
    the university model, 77
Whitney, William Dwight, 13
Wolterstorff, Nicholas, 122–23
Woodberry, George, 63, 65

Yale University
    English literature at, 59
    Ph.D. program, 88
    School of Fine Arts, 64
    Sheffield School, 56, 59, 170n16
Yale University Report of 1828, 73, 75, 77, 180n13